Interweaving Patterns in the Works of Joseph Conrad

Studies in Modern Literature, No. 81

A. Walton Litz, General Series Editor
Professor of English
Princeton University

Consulting Editor:
Thomas C. Moser
Professor of English
Stanford University

Other Titles in This Series

No. 39	*Conrad's Endings: A Study of the Five Major Novels*	Arnold E. Davidson
No. 40	*Theories of Action in Conrad*	Francis A. Hubbard
No. 41	*The Ludic Imagination: A Reading of Joseph Conrad*	Kenneth Simons
No. 42	*Conrad's Rebels: The Psychology of Revolution in the Novels from* Nostromo *to* Victory	Helen Funk Rieselbach
No. 45	*The Indestructible Woman in the Works of Faulkner, Hemingway, and Steinbeck*	Mimi R. Gladstein
No. 46	*Joseph Conrad, Ford Madox Ford, and the Making of* Romance	Raymond Brebach
No. 56	*The Museum World of Henry James*	Adeline Tintner

Interweaving Patterns in the Works of Joseph Conrad

by
Gail Fraser

Research Press

Ann Arbor / London

Copyright © 1988
Caroline Gail Fraser
All rights reserved

Produced and distributed by
UMI Research Press
an imprint of
University Microfilms Inc.
Ann Arbor, Michigan 48106

Library of Congress Cataloging in Publication Data

Fraser, Gail, 1939-
 Interweaving patterns in the works of Joseph Conrad / by Gail Fraser.
  p. cm.—(Studies in modern literature ; no. 81)
  Bibliography: p.
  Includes index.
  ISBN 0-8357-1828-X (alk. paper)
  1. Conrad, Joseph, 1857-1924—Technique. I. Title. II. Series.
PR6005.O4Z727   1988
823'.912—dc19   87-23283
                                                                 CIP

British Library CIP data is available.

To the memory of my father, Hugh Mackenzie Morrison

Contents

Acknowledgments   *ix*

1 Introduction   *1*

2 "An Outpost of Progress" and *The Secret Agent*   *7*

3 "The Lagoon," "Karain," and *Lord Jim*   *27*

4 "Youth," "Heart of Darkness," and *Lord Jim*   *49*

5 "Heart of Darkness" and *Lord Jim*   *85*

6 "The Secret Sharer" and *Under Western Eyes*   *111*

7 Conclusion   *135*

Notes   *143*

Bibliography   *157*

Index   *165*

Acknowledgments

I am very grateful to Andrew Busza, who supervised the initial version of this book with patience, humour, and insight. I would also like to thank Thomas Moser for his helpful suggestions about the manuscript, and my husband, our three children, and my mother for their unfailing interest and support.

Thanks are also due to the Trustees of the Joseph Conrad Estate and to J. M. Dent and Sons Ltd. for their kind permission to quote from Conrad's works; to the Henry W. and Albert A. Berg Collection, The New York Public Library, Astor, Lenox, and Tilden Foundations; The Beinecke Rare Book and Manuscript Library, Yale University; and Colgate University Library for permission to quote from unpublished manuscripts in their possession; to the Estate of Joseph Conrad and Cambridge University Press for permission to quote from the published and unpublished letters of Conrad.

I also wish to thank Bruce M. Brown, archivist of Colgate University Library for his prompt and friendly assistance, and Owen Knowles, editor of *The Conradian* (Journal of the Joseph Conrad Society, U.K.) for permission to reprint a large portion of chapter 2, which appeared as "Conrad's Irony: 'An Outpost of Progress' and *The Secret Agent*" in *The Conradian* 11 (1986): 155–69.

1

Introduction

In contrast to other major novelists like Henry James and Virginia Woolf, Conrad provided us with very few critical statements concerning his own writing. Moreover, with the exception of his preface to *The Nigger of the "Narcissus,"* the explanations he did offer are fragmentary and often misleading. Not until 1919 and 1920, several years after his best fiction had been completed, did he write the "Author's Notes" for the separate volumes of Doubleday's collected edition. Although these prefaces occasionally contain hints about Conrad's intentions at the time he wrote the fiction, they also display his tendency to mythologize about his life and art.

For example, in the "Author's Note" to *Tales of Unrest* he says that he wrote "The Lagoon" immediately after *An Outcast of the Islands*. The two works were "seen with the same vision, rendered in the same method"—even written with the same pen.[1] In actual fact, Conrad completed *An Outcast of the Islands* on September 17, 1895; he began *The Sisters* toward the end of the year and abandoned it in April 1896, and wrote "The Idiots" and "An Outpost of Progress" in May and July, respectively, before completing "The Lagoon" in August. By claiming to have written "The Lagoon" before "The Idiots" and "An Outpost of Progress" and failing to mention the abandoned novel, Conrad could give the first years of his writing career an imagined order and direction: they became "my first phase, the Malayan phase with its special subject and its verbal suggestions" (v). The "Notes" contain other similar instances of Conrad's mythologizing, such as the story he put forth in the preface to *An Outcast of the Islands* indicating that Edward Garnett had been responsible for his writing a second novel. This story suggests a correspondence between Conrad's sailing and writing careers, for, as he demonstrates in *A Personal Record*, each is perceived to have its origin in a mysterious impulse or set of circumstances.

In a letter of 1923 Conrad claimed that the "Author's Notes" were not intended to explain the factual origins or the formal aspects of his works. He told Richard Curle, who had "summarized" the prefaces for a comprehensive article on Conrad's writing, that the "Notes" should be treated as "an intensely personal expression": "the summarizing of Prefaces . . . has got this disadvantage that it doesn't give their atmosphere, and indeed it cannot give their atmosphere, simply because those pages are an intensely personal expression, much more so than all the rest of my writing, with the exception of the Personal Record perhaps."[2] In fact, the chief myth that Conrad puts forth in the "Notes" is that he did not consciously plan his artistic effects. Consequently, he plays down the formal aspects of his writing, offering the reader entertaining analogies rather than explanations of his methods.

In the preface to the *Youth* volume, for example, he comments with good-humoured irony on contemporary critical attempts to describe Marlow's function:

> The origins of that gentleman . . . have been the subject of some literary speculation of, I am glad to say, a friendly nature.
> One would think that I am the proper person to throw a light on the matter; but in truth I find that it isn't so easy. It is pleasant to remember that nobody had charged him with fraudulent purposes or looked down on him as a charlatan; but apart from that he was supposed to be all sorts of things: a clever screen, a mere device, a "personator," a familiar spirit, a whispering "daemon." I myself have been suspected of a meditated plan for his capture.
> That is not so. I made no plans. The man Marlow and I came together in the casual manner of those health-resort acquaintances which sometimes ripen into friendships. This one has ripened.[3]

On the whole, Conrad's commentary on his work in the other "Notes" is similar in tone and substance to this passage. In contrast to the prefaces of Henry James, the "Author's Notes" do not shed much light on the individual novels and stories.

Conrad's letters to friends and publishers about his writing are more revealing, since they provide us with a record of his work in progress. Despite the fragmentary nature of these comments, they impress the reader as reliable indications of his immediate problems and goals. However, there was a great deal that Conrad was either unable or unwilling to say about his work in a letter. For example, in his correspondence with William Blackwood at a time when he was "devoting himself exclusively" to *Lord Jim* he tends to obscure his overall intentions rather than illuminate them. In the following passage, he refers to his "guiding idea":

> I am glad you like Jim so far. Your good opinion gives one confidence. From the nature of things treated the story can not be as dramatic (in a certain sense) as the *H of D*. It is certainly more like *Youth*. It is however longer and more varied. The structure of it is a little loose—this however need not detract from its interest—from the "general reader" point of view. The question of *art* is so endless, so involved and so obscure that one is tempted to turn one's face resolutely away from it. I've certainly an idea—apart from the idea and the subject of the story—which guides me in my writing, but I would be hard put to it if requested to give it out in the shape of a fixed formula. After all in this as in every other human endeavour one is answerable only to one's conscience.[4]

Here, Conrad's desire to assure Blackwood (and himself) of a popular success with his new "story" is evident,[5] as is his inability or reluctance to discuss in detail a creative process that was partly instinctual. Thus, he insists upon a central "idea . . . which guides me in my writing," but refuses to define it. If we wish to understand the artist's methods, and his intentions in general, we must turn to the works themselves.

From the large and complex body of Conrad's fiction a suggestive pattern emerges, made up of the formal and thematic links between shorter works and certain major novels. By exploring these links, we can gain a better understanding of his writing without proposing systems or theories which might obscure his intentions even further. From his preface to *The Nigger of the "Narcissus"* we know that Conrad was an avowed enemy of such theories: "The changing wisdom of successive generations discards ideas, questions facts, demolishes theories. But the artist appeals to that part of our being which is not dependent on wisdom; to that in us which is a gift and not an acquisition—and, therefore, more permanently enduring."[6] And a little later, he writes:

> It is evident that he who, rightly or wrongly, holds by the convictions expressed above cannot be faithful to any one of the temporary formulas of his craft. The enduring part of them—the truth which each only imperfectly veils—should abide with him as the most precious of his possessions, but they all: Realism, Romanticism, Naturalism, even the unofficial sentimentalism (which like the poor, is exceedingly difficult to get rid of,) all these gods must, after a short period of fellowship, abandon him—even on the very threshold of the temple—to the stammerings of his conscience and to the outspoken consciousness of the difficulties of his work. (x-xi)

Not surprisingly, Conrad displays the same lack of respect for the "formulas of [the] craft" in his critical essays about other authors. He is always concerned with the writer's conception of his art, his craftsmanship, and his "attitude towards our world"[7] rather than his place within a historical or aesthetic scheme.

In discussing the most provocative links between works of different lengths, I have not tried to prove that the shorter fiction gave rise to the novels. Nor have I taken the conventional position when writing about the former that "the highest level of Conrad's art exists in the short fiction."[8] Instead, one of my guiding principles has been a remark that Conrad made to Marguerite Poradowska in 1893 suggesting that the form and style of the writer are more clearly displayed in his short fiction than in his longer works: "It takes a small scale narrative (short story) to show the master's hand."[9] In this statement Conrad resembles most other masters of the form from Edgar Allan Poe, who claimed that the writer could achieve "totality of effect" through technique in short fiction, to Henry James, whose *Notebooks* document the artist's attempts to make his style express an idea within the "brief compass" of the short story. In Conrad's shorter fiction "the master's hand" is displayed in action: formal elements like symbols, images, the arrangement of details and events, and point of view are foregrounded so that we can see how the writer's style reflects his view of the world.

The vital relationship of technique to content is stressed in an important letter Conrad wrote to Ford, dated by Karl and Davies as June 13, 1901:

> The value of creative work of any kind is in the *whole* of it. Till that is seen no judgment is possible. Questions of phrasing and such like—*technique*—may be discussed upon a fragmentary examination; but phrasing, expression—*technique* in short has importance only when the Conception of the whole has a significance of its own apart from the details that go to make it up—if it (the Conception) is imaginative, distinct and has an independent life of its own—as apart from the "life" of the style.[10]

Because Conrad's short fiction provides such a clear, concentrated view of "the whole," technique often reveals the "Conception" in striking and unusual ways.

Another factor which can help us interpret Conrad's work is the interrelationship of certain stories and novels written within the same period of time. This relationship is not manifested in the obvious way that some of Faulkner's short stories are linked to his novels; that is, by the recurrence of specific characters, settings, and even events.[11] Instead, some of Conrad's stories and novels are linked by common themes and moral preoccupations, which are emphasized by common motifs. Unlike the usual repetition and development of certain themes that we find throughout the works of any major writer, these thematic connections comprise a dialectical method of exploring a central idea. Therefore, a study of the connecting links will yield a more comprehensive understanding of Conrad's meaning than analyzing the works separately. Moreover, because Conrad explores one aspect of his idea in a more concentrated form in the short fiction than in the corresponding novel, a close look at the former will help us to see the larger pattern of his intentions.

In general, Conrad's critics have not focussed on the links between short fiction and novels in order to interpret his major themes and explore the nature of his originality. Some of the differences between Marlow as a narrator in "Youth," "Heart of Darkness," and *Lord Jim* have been analyzed, but there has been no comprehensive study of the influence on the longer fictions of Conrad's experiments with form and technique in "Youth." In fact, most critics treat the connections between the works as cursorily as Ian Watt when he writes that "there are too few examples in literature of a simple thing beautifully done to make us value it only for the way it leads into the later Marlow stories. Yet lead it does."[12]

In other cases, critics have pointed out specific correspondences between characters, motifs, themes, or settings, but have not considered the total relationship of one work to another. For example, Ted Boyle remarks that the white man's glimpse of Arsat standing in the sunlight against "the darkness of a world of illusions" in "The Lagoon" anticipates Marlow's last view of Patusan, but his discussion is limited to the symbolic implications of the "darkness."[13] Other critics have commented on the fact that Kurtz and Jim are both imaginative egoists, and so on. Neither of the two book-length studies of Conrad's short fiction analyzes the stories in relationship to the novels in order to explore the writer's themes and techniques as a whole. Edward Said's *Joseph Conrad and the Fiction of Autobiography* (1966) relates the short fiction to Conrad's letters, and Lawrence Graver's

Conrad's Short Fiction (1969) evaluates the individual works on the basis of how well they present the conflict between egoism and altruism. To some degree, both studies attempt to systematize the shorter fiction.

Instead of imposing a set of assumptions on Conrad's work, we can use the creative process to illuminate the writer's ideas and methods. Conrad's revisions give us some fascinating insights into the structure of his imagination; they also help to interpret individual stories. In his essay on Maupassant Conrad himself compares earlier and later stages of a writer's work to explain his originality. Commenting on the publication of Maupassant's posthumous fiction, he says: "On looking at the first feeble drafts from which so many perfect stories have been fashioned, one discovers that what has been matured, improved, brought to perfection by unwearied endeavour is not the diction of the tale, but the vision of its true shape and detail."[14] Conrad's revisions at both the manuscript and typescript stages show us how he developed "the true shape" of his work in the process of composition. They also reveal his painstaking attention to detail, illustrating in a concrete form his advice to Sir Hugh Clifford in a letter of 1899:

> True, a man who knows so much (without taking into account the manner in which his knowledge was acquired) may well spare himself the trouble of meditating over the words, only that words, groups of words, words standing alone, are symbols of life, have the power in their sound or their aspect to present the very thing you wish to hold up before the mental vision of your readers. The things "as they are" exist in words; therefore words should be handled with care lest the picture, the image of truth abiding in facts, should become distorted—or blurred.
>
> These are the considerations for a mere craftsman—you may say; and you may also conceivably say that I have nothing else to trouble my head about. However, the *whole* of the truth lies in the presentation. . . .[15]

Conrad's reference to "the image of truth abiding in facts" which must be "held up before the mental vision" of one's readers echoes one of the most familiar passages in the preface to *The Nigger of the "Narcissus."* There, Conrad said that the ultimate aim of literary craftsmanship is solidarity with the reader:

> The task approached in tenderness and faith is to hold up unquestioningly, without choice and without fear, the rescued fragment before all eyes in the light of a sincere mood. It is to show its vibration, its colour, its form; and through its movement, its form, and its colour, reveal the substance of its truth—disclose its inspiring secret: the stress and passion within the core of each convincing moment. In a single-minded attempt of that kind, if one be deserving and fortunate, one may perchance attain to such clearness of sincerity that at last the presented vision of regret or pity, of terror or mirth, shall awaken in the hearts of the beholders that feeling of unavoidable solidarity; of the solidarity in mysterious origin, in toil, in joy, in hope, in uncertain fate, which binds men to each other and all mankind to the visible world. (x)

In both of these statements (but more explicitly and movingly in the second) Conrad defines craftsmanship as an ethical imperative; that is, the writer's task is to rescue "the image of truth" from the flux of reality, thereby communicating to the reader a sense of human continuity and fellowship. The emphasis on *endeavour* points to the larger, moral context of Conrad's ongoing struggles with his material. In his correspondence with J. B. Pinker there are several instances of his asking for a typescript to be returned for additional changes after he had already revised it.

Manuscript and typescript revisions can be particularly illuminating in the case of a partly "instinctual" writer like Conrad. Most of his works underwent major changes in form and structure during the process of composition. Of the short fiction we shall look at, only "The Lagoon" was conceived with a clear idea as to its length, because *The Cornhill* had asked for a story of from 6,000 to 8,000 words. Therefore, Conrad's revisions help us to see his intentions as they evolve, requiring the addition or cancellation of material. (In "Youth," for example, he added an entire episode at the typescript stage.) The revisions also show us how he sharpened the focus of descriptions, images, and so on to emphasize his ideas and moral concerns. Finally, an understanding of Conrad's working methods helps to clarify the nature of his originality. "There is nothing in me but a turn of mind which whether valuable or worthless can not be imitated," he once wrote to J. B. Pinker.[16]

Exploring the links between short fiction and major novels reveals this "turn of mind" in Conrad's earliest, most experimental stories as well as the later masterpieces like *The Secret Agent,* "The Secret Sharer," and *Under Western Eyes*. In an often-quoted letter to Sidney Colvin, a friend and influential critic, Conrad wrote: "Perhaps you won't find it presumption if, after 22 years of work, I may say that I have not been very well understood." He went on to tell Colvin that his chief aim—to portray "the 'ideal' value of things, events and people"—had been obscured by the critics' attempts to categorize his writing: "I have been called a writer of the sea, of the tropics, a descriptive writer, a romantic writer—and also a realist."[17] Yet Zdzisław Najder points out that even the author's self-interpretation ("all my concern has been with the 'ideal' value of things") is partly obscured by the words he chooses.[18] In the following chapters, I have tried to provide a different sort of context for the individual stories and novels—one that relies neither on "categorization" nor on Conrad's suggestive but often ambiguous and sometimes misleading statements.

2
"An Outpost of Progress" and *The Secret Agent*

Although Conrad critics usually relate "An Outpost of Progress" to "Heart of Darkness,"[1] there are also significant links between this early story and *The Secret Agent*. In both narratives Conrad explores political and moral issues by constructing a network of ironic parallels, juxtapositions, and allusions. Moreover, in each work the reader is controlled by an omniscient narrator whose sardonic perspective of events and characters probes beneath the surface of appearances and emphasizes the impossibility of realizing ideal human values. In Conrad's revisions to the manuscript and serial versions of the shorter fiction he intensifies its ironic impact, foregrounding the grotesque elements and adding concrete descriptive details.[2] As a result, "An Outpost of Progress" demonstrates with remarkable clarity some of the techniques Conrad used later to create his vision of social and moral disorder in *The Secret Agent*.

"An Outpost of Progress" was not Conrad's first attempt to write a short narrative in the manner of Maupassant or Flaubert. Two months earlier, he had completed "The Idiots," a melodramatic story about a Breton peasant who kills her husband and then throws herself over a cliff because she thinks his ghost is haunting her. Although this story is written in the ironic mode like "An Outpost of Progress," it lacks the latter's concentrated economy. In the following discussion a brief comparison of the two works will indicate why Conrad achieved a greater degree of artistic control in "An Outpost of Progress." In the process, I shall also point out an important thematic correspondence between that short story and the novel, *The Secret Agent*.

In "The Idiots" Conrad's chief protagonists are the helpless victims of circumstances and social conditions. As peasants who must live in harmony with "the earth beloved and fruitful,"[3] Susan and Jean-Pierre Bacadou are doomed to suffer because a "high and impassive heaven" has decreed that Susan bear only idiot children. Five years later in "Amy Foster" Conrad introduced a sympathetic narrator to tell the story of Yanko Goorall, an archetypal scapegoat like Susan, and the result was a moving narrative with universal appeal. "The Idiots" is not a success because it lacks a narrator within the peasant community who can describe

Susan's despair from a sympathetic point of view. At the same time, Conrad cannot adopt a Maupassant-like detachment from his subject. Whereas Maupassant records the events of his "Aux champs" and "Histoire d'une fille de ferme" with realistic objectivity,[4] Conrad experiments with Gothic effects such as a moonlit graveyard, "unearthly" shrieks, a darkly sinister church tower, and a ghost. He also tries to enhance the pathos of his characters' plight by using emotive terms to describe the setting (for example, the bare trees on the hillside sway "sadly" in the wind, "as if contorted with pain" [70]). As a result, his writing tends to be melodramatic rather than concrete and suggestive.

In "An Outpost of Progress" Conrad has no such problems with narrative perspective. Kayerts and Carlier, the incompetent protagonists, can be viewed with detachment because they represent a society determined to sacrifice ethical values for material profit. Thus, Conrad extends his criticism of individual Europeans such as Almayer, Willems, and even Lingard (who seek wealth and influence in the colonial world) to include the materialistic aspects of European society as a whole. Kayerts is a state bureaucrat and Carlier, a soldier: together, they stand for the very foundations of an "enlightened" social order. Moreover, the Director's references to the home office and the emphasis on the Company as a symbol of civilized greed expose the economic system behind the individual colonialist: "The men being Company's men the ivory is Company's ivory" is Carlier's rationalization of the slave trade (106). In *The Secret Agent* Conrad explores the soulless materialism at the heart of civilized society "at home" in London.[5] As Mr. Verloc walks past Hyde Park on his way to meet with Vladimir, he surveys

> the evidences of the town's opulence and luxury with an approving eye. All these people had to be protected. Protection is the first necessity of opulence and luxury. They had to be protected; and their horses, carriages, houses, servants had to be protected in the heart of the city and the heart of the country; the whole social order favourable to their hygienic idleness had to be protected against the shallow enviousness of unhygienic labour.[6]

The changes Conrad made to the story's title in the manuscript of "An Outpost of Progress" trace the evolution of this satirical focus. Thus, on page 1 the title reads "A Victim of Progress," referring to Kayerts, the station chief. Conrad apparently decided to include Carlier when he was writing page 5, because the title "Two V. of P." is noted in the top left-hand corner. The more inclusive final version, "An Outpost of Progress," appears on the title page, which (according to Robert Hobson)[7] postdates the manuscript revisions and was probably added when Conrad prepared the typescript. The implications of this phrase and the deceptively innocent opening sentence ("There were two white men in charge of the trading station") may have led the contemporary reader to expect a story justifying English imperialist morality. After all, Kipling's "Slaves of the Lamp" had been featured in the preceding issue of *Cosmopolis,* where "An Outpost of Progress" first appeared in print.[8] However, the description of Kayerts and Carlier that follows the opening sentence establishes the narrator's ironic intention quickly and decisively. In *A Rhetoric of Irony* Wayne Booth describes "stable irony" as a process in which the reader is first asked to reject the literal meaning and then, following clues in the text, to reconstruct the statement in harmony with the implied author's intention.[9] In "An Outpost of Progress" and *The Secret Agent,* this reconstruction takes place within the first few sentences and guarantees the reader's confident discrimination of shades of meaning throughout the work.

In summary, the style of "An Outpost of Progress" can be distinguished from that of "The Idiots" by its satiric thrust. In contrast to the heavy situational irony in the earlier story, Conrad's rhetoric in "An Outpost of Progress" falls into D. C. Muecke's category of "verbal irony."[10] The author's ironic intention is sustained for the most part by an omniscient narrator (more sardonic than any of the narrators in the works of Maupassant or Flaubert) who guides our interpretation of events by pointing out comic juxtapositions, parallels, and discrepancies. The rhetorical significance of this technique should not be underrated, as it is by some critics who find the short story too much like Kipling's "The Man Who Would Be King." Lawrence Graver, for example, maintains that

> the similarities between "The Man Who Would Be King" and "An Outpost of Progress" are too close to be wholly accidental. Aside from the occasional tonal likeness, both stories describe the breakdown of two European egoists who had hoped to get rich quickly in a primitive society, and both end with scenes of slaughter and crucifixion. At the close of Kipling's tale, Peachey Carnehan pulls the dried, withered head of his friend Dravot from a paper bag, an act similar in grotesque impact to Kayerts' suicide on the cross. Conrad's use of high-spirited gallows humor to treat squalid materials seems like an attempt to capitalize on a fictional fashion which Kipling had established by himself.[11]

In order to see Conrad's relationship to Kipling in its true light, however, we must consider the moral impact of their stories on the reader.

The chief protagonist of "The Man Who Would Be King" is Dan Dravot, a white man who achieves kingship over remote Himalayan tribesmen by pretending to be a god. When he insists on marrying a native girl, he loses his "divinity," and his subjects respond by casting him into a gully. With the comic bravado that has characterized his conduct up to this point, Dravot asks Peachey Carnehan (his cohort) for forgiveness, and challenges his captors to cut the ropes. Peachey returns to civilization (a Bombay pressroom) to provide an eye-witness account for the "respectable" journalist who is the author's surrogate. Although Kipling pokes fun at the hero's grandiose schemes and ambitions, Peachey's narration is sympathetic to Dravot and elegiac in tone. Moreover, the journalist-listener does not contradict Peachey's depiction of Dravot as a resourceful rogue who is redeemed by the manner of his death. In other words, Kipling's narrative technique (the limited perspective) allows him to endorse the contemporary paternalistic attitude towards the Indians, for Peachey's testimony indicates that although Dravot becomes a reasonably effective king, the natives require an omnipotent "god" to rule them.

In contrast, the narrator of "An Outpost of Progress" distances us from the protagonists; like the omniscient narrator of *The Secret Agent,* he discriminates among various degrees of criminality and stupidity, and permits no heroes. Moreover, from the opening description of Kayerts and Carlier, the ludicrously mismatched agents who are "in charge" of the station, to the final irony that exposes the Director to a grotesque form of his own grim humour this narrator guarantees our silent participation in his uncompromising evaluation of the imperialist myth. "I am sure You will understand the reason and meaning of every detail," Conrad wrote when he sent the typescript of the story to Edward Garnett.[12]

As we have seen, "stable irony" involves the sharing of values and beliefs between the reader and the implied author. In fictions such as "An Outpost of Progress" and *The Secret Agent,* which emphasize the folly and hopelessness of man's attempt to organize his world, this silent complicity takes on a certain defensiveness, illustrated by Cunninghame Graham's response to "An Outpost of Progress." He praised the story because it was "true to life—; therefore unpopular."[13] *The Secret Agent* was similarly unpopular with the reading public of the day, who found the novel "sordid" and objected to "the moral squalor of the tale."[14] The ironic narrative perspective, which we identify with the implied author because it is reliably supported by the text as a whole, seeks to control and persuade us by inviting our recognition of significant incongruities and parallels. We are not asked to interpret, to fill in hermeneutic gaps, but to take a moral stand with the author. In "An Outpost of Progress," this stand is against the imperialist writers in *Blackwood's Magazine* and journalists in the daily papers. Thus, although the setting, themes, and some motifs in "An Outpost of Progress" are similar to Conrad's later story "Heart of Darkness," the narrative method invites the reader to recognize meanings rather than create them.

In his study of "Heart of Darkness" Cedric Watts points out that the title of the longer story balances two profoundly metaphoric terms in an ambiguous relationship, from which the reader can infer both "a mysterious or evil human heart" and "the core of a metaphysical darkness."[15] For his title "An Outpost of Progress," however, Conrad selected a familiar phrase from imperialist rhetoric, thus ironically turning the enemy's own words against him. Indeed, this tactic yields some of the more blatant of the story's multiple ironies, and it never fails to alert the reader to the bitter discrepancies between idealistic words and reality. Thus, Kayerts and Carlier, at ease on their verandah, are described in contemporary journalese as "the two pioneers of trade and progress" (93). Even more destructive is Conrad's parody of the newspaper report from "home" which eulogizes "those who went about bringing light, and faith, and commerce to the dark places of the earth" (94). Here, the sardonic emphasis on "commerce" subverts the idealistic rhetoric, censuring both "masquerading philanthropy"[16] and those who believe in its flattering disguises.

Carlier, then, is ridiculed because he is moved by the "high-flown language" in the newspaper to dream of "Quays, and warehouses, and barracks, and—and—

billiard-rooms. Civilization, my boy, and virtue—and all'' (95). The irony deepens when he responds to his first real test, as supplies run short, by talking about "the necessity of exterminating all the niggers" (108), but a protagonist who equates billiard rooms with virtue and civilization cannot be taken very seriously. One of the reasons we find Kurtz's postscript—"Exterminate all the brutes!"—so shockingly ironic is that it follows an account of "burning, noble words" which (after the first two phrases) we never hear. Marlow interprets this silence for us, scornfully, as "the notion of an exotic Immensity ruled by an august Benevolence"; and his terms, because they must suggest the ineffable, defy an analysis of Kurtzian "ideas" and "plans." Yet, like the "unspeakable rites" in the wilderness, and like Marlow's conception of Kurtz himself, the imprecise and the metaphoric involve us in a process of definition. "Make him [the reader] *think* the evil, make him think it for himself," writes Henry James in his preface to *The Aspern Papers,* "and you are released from weak specifications." In contrast, Carlier's enthusiasm for "the sacredness of the civilizing work" and "Our Colonial Expansion" is mocked because he specifies "barracks" and "billiard-rooms." The discrepancy between this "civilizing work" and "exterminating the niggers" is comic, and the reader is invited to judge and condemn rather than speculate or participate.

The omniscient narrator of "An Outpost of Progress" is telling a cruel joke, and arranges his material so that the "point" is pressed home relentlessly from the beginning of the story to its appallingly grotesque climax. Unlike Marlow, who is self-consciously aware of the ambiguity and inadequacy of his words, and who corrects and contradicts himself in the narrative process, he seeks to convince and persuade. In fact, at certain times the narrator strategically underlines the ironic discrepancies and other indirect information in the text with passages of straightforward commentary.

The opening description of Kayerts and Carlier and their arrival at the outpost, for example, gives us the impression of their childish incompetence indirectly, through ironic contrasts. The two white men are "in charge of" the station, but Makola, the native assistant, is in charge of the trading. Similarly, Kayerts and Carlier are described in terms of their ungainly physical features, while Makola is credited with a catalogue of practical accomplishments. Even the white men's untidy litter reflects obliquely on their hapless situation, for the agents themselves have been thrown on shore by the Director like rubbish, along with the cotton goods and the provisions, and the scornful remark, "At any rate, I am rid of them for six months" (88). Conrad also derides the usefulness of their past careers in the cavalry and the Administration of Telegraphs by placing their professional behaviour in a wilderness setting. In the midst of forests and impenetrable bush "that seemed to cut off the station from the rest of the world," Carlier wonders about commissions, and Kayerts expresses himself "correctly" in bureaucratic slogans.

Confirming our impression of the agents' disabling helplessness, the narrator tells us that Makola "despised" the two white men, and the Director elaborates:

"I always thought the station on this river useless, and they just fit the station!" (88). At this point, Conrad speaks to us directly in a passage which recapitulates all the preceding information: Kayerts and Carlier have always been "under the eye and guidance of their superiors," they are "dull . . . to the subtle influences of surroundings," they feel abandoned when "suddenly left unassisted." Thus, we are led inexorably to the conclusion that civilized society necessarily fosters a dangerous dependence: "They were two perfectly insignificant and incapable individuals, whose existence is only rendered possible through the high organization of civilized crowds" (89). In this explicit statement of the main theme, Conrad satirizes the social structure that has produced the incompetent agents.

An attentive reader might suspect, however, from the tone of the narrator's "They were two perfectly insignificant and incapable individuals [just as we are]" the intention to involve him by invoking his own membership in the "civilized crowds." The sentence that immediately follows confirms this suspicion: "Few men realize that their life, the very essence of their character, their capabilities and their audacities, are only the expression of their belief in the safety of their surroundings." Conrad abandons Kayerts and Carlier and the rueful details of their predicament and, as the passage continues, appeals to his readers directly, using inclusive terminology such as "one's thoughts" and "one's sensations" to describe a universal heart of darkness ruled by primitive fear. Because life at the outpost tests "the foolish and the wise alike," the narrator urges the reader who identifies himself with civilized wisdom (the two agents having been cast as the fools) to recognize the hypocrisy of his attitudes.

The narrator speaks to us directly again, when the white men discover Makola's "business deal":

> They believed their words. Everybody shows a respectful deference to certain sounds that he and his fellows can make. But about feelings people really know nothing. We talk with indignation or enthusiasm; we talk about oppression, cruelty, crime, devotion, self-sacrifice, virtue, and we know nothing real beyond the words. Nobody knows what suffering or sacrifice mean—except, perhaps, the victims of the mysterious purpose of these illusions. (105-6)

The initial mention of Kayerts and Carlier introduces a rhetorical plea which makes effective use of repetition, a cumulative word-series, and the all-inclusive "we," in order to involve us. And, in the manner of Marlow's appeals to his listeners on board the *Nellie* ("You can't understand. How could you?") this passage, like the earlier one, tries to provoke the reader by exposing conventional escapes from reality.

In shifting the point of view from sardonic detachment to rhetorical persuasion, Conrad deliberately sacrifices the "scrupulous unity of tone" for which he tells us he strove in this story.[17] The effects of the technique, however, are more obvious in *The Secret Agent,* which contains brilliantly executed modulations such as the familiar passage on revolutionary reformers that begins with Mr. Verloc's thoughts in free indirect style:

As to Ossipon, that beggar was sure to want for nothing as long as there were silly girls with savings-bank books in the world. And Mr. Verloc, temperamentally identical with his associates, drew fine distinctions in his mind on the strength of insignificant differences. He drew them with a certain complacency, because the instinct of conventional respectability was strong within him, being only overcome by his dislike of all kinds of recognized labour—a temperamental defect which he shared with a large proportion of revolutionary reformers of a given social state. For obviously one does not revolt against the advantages and opportunities of that state, but against the price which must be paid for the same in the coin of accepted morality, self-restraint, and toil. The majority of revolutionists are the enemies of discipline and fatigue mostly. There are natures, too, to whose sense of justice the price exacted looms up monstrously enormous, odious, oppressive, worrying, humiliating, extortionate, intolerable. Those are the fanatics. The remaining portion of social rebels is accounted for by vanity, the mother of all noble and vile illusions, the companion of poets, reformers, charlatans, prophets, and incendiaries.

Lost for a whole minute in the abyss of meditation, Mr. Verloc did not reach the depth of these abstract considerations. (53)

The narrator shifts from Verloc's criticism of his friends, a device by which Conrad can satirize the revolutionists and Verloc at the same time, to sardonic omniscient commentary on the latter's character. From here, he moves easily into more provocative, paradoxical references, culminating in a consideration of the "social rebels" motivated by vanity—the universally human trait displayed by most characters in the novel as well as (presumably) the reader himself. At the end of the passage, however, the narrator resumes his satire of Verloc, and the agent's "meditation" (that is, his preoccupation with thinly disguised personal worries) is ironically juxtaposed with the "abstract considerations" that treat his case as just one of many.

These modulations from specific satirical foci to general commentary in *The Secret Agent* have a further rhetorical function. Through them, Conrad can guarantee the reader's condemnation of some characters more than others. For example, he satirizes the Assistant Commissioner's faults with relatively mild irony, which often modulates into general commentary. In the following passage, the narrator shifts from verbal play with the term "natural" to a grotesque figure of speech, and then to a gnomic phrase ("We can never cease to be ourselves") that modifies the reader's sense of ironic detachment by making a direct appeal: "It was natural. He was a born detective. It had unconsciously governed his choice of a career, and if it ever failed him in life it was perhaps in the one exceptional circumstance of his marriage—which was also natural. It fed, since it could not roam abroad, upon the human material which was brought to it in its official seclusion. We can never cease to be ourselves" (117–18).

In the same episode the narrator dramatizes Chief Inspector Heat's thoughts so that his personal predicament has the widest possible human reference. Thus, Heat is likened to a tightrope walker having his rope shaken in the middle of a performance by the manager of the Music Hall:

> Indignation, the sense of moral insecurity engendered by such a treacherous proceeding joined to the immediate apprehension of a broken neck, would, in the colloquial phrase, put him in a state. And there would be also some scandalized concern for his art, too, since a man must identify himself with something more tangible than his own personality, and establish his pride somewhere, either in his social position, or in the quality of the work he is obliged to do, or simply in the superiority of the idleness he may be fortunate enough to enjoy. (116–17)

Incidentally, Conrad used the image of the tightrope walker in a letter of August 31, 1898[18] to describe his attitude toward his own art. He also echoed the reference to the Assistant Commissioner's plight ("We can never cease to be ourselves") in his "Author's Note" to *Tales of Unrest*. Writing about the personal aspect of style, he said "We cannot escape from ourselves." In *The Secret Agent* Conrad introduces general commentary to make sympathy possible for characters such as Heat, the Assistant Commissioner, and even Verloc, whose motives, being familiar to the reader, are perhaps more easily shared, but rarely for the extremist Professor and never for the "sham revolutionaries"[19] (Michaelis, Ossipon, and Yundt) or Vladimir. At the same time, as in "An Outpost of Progress" this narrative technique challenges us to recognize our own membership in a civilized "herd" that stifles individuality and passionate feeling.

The narrative structure of "An Outpost of Progress," which recalls Maupassant, contributes to the ironic impact of the story. In a letter objecting to the proposed publication in two installments Conrad wrote: "All the sting—so to speak—is in the tail,"[20] alluding to the favourite Maupassant ending, climactic irony. The fact that Conrad revised Carlier's advice to Kayerts at the end of part 1 in the serial and the subsequent book editions before he learned that "the unspeakable idiots" planned to divide the story is significant. The manuscript reads: "Keep all our men together to-day" (MS 16), and the revision, "Keep all our men together in case of some trouble," has been traced to the missing typescript,[21] which predates the serial version. Thus, Conrad made the change in order to heighten the sense of an inevitable working out of events rather than accommodate a proposed division. In fact, his practice of "chaptering" his novels after the first draft had been completed indicates that he tended to think in terms of blocks of action; that is, with a sense of dramatic effect.[22] Tightness of construction is particularly evident in *The Secret Agent,* where dramatic irony seems to circumscribe and compress the characters' actions from chapter 8 to the end of the novel.

In the first part of "An Outpost of Progress" all the elements of a potentially disastrous situation are present: the isolation, the climate, Makola's cunning, the white men's stupidity and sloth. Then, as if in a Maupassant story, "one morning" the outside world impinges upon the quiet scene, and "a knot of armed men came out of the forest and advanced towards the station" (97). The resulting chain of events is therefore inevitable, but it is not predictable, as the resolutions of Maupassant's tales often are. The ironic parallels in "An Outpost of Progress" add complexity and richness to the climactic form as the reader discovers more and more evidence of Conrad's moral attitude towards soulless materialism. Also, the modulations in the narrator's ironic tone create significant contrasts. We cannot condemn the friendly Gobila, for example, although Conrad takes care, in his manuscript revisions, to underline the native's childish lack of discrimination. Thus, "Gobila loved the white men" becomes "Gobila's manner was paternal and he seemed really to love (the) all white men" (MS 12). However, the satirical irony directed toward the old chieftain rebounds on Gobila's two "brothers" whom he considers "immortal": they are only fond of him "in a way" (unfraternally, that is) and their mysterious powers consist of striking matches "recklessly"[23] and offering ammonia bottles for sniffing (96). The white men's attitude of superiority toward their host is emphasized along with the chief's comically naive speculations.

The narrative straightforwardness of "An Outpost of Progress" does not preclude complexity, but it does eliminate ambiguity. In "Heart of Darkness" the meanings of terms such as "efficiency," "idea," and "belief" shift as Marlow's audience in the narrative present interrupts his telling of past events. What Conrad means by "progress" in the earlier story, on the other hand, is clear at the beginning, and becomes emphatic at the end. The "sting in the tail" is the antithesis of the ever-widening circle that opens out when Marlow falls silent and the forgotten "I" on board the yawl takes us into "the heart of an immense darkness" that is past and present, private and public, metaphoric as well as palpable.

In "An Outpost of Progress" Conrad controls our responses by reserving the broader implications of his irony for the latter half of the story, after the native workers have been traded for ivory. In the beginning, for example, the narrator's portrayal of Makola is playfully sardonic. The assistant is a grotesque blend of savagery and sophistication. He affects the white men's culture by calling himself "Henry Price" (and his wife "Mrs. Price") but his native name has "stuck to him" in spite of his efforts and his travels. Similarly, his civilized accomplishments (foreign languages, beautiful handwriting, and bookkeeping) are only skin-deep, for "in his innermost heart" he cherishes "the worship of evil spirits" (86). Moreover, while he maintains a neat, correct appearance and a studied indifference to events, his wife is embarrassingly large, noisy, and excitable. To compound the comic incongruities, Mrs. Makola appears to be in charge of her husband when the slave traders arrive. All in all, the irony is biting, but limited in scope.

On the night of the kidnapping and afterwards, however, Makola's diligence is linked to the ruthless greed of the Great Trading Company. "I know my business," he whispers to the confused Kayerts while the men are being captured and shot (102). When the "business" is exposed the next morning, his parody of the faithful servant confirms the true role of the Company and its absent Director: "I did my best for you and the Company" (104). At this point, the narrator depicts Makola as a family man, in a fiercely ironic cliché: "Makola retired into the bosom of his family; and the tusks, left lying before the store, looked very large and valuable in the sunshine" (104). The children are particularly emphasized, as "he lay full-length on a mat outside his door, and the youngsters sat on his chest and clambered all over him." Later, he bathes them in the river.

There are many ironic references to family relationships in "An Outpost of Progress," but the domestic scene picturing a father playing contentedly with his children in the sun is the most savage. Because Conrad juxtaposes this scene with the discovery of one of Gobila's men, who has been shot through the body, he underlines even more heavily his condemnation of the exploiters and the absence of human solidarity at the outpost. Kayerts's platitude from colonialist rhetoric, "We took care of them [the station men] as if they had been our children," is also scathing, because in the first half of the story he and Carlier are portrayed metaphorically as children themselves, fresh from "the fostering care" of bureaucrats in Europe (91). When they arrive at the station, for example, they face the dangers of the unknown by "drawing close to one another as children do in the dark," and their first day is spent playing house, "pottering about with hammers and nails and red calico" (90).

And so, as the events that will end in the disintegration of the "brotherhood" between Kayerts and Carlier are set in motion by the trade, the narrator's irony becomes more censorious. Makola betrays his fellows because of his "civilized" ties to the Company; and the white men in their "paternal" role toward the native workers speak for the "progress" that denies traditional bonds of love, respect, and responsibility. Thus, the ironic mode, which distances us from the characters so that we can judge them, works well within the climactic shape of "An Outpost of Progress" in order to make us see with increasing intensity the horrifying gulf between idealistic illusions and the nightmarish reality.

In "Heart of Darkness" we share Marlow's moral perspective when he describes the efficient chief accountant at the Outer Station (who makes "correct entries of perfectly correct transactions" while men are dying nearby) or the native guarding his fellow natives with a gun and a "large, white, rascally grin" (16). Either one of these could be Makola, and each one of them, we condemn. In addition to Marlow's irony, however, the narrative form of "Heart of Darkness" permits Conrad to affirm some essential, human ties—through our identification with Marlow, for example, when he offers a ship's biscuit to the dying worker; through the conflation of times and places that gives the men on board the *Nellie* (who have worked with others at sea) an understanding of the native helmsman who was learning, under Marlow, how to navigate; and through the expressiveness of archetypal symbols, such as the journey.

"An Outpost of Progress," in contrast, focusses on the ironic incongruities that deny such affirmations. In the closing section, after Kayerts wakes into the nightmare of reality beside Carlier's corpse, Conrad uses grotesque dramatized images to shock us into seeing Kayerts's position. First, the agent's cry of prayer—"Help! . . . My God!"—is answered by the screeching steamer, which is "Progress":

> A shriek inhuman, vibrating and sudden, pierced like a sharp dart the white shroud of that land of sorrow. Three short, impatient screeches followed, and then, for a time, the fog-wreaths rolled

on, undisturbed, through a formidable silence. Then many more shrieks, rapid and piercing, like the yells of some exasperated and ruthless creature, rent the air. Progress was calling to Kayerts from the river. *Progress and civilization and all the virtues.* Society was calling to its accomplished child to come, to be taken care of, to be instructed, to be judged, to be condemned; it called him to return to that rubbish heap from which he had wandered away, so that justice could be done. Kayerts heard and understood. (116; my italics)

The unexpectedness of the distortion (the bestial steamer) and the juxtaposition of an inhuman shriek with a human prayer forces the reader (by disorienting him) to share Kayerts's sense of helplessness before the parental monster, civilized materialism. In fact, the dramatization of cruel implacability is considerably more effective than the narrator's explication following it, although the echo from Carlier's earlier eulogy ("Civilization, my boy, and virtue—and all") is fine irony.

Conrad uses a grotesquely elaborated image again for the "sting in the tail," thus exaggerating the impact of the ironic surprise at the climax. Dangling from the cross at his predecessor's grave, Kayerts presents us with a violent fusion of marionette and human corpse, or inanimate form and animate gesture. The conventional Maupassant ending seems decorous in comparison with this macabre conclusion: "His toes were only a couple of inches above the ground; his arms hung stiffly down; he seemed to be standing rigidly at attention, but with one purple cheek playfully posed on the shoulder. And, irreverently, he was putting out a swollen tongue at his Managing Director" (117). In the dramatized image of Kayerts as the puppet of Progress, Conrad uses grotesque distortion to focus the critical ironies of the story on a single target: the Great Trading Company. In the end, the "joke" is on the Director—a man who, as we have seen in his earlier address to the new chief, "at times, but very imperceptibly, indulged in grim humour" (87). And, as he fumbles ineptly in his pockets, his discomposure reflects the reader's sudden displacement from a safe, ironic detachment to an uneasiness that results from the mingling of horror with a practical joke. Our ambivalence involves us in the narrator's derisive protest.

Conrad revised both of these images to make them more concrete and immediate. In the manuscript he altered the description of the steamer's shrieks from "like yells of a masterful exasperation" to "like the yells of an exasperated and fabulous animal," and finally to "like the yells of some exasperated and ruthless creature" (MS 35). Thus revised, the simile fuses animal and machine, and the substitution of "ruthless" for "fabulous" changes the tone of the grotesque from fantasy to menace. The impression of sharpness is added, figuratively and aurally, by changing the verb "followed" to "rent," which immediately follows the simile. Conrad polished the final image in the manuscript and also before the book version of the story. In the manuscript he revised "He seemed to be standing rigidly at attention but with his head playfully on the shoulder" to "He seemed to be standing rigidly at attention but with one purple cheek playfully posed on the shoulder" (MS 36). Thus, he achieves visual immediacy as well as a nice anticipation of the last gesture (putting out the tongue) in the suggestion of Kayerts "posing" himself. Finally, preparing the story for *Tales of Unrest,* Conrad changed "feet" to "toes" so that the sentence read "His toes were only a couple of inches above the ground," yielding a more concrete metaphor—a visual image of the human puppet stretched out and dangling.

Modulations from irony to the grotesque involve a shift for the reader from intellectual engagement to sense experience and emotional response. In "An Outpost of Progress" the grotesque images achieve the result Conrad perhaps was hoping for when he experimented with Gothic effects in "The Idiots." However, as we have seen, the narrator also comments ironically in the climactic scene of "Outpost," controlling us crudely with sarcasm.[24] In *The Secret Agent* Conrad creates a narrative point of view that modulates more skilfully and more consistently from rhetorical irony to a grotesque vision of a chaotic and fragmented world. Moreover, as the ironic mode shifts from comic (or satiric) to tragic, and the Verlocs' "domestic drama" becomes the central focus, Conrad combines grotesque elements with dramatic irony in order to involve the reader more directly.

Scenes in the latter part of the novel such as the cab ride and the murder of Verloc contain many grotesque elements that include both subject matter (the cab driver whose body is partly flesh and partly "hooked iron contrivance") and technique (the narrator suddenly focusses on a detail, for instance, and enlarges it beyond realistic proportions, as when Winnie's mother's big cheeks glow orange in the gaslight). As our reaction to the hanging puppet at the end of "An Outpost of Progress" shows, stable communication based on shared values between reader and narrator dissolves under the influence of the grotesque, and we lose our safe vantage point from which to criticize the characters' actions. In *The Secret Agent* more than in "An Outpost of Progress" Conrad constructs a delicate balance between stable irony and the grotesque. Moreover, the concentration of grotesque elements in the latter part of the novel accompanies an ironic structure from chapter 8 to the end that directs our attention to the situation of the victims rather than their deviation from a moral standard of behaviour. When the narrator tells us that Winnie's mother "would avoid the horrible incertitude on the death-bed" because she would know then the results of her heroic sacrifice, he exploits this dramatic irony. We see that although Winnie and her mother have been guilty of narrow-mindedness and secrecy, they are overwhelmed by a predetermined catastrophe out of proportion to their guilt.

In contrast, despite the grotesque images and the sudden shift in perspective when Kayerts realizes that he has shot Carlier, "An Outpost of Progress" engages the reader most effectively on an intellectual level. The verbal irony of the narrator and the Flaubertian juxtapositions and parallels comprise a rhetoric that expresses an intensely critical view of society with sardonic energy. In the "Author's Note" to *Tales of Unrest* Conrad says: "I seemed able to capture new reactions, new suggestions, and even new rhythms for my paragraphs." Frustrated in his attempts to finish *The Rescue* and doubting his abilities,[25] Conrad wrote this story "with pleasure," as he told Garnett. He returned to the ironic narrative perspective a decade later when, in a similarly unsettled time, he was unhappy with his work on *Chance,* troubled by his lack of creative productivity since *Nostromo,* and even considering writing a play.[26]

Critics have largely neglected the "stable irony" in *The Secret Agent,* focussing instead on ironies of situation or on the "ironic perspective," as J. Hillis Miller calls Conrad's motifs of disjunction and chaos. Those who, like Albert Guerard, find the narrator's irony limited have failed to explore its rich variations in tone. In fact, except for Wayne Booth, recent critics tend to disparage ironic techniques in general as "secondary" and "derivative" compared with "irony as a mode of consciousness" or "metaphysical irony," presumably because reliable ironic narrators are difficult to find in modern fiction.[27] Even in a historical overview such as "Theory of Modes" from *Anatomy of Criticism,* Northrop Frye excludes the rhetorical ironist from his definition of the mode. He writes: "When we try to isolate the ironic as such, we find that it seems to be simply the attitude of the poet as such, a dispassionate construction of a literary form, with all assertive elements, implied or expressed, eliminated."[28] Yet the relationship between the implied author and the reader in this novel is certainly "assertive," for the narrator does not function as a lifeless mask or a detached historian. The difference between *The Secret Agent* and a less assertive novel such as Faulkner's *Sanctuary,* which gives us a similar impression of a fragmented, grotesque world, is that in the former, the narrator's rhetorical tone and strategies keep us from remaining uncritically fascinated or repelled by this world.

The narrator's tone in *The Secret Agent* ranges from dry understatement, which is calculated to provoke the reader into examining words, impressions, and appearances more closely, to savage indignation. Control over the reader is exercised through stylistic features such as qualifying words and phrases, oxymoron, figures of speech, refrains, repetitions, and epithets. The narrator's use of the latter illustrates the moral effectiveness of his irony, since epithets discriminate between characters like Winnie's mother, "the heroic old woman" despite her trappings, and the great lady who, despite *hers,* is only "the aged disciple of Michaelis." In fact, the narrator's ironic tone even determines the prose rhythm of the novel.[29] In the opening description, for example, the paragraphs from the third through the sixth are linked schematically, with the first sentence of each repeating the last words of the paragraph before, to give an ironic impression of neatness and order.

Thus, the first sentence of the fourth paragraph begins, "These customers were either very young men . . . ," which takes up the concluding phrase of the third paragraph: ". . . for the sake of the customers." Similarly, the first sentence of paragraph 5—"The bell, hung on the door by means of a curved ribbon of steel, was difficult to circumvent"—is linked to the last sentence of paragraph 4, which ends " . . . as if afraid to start the bell going." Finally, the first sentence of the sixth paragraph repeats the phrase "it clattered" from the preceding sentence, which ends, "it clattered behind the customer with impudent virulence": "It clattered; and at that signal, through the dusty glass door behind the painted deal counter, Mr. Verloc would issue hastily from the parlour at the back'' (4). As I have suggested, the cumulative effect of these links is ironic because Conrad uses a schematic pattern to describe a scene of disorder: the cluttered shop window, for example, and Mr. Verloc himself, who "had the air of having wallowed, fully dressed, all day on an unmade bed." Moreover, the insistent repetitions draw our attention to the narrator as a source of meaning in the text.

Ironic parallels are another source of meaning in *The Secret Agent* through which Conrad explores the materialism and lack of real solidarity in this society. In the opening description of the shop, Mr. Verloc's customers bear a striking resemblance to their soiled, worthless purchases; and Winnie's provocative charms, which have bought security for Stevie, are juxtaposed with the "faded, yellow dancing girls" sold across the counter. A network of such parallels connects the various characters and episodes in the novel. For example, Chief Inspector Heat and Verloc each try to defend their comfortable position against attack from a superior,[30] and neither Winnie nor the wife of the Assistant Commissioner will risk "going abroad." The same conservatism pervades the entire social organization. One of Conrad's most provocative insights into the workings of a stable democratic society involves the underlying ironic similarity between the burglar and the police officer:

> the mind and the instincts of a burglar are of the same kind as the mind and the instincts of a police officer. Both recognize the same conventions, and have a working knowledge of each other's methods and of the routine of their respective trades. They understand each other, which is advantageous to both, and establishes a sort of amenity in their relations. Products of the same machine, one classed as useful and the other as noxious, they take the machine for granted in different ways, but with a seriousness essentially the same. (92)

Threatening this status quo are the two extremists: the reactionary Vladimir, who instigates a senseless, "inexplicable" act of destruction because he believes that "madness alone is truly terrifying, inasmuch as you cannot placate it either by threats, persuasion, or bribes" (33), and the anarchist Professor, who states: "Madness and despair! Give me that for a lever and I'll move the world!" Like the burglar and the policeman—"one classed [by society] as useful and the other as noxious"—Vladimir and the professor are completely different in their social roles, but on close examination they display a sinister moral and political resemblance.

Another of Conrad's techniques to reveal the disjunction between appearances and reality in *The Secret Agent* is ironic incongruity. Vladimir, the Russian *agent provocateur,* frequents the drawing rooms of the upper classes, where he becomes "the favourite of intelligent society women." However, in grotesque contrast to his urbane mannerisms, Latin phrases, and blue silk socks, Mr. Vladimir's true nature is uncivilized—even savage:

> Then he turned, and advanced into the room with such determination that the very ends of his quaintly old-fashioned bow necktie seemed to bristle with unspeakable menaces. The movement was so swift and fierce that Mr. Verloc, casting an oblique glance, quailed inwardly.
> "Aha! You dare be impudent," Mr. Vladimir began, with an amazingly guttural intonation not only utterly un-English, but absolutely un-European, and startling even to Mr. Verloc's experience of cosmopolitan slums. "You dare! Well, I am going to speak plain English to you. Voice won't do. We have no use for your voice. We don't want a voice. We want facts—startling facts—damn you," he added, with a sort of ferocious discretion, right into Mr. Verloc's face.
> "Don't you try to come over me with your Hyperborean manners," Mr. Verloc defended himself, huskily, looking at the carpet. (24–25)

Similarly, Verloc, the "celebrated" secret agent of the book's title, whose confidential reports "had the power to change the schemes and the dates of royal, imperial, grand-ducal journeys, and sometimes cause them to be put off altogether," is revealed as thoroughly domesticated and conventional—*l'homme moyen sensuel.* And Sir Ethelred, a Liberal politician engaged in the "revolutionary" task of nationalizing the fisheries, symbolizes the aristocracy's reluctance to see beyond the established order: consider his weak eyesight and his aversion to details. Like the ironic parallels in the novel, the web of incongruities alerts the reader to Conrad's central moral theme: the tragic disjunction between the comfortable world of appearances and the "madness and despair" beneath the surface.

In a much more limited way, Conrad experiments with similar techniques in "An Outpost of Progress." Revisions to the story in the manuscript and typescript versions show an ongoing process that enhances the ironic impact on the reader. He took particular care with the long descriptive passage at the beginning of the story, and to Garnett's criticism that the opening destroyed the reader's interest in the characters, he replied that the ironic technique had been "a matter of conscious decision."[31] Revisions to this passage intensify the mocking tone of the omniscient narrator, concentrating on the selection and arrangement of details for ironic effect. In the manuscript Carlier is originally described as having "a very broad trunk and a large head on a long pair of thin legs" (MS 1). Conrad reversed the first two features and substituted "perched upon" for "on" to create a comic "top to bottom" order in which Carlier's weight balances precariously on the cranelike legs: "Carlier, the second, was tall with a large head and a very broad trunk perched upon a long pair of thin legs." In another revision he replaced explicit commentary on the agents' lack of moral fibre with concrete details and the sardonic modifier "mysteriously," to suggest the point less crudely. Thus, the litter of "open boxes, belongings of the white men who were untidy having no inducement to be otherwise" became "open half empty boxes, torn wearing apparel, old boots—the things dirty, and the things broken that accumulate mysteriously round untidy men" (MS 1–2).

The initial description of Makola was also revised in the manuscript. In the following sentence Conrad added to the list of his accomplishments and changed the word order of the last phrase to make it parallel with the others. The final result emphasizes the contrast between Makola's civilized appearance and his savage nature: "He *spoke English and French with a warbling accent,* wrote a beautiful hand, understood book-keeping and (in his innermost heart cherished the worship of) cherished in his innermost heart the worship of evil spirits" (MS 1).* A similar revision later in the paragraph reinforced this ironic juxtaposition: "Then (in the intervals of bookkeeping he communed alone with the Evil) for a time he dwelt alone with his family, his account books, and with the Evil Spirit that rules the lands under the equator" (MS 2). With the addition of the phrase "pretended to," Conrad also alerted the reader to Makola's trickery within the first few sentences: "He had charge of a small clay storehouse with a palm-leaf roof and *pretended to* keep *a* correct account of beads, cotton cloths, red kerchiefs, brass wire, *and other trade goods it contained"* (MS 1).

Subsequent changes to the same paragraph at the typescript stage included the addition of a brief sentence, "He got on very well with his god," that emphasizes Makola's unholy communion with the Evil Spirit and establishes an ironic comparison with Kayerts's despairing cry for help to an "invisible heaven" at the end of the story. Conrad also continued to experiment with rhythm and diction in order to emphasize his ironic intention. Thus, "Perhaps he promised him more white men to play with" became, probably at the typescript stage, "Perhaps he had propitiated him by a promise of more white men to play with, by and by." By the time the story appeared in *Cosmopolis* the opening paragraph (one of the longest Conrad ever wrote) had been painstakingly revised to set the tone for the events that follow.

Similarly, the ironic parallels in "An Outpost of Progress" anticipate those in *The Secret Agent.* For example, the narrator does not introduce the group of ten native workers until the pivotal point in the story, when the arrival of the slave traders has instigated the action involving Makola and the agents. In the manuscript Conrad cancels a reference to "the working hands of the station" (MS 2) in the opening paragraph—apparently the advantages of withholding mention of the men occurred to him as he was writing. The delay allows us to connect the workers' miserable plight with that of Kayerts and Carlier, who provide useless medical attention while trying to get the men to work. The narrator describes the natives' exile with sardonic detachment: "They were not happy, regretting the festive incantations, the sorceries, the human sacrifices of their own land; where they also had parents, brothers, sisters, admired chiefs, respected magicians, loved friends, and other ties supposed generally to be human" (100). We must recognize, in this commentary, the ironic bond between exploiters and exploited, for the white men are like the natives in their exile from their own land, in their prison fare (the rice rations), in their illness, and in their spiritless lethargy. Like the tribal warriors, they have been cut off from the once-daily rhythm of their activities and like the natives too, this has been by their own "agreement," for Kayerts is so easily

---

*Throughout this book certain conventions have been employed when quoting passages from Conrad's manuscripts. Italic type indicates words or phrases interlined (added between the lines) and text enclosed in parentheses indicates material that was deleted.

manipulated by the Director that he might as well have engaged himself without understanding the terms of his contract.

We have already learned that Kayerts, like the native men, has his list of regrets: "He regretted the street, the pavements, the cafes, his friends of many years; all the things he used to see, day after day; all the thoughts suggested by familiar things—the thoughts effortless, monotonous, and soothing of a Government clerk; he regretted all the gossip, the small enmities, the mild venom, and the little jokes of Government offices" (91). And Carlier, also, "like Kayerts, regretted his old life. He regretted the clink of sabre and spurs on a fine afternoon, the barrack-room witticisms, the girls of garrison towns" (92). Thus, the narrator emphasizes the common lot of all the victims, while the comic parallelisms reveal that the petty rituals of the white men are much less attractive or admirable than the savage rites of the tribe. As the two agents degenerate into animals fighting each other over fifteen lumps of sugar, their situation becomes pitiable. Unlike the station men, however, Kayerts and Carlier are severely judged.

As the white men examine the visiting native traders from the superior height (and safety) of their verandah, they are themselves examined with Flaubertian irony. The stately movements of the warriors are compared with Carlier's swaggering and moustache-twirling; and Kayerts's dull, blue-eyed stare is juxtaposed with the natives' "quick, wild glances." Sharing the narrator's Olympian view of the two men, we share, as well, his silent contempt—particularly when he dramatizes their complacency in direct dialogue. Carlier's criticism of the warriors (who are "perfect of limb") reduces the agent to a figure of fun: "Fine arms, but legs no good below the knee. Couldn't make cavalry men of them" (93). Furthermore, both men's haughty references to "the funny brute," "fine animals," and "that herd" are crude exaggerations of the social Darwinism popular among contemporary expansionists. Without the aid of narrative commentary, the scene exposes civilized pretensions with a deliberation that guarantees the reader's contempt and forbids identification.

Another scene that exhibits Flaubertian economy is the discovery of the station men's disappearance. Ian Watt refers to the similarity in theme between "An Outpost of Progress" and *Bouvard et Pécuchet,* the novel about two clerks who embody the *idées réçues* and the practical incompetence of bourgeois society.[32] In style also, on occasion, Conrad's reduction of his two heroes reminds one of Flaubert's deliberately flat use of language. As Kayerts and Carlier emerge on the morning after the raid, their movements are synchronized: "In the morning Carlier came out, very sleepy, and pulled at the cord of the big bell. The station hands mustered every morning to the sound of the bell. That morning nobody came. Kayerts turned out also, yawning" (102). The mechanical repetitions of "morning" and "bell," and the short, simple, parallel structures establish a rhythm for the marionette movements of the two men.

The dialogue is similarly patterned. When Kayerts and Carlier learn about the men's mysterious disappearance, their gestures and speech mirror each other like theatrical "stock" responses, emphasizing their ineptness: "They heard him plainly, but in their surprise they both yelled out together: 'What!' Then they stared at one another. 'We are in a proper fix now,' growled Carlier. 'It's incredible!' muttered Kayerts'' (103). The white men's dependence on the "herd" at home is reflected in the safe, automatic platitudes of their speech. They are, in fact, masters of the *idées réçues,* as the following dialogue indicates. This exchange occurs when the agents discover that the men have been traded for ivory, and its artificially neat structure mocks the hollow principles of the men:

> "We can't touch it, of course," said Kayerts.
> "Of course not," assented Carlier.
> "Slavery is an awful thing," stammered out Kayerts in an unsteady voice.
> "Frightful—the suffering," grunted Carlier with conviction. (105)

The narrator's concentration on the external view of his characters makes a silent statement to the reader, for (as we see in their sentimental reactions to the old novels and papers left behind by their predecessor) there is nothing of the inner life to be found in Kayerts and Carlier. Conrad projects their blindness symbolically onto the landscape surrounding the tiny clearing of the outpost: "The river, the forest, all the great land throbbing with life, were like a great emptiness. . . . The river seemed to come from nowhere and flow nowhither. It flowed through a void" (92). Similarly, the courtyard is empty for days at a time in the blinding sunlight, while "stretching away" from the immobile scene are "immense forests, hiding fateful complications of fantastic life" (93-94).

When the pathetic struggle between Kayerts and Carlier begins, however, the narration takes us, all at once, inside Kayerts's awakening intelligence. Just before the agent shoots Carlier, he has "the sudden perception that the position was without issue—that death and life had in a moment become equally difficult and terrible" (112). The shooting is at first simply "a loud explosion," and then "a roar of red fire, thick smoke."[33] The reader must think along with Kayerts as he tries to assemble the pieces and create meaning. It is as if we were present at the birth of a thinking, perceiving imagination, one suddenly capable of interpreting signs. This internal narration culminates in the aftermath of the shooting, when the "fateful complications" which have been hidden in the forests appear before him as sentient ideas: "He sat by the corpse thinking; thinking very actively, thinking very new thoughts. He seemed to have broken loose from himself altogether" (114).

Like Kurtz, who "kicked himself loose from the earth," Kayerts has been a "believer," and his "very new thoughts" are ironically juxtaposed with the ideals he once shared with "the rest of mankind—who are fools." Thus, although Kayerts only begins a journey of self-understanding he has travelled a significant distance from his first mechanical response to danger, when he feared Carlier's death by overexposure because he was incapable of imagining his own. On the edge of madness he barely retains his own identity, for "by a clever and timely effort of mind he saved himself just in time from becoming Carlier" (115). The return of "reason" is celebrated by self-congratulatory cunning, and the careful balancing of the phrase keeps us inside Kayerts's precarious state of mind.

Like Winnie Verloc's descent into an inner world when she learns about Stevie's death in *The Secret Agent,* Kayert's self-examination becomes tranced and depersonalized. The agent, like a corpse himself, sits unmoving beside the dead man through the night: "He sat quiet as if he had taken a dose of opium. The violence of the emotions he had passed through produced a feeling of exhausted serenity. He had plumbed in one short afternoon the depths of horror and despair, and now found repose in the conviction that life had no more secrets for him: neither had death!" (114). Kayerts's "new wisdom" does not evolve from his past experience and bears no resemblance to the pathos of Winnie's thoughts and feelings, but the function of these scenes is similar. Like a brilliantly lit inner stage, they open out another dimension of the perspective at a climactic moment in the action.

In *The Secret Agent* Conrad uses the narrative shift to involve us in Winnie's personal tragedy. Until she learns about Stevie's death, the secrets of Winnie Verloc's inner life are merely intimated, either from the narrator's point of view or her mother's. In this way, Conrad maintains his narrator's sardonic undercutting of the character, while keeping the reader intrigued. Later, confronted with the news about Stevie, Winnie's tragic awareness coincides with the reader's recognition of her life as a rounded whole. The past impinges on the present in the form of concrete images, beginning with Winnie's first memories of Stevie:

> With the rage and dismay of a betrayed woman, she reviewed the tenor of her life in visions concerned mostly with Stevie's difficult existence from its earliest days. It was a life of single purpose and of a noble unity of inspiration, like those rare lives that have left their mark on the thoughts and feelings of mankind. But the visions of Mrs. Verloc lacked nobility and magnificence. She saw herself putting the boy to bed by the light of a single candle on the deserted top floor of a "business house," dark under the roof and scintillating exceedingly with lights and cut glass at the level of the street like a fairy palace. (241-42)

Continuing the pattern of light and dark imagery in the last sentence, Conrad suggests the quality of his character's life: the "dreary shadow of the Belgravian mansion" with its "grimy" kitchen, the suitor ("a fascinating companion for a voyage down the sparkling stream of life") and the lodger, Mr. Verloc ("There was no sparkle of any kind on the lazy stream of his life. It flowed through secret places"). By revealing Winnie's inner thoughts at the very moment when she is torn from the community of the civilized and familiar, Conrad involves us in her catastrophe. Kayerts's self-analysis in "An Outpost of Progress" adumbrates this episode, but it does not engage us in the same way because it involves conventional abstractions ("Life had no more secrets for him") rather than concrete images from a past rich in "fidelity of purpose."

After "An Outpost of Progress" Conrad explored his characters' thoughts and feelings through narrators such as the anonymous crew member of the *Narcissus* and Marlow. In "Heart of Darkness" and *Lord Jim,* for example, Marlow's subjective impressionism draws the reader into a process of interpretation as complex and incomplete as actual experience. The ironic mode, on the other hand, reveals the author's intention clearly instead of suggesting different possible meanings. Although Conrad turned away from the "new reactions, new suggestions, and even new rhythms" he had rehearsed in this early story, the sardonic narrative voice returns in *The Secret Agent*. "An Outpost of Progress" anticipates this masterpiece in its control of the reader through stable irony, sudden shifts in perspective, and grotesque elements. Unlike "Heart of Darkness," with its suggestive ambiguities, the ironic perspective of "An Outpost of Progress" invites our moral judgment of an inhumane and materialistic society.

3

"The Lagoon," "Karain," and *Lord Jim*

In contrast to "The Idiots" and "An Outpost of Progress," "The Lagoon" and "Karain" demonstrate that in his earliest short stories Conrad was also experimenting with a narrative technique that would allow him to affirm certain human values, or "illusions." In this chapter we shall look at the Conradian version of the "told-tale" device in its embryonic form. Moreover, when we compare the narrative mode of these two stories with "An Outpost of Progress" we can see the different aspects of Conrad's thought reflected quite clearly in his art. Whereas the ironic style emphasizes the disjunction between the ideal world and reality, the "teller and listener" mode explores the ways in which human beings can introduce some kind of moral order into their lives. It also expresses, indirectly, Conrad's concern and sympathy for his characters in spite of their limitations.

Let us consider the earliest illustration of the told-tale mode, in a story which Conrad wrote immediately after he had completed "An Outpost of Progress."[1] "The Lagoon" is the first of Conrad's stories about betrayal and redemption. Arsat, the Malay protagonist, has sacrificed his brother so that he and his lover, Diamelen, could escape their enemies and seek refuge. As he tells the story of the betrayal to a visiting white friend, he interrupts himself several times to mourn the woman, who is close to death inside their hut. This evidence of human death and grief provides an ironic context for a story about escape from the real world to "a country where death is forgotten—where death is unknown."[2] Anticipating his juxtaposition of past and present in order to dramatize the passing of illusions in "Youth" and "Heart of Darkness," Conrad has Arsat discover the moral significance of his life as he reconstructs it for a listener in the fictional present. At the end of his story the protagonist rejects the dream of escape and vows to redeem the betrayal with his actions:

> "I shall not eat or sleep in this house, but I must first see my road. Now I can see nothing—see nothing! There is no light and no peace in the world; but there is death—death for many. We are sons of the same mother—and I left him in the midst of enemies; but I am going back now."

> He drew a long breath and went on in a dreamy tone: "In a little while I shall see clear enough to strike—to strike." (203-4)

The anonymous white man who listens involves the reader indirectly in Arsat's tragedy, for his relationship to his friend changes during the course of the tale and his remarks, which are of an interpretive and gnomic nature, suggest a struggle to comprehend. In fact, Conrad's first experiment with tale-telling as a rhetorical device to develop the reader's sympathetic understanding in "The Lagoon" looks forward to Marlow's complex oral performances in "Heart of Darkness" and particularly, *Lord Jim*.

Despite its sketchiness, the relationship between teller and listener in this story deserves attention because it demonstrates clearly, in a simple form, some effects Conrad was to achieve by giving up the omniscient narrative point of view of his earliest works. As Albert Guerard and Ian Watt have shown, Conrad is most effective in *Almayer's Folly* and *An Outcast of the Islands* when, through retrospective narration and techniques of ironic indirection, he distances himself from his characters' inner lives.[3] His attempts to render subjective experience sympathetically are unconvincing because the narrative mode reveals Conrad at his most self-conscious. In these first two novels internal analyses in the omniscient voice tend to be melodramatic, and narrated monologues (in which words and tone are presumed to be the character's) are awkwardly integrated and overstated. The narrator is more confident when he undercuts the protagonists and their illusions: " . . . Almayer . . . would hear the deep and monotonous growl of the Master, and the roared-out interruptions of Lingard—two mastiffs fighting over a marrowy bone. But to Almayer's ears it sounded like a quarrel of Titans—a battle of the gods."[4] As we have seen, the rhetorical ironies of "An Outpost of Progress" distance us even more insistently from Kayerts and Carlier, and invite our critical judgment.

Only a few months before writing this story and "The Lagoon" Conrad had abandoned a novel in which he described the thoughts and emotions of Stephen, a young Russian artist who cannot reconcile his native tendences towards mysticism with the self-centered materialism he finds in western Europe. As an attempt to represent aspects of the author's personal experience and temperament, *The Sisters* displays even more problems with the omniscient narrative mode than *Almayer's Folly* and *An Outcast of the Islands*. In each of these works Conrad was seeking to render his characters' inner lives sympathetically when appropriate, but neither internal analysis (which was too authorial) nor the narrated monologue[5] of a protagonist who shared some of the writer's feelings, offered the rhetorical stance he required in order to explore without self-consciousness. In *The Nigger of the "Narcissus,"* for example, the narrator becomes a member of the crew, reporting thoughts and attitudes collectively and individually from a dramatic point of view within the text.

"The Lagoon," "Karain," and Lord Jim   29

Although "The Lagoon" employs a framing narrator who is partially omniscient, the teller and listener relationship between Arsat and the white man represents Conrad's first attempt to suggest subjective experience dramatically. Abandoning the attempt to explore the feelings of his protagonist authorially, he creates the "raw material" for a narrator like Marlow, who interprets the meaning of a character's experience while dramatizing its mysterious uniqueness. Thus, in *Lord Jim* Marlow's limited perspective prevents us from fully understanding Jim, but the impressionistic structuring of his narration involves us in his changing attitude toward the other's moral point of view. In "The Lagoon" the functions of a narrator who interprets an individual's experience without privileged information about his inner life are divided between Arsat's friend, who listens and responds, and the framing narrator, who describes the scene and comments. Albert Guerard writes perceptively about the significance of the former:

> As yet the white man is only a listener, who can interrupt the adventure narrative (and so lend it suspense) by looking out at the landscape. And as yet he is probably only a half-conscious projection of the author, and only incidentally a "brother" of the criminal. But no very long technical step would need to be taken to a first-person narrator directly responding alike to a soulless universe and to a brother's marginal unintended crime.[6]

Although the white man is "only" a listener, his role is essential because it allows Conrad to dramatize his character's motivations rather than analyze them as he does in previous works. Like Jim when he tries to justify his desertion of the *Patna* to Marlow, Arsat chooses his words for an audience.

Describing the abduction of Diamelen, Arsat appeals to his friend, implicating him indirectly as a "secret sharer" in the action: "'We are of a people who take what they want—*like you whites*. There is a time when a man should forget loyalty and respect. Might and authority are given to rulers, but to all men is given love and strength and courage'" (196; my italics). Even before we know the true nature of Arsat's crime, the claim that "there is a time when a man should forget loyalty" has an unmistakable ring of self-justification. From the beginning of the story, in fact, when the Malay alludes to the adventures the two men have shared in "the time of trouble and war," Arsat draws his listener into the events through their common memories of his brother, of Si Dendring, the Ruler, and Inchi Midah, his wife. "Tuan, do you remember the old days? Do you remember my brother?" he asks, as if the other's affirmation were necessary in order to authenticate his own past and his present moral identity.

In its emphasis on human solidarity and its suggestion of a will to believe on the listener's part, the prologue to Arsat's tale is an early version of the epigraph to *Lord Jim* ("It is certain my conviction gains infinitely the moment another soul will believe in it"):

> "for where can we lay down the heaviness of our trouble but in a friend's heart? A man must speak of war and of love. You, Tuan, know what war is, and you have seen me in time of danger

seek death as other men seek life! A writing may be lost; a lie may be written; but what the eye has seen is truth and remains in the mind!"

"I remember," said the white man, quietly. (194)

Jim prefaces his narration with a similar appeal for a witness to his truth: "I don't want to excuse myself; but I would like to explain—I would like somebody to understand—somebody—one person at least! You! Why not you?"[7] Later, when Marlow responds by remembering Jim's story "at length, in detail and audibly," he acts as a creative historian, confirming the validity of past memories.

The underlying rhetorical purpose of Arsat's tale, then, is his attempt to share the burden of guilt by making it fully comprehensible to others as well as himself. Conrad suggests the nature of this understanding between teller and listener by dramatizing its dynamic process. Before Arsat begins his story, the first narrator describes the relationship between the two from the white man's point of view:

He liked the man who knew how to keep faith in council and how to fight without fear by the side of his white friend. He liked him—not so much perhaps as a man likes his favourite dog—but still he liked him well enough to help and ask no questions, to think sometimes vaguely and hazily in the midst of his own pursuits, about the lonely man and the long-haired woman with audacious face and triumphant eyes, who lived together hidden by the forests—alone and feared. (191-92)

The mildly sardonic tone of the comparison between the useful Malay and a man's faithful dog suggests that the narrator's conception of friendship is not as limited by racial bias as the white man's. At the end of the story, the listener (and indirectly, the reader) seems to see that his "own pursuits" are not unconnected to Arsat's trouble. Thus, the Malay's confession of betrayal and his statement, "Tuan, I loved my brother," evokes a thoughtful response: "We all love our brothers."

The white man's offer of assistance to Arsat is a more explicit indication that the listener's sympathetic imagination has been affected by the story. Conrad juxtaposes this offer ("If you want to come with me, I will wait all the morning") with nature's indifference to human suffering: "In the merciless sunshine the whisper of unconscious life grew louder, speaking in an incomprehensible voice round the dumb darkness of that human sorrow" (203). Moreover, Conrad uses the white man's gesture of solidarity to clarify Arsat's moral position; that is, it gives the protagonist a choice between escape and fidelity to a personal ideal of conduct. In this respect also, "The Lagoon" anticipates *Lord Jim*. Jim's refusal to "clear out" when urged by Marlow not to submit to certain punishment in the courtroom convinces the older man of his moral superiority to the German captain of the *Patna* and his second engineer. It also initiates a sequence of willed actions (ending when Jim goes to his death) that replaces the earlier pattern of desertion and evasion. The Malay's decision to return to the place of his brother's death ("We are sons of the same mother—and I left him in the midst of enemies; but I am going back now") marks a similar assertion of self-respect through action.[8] Thus, the relationship between teller and listener is used to emphasize Arsat's determination to uphold an ideal of personal honour, even though for him "there is no light and no peace" in the world.

Writing to Edward Garnett about "The Lagoon," Conrad described the narrative mode rather than the theme or plot: "I've sent a short thing to the *Cornhill.* A malay [*sic*] tells a story to a white man who is spending the night at his hut."[9] Two features of this mode distinguish "The Lagoon" from Conrad's previous work and anticipate the Marlow stories, *Lord Jim* in particular. First, Conrad can express sympathy with the protagonist indirectly, by emphasizing the common ground between the narrator and listener. For this reason, the bond between Arsat and the white man is stressed at the beginning of the story: "He liked the man who knew how to keep faith in council and how to fight without fear by the side of his white friend" (191). In *Lord Jim* Marlow is first attracted to Jim because his bearing reminds him of the generations of "young So-and-So's" who have kept faith with the maritime code of service. Jim is "one of us." In fact, in "The Lagoon" we can see the genesis of the technique by which Conrad explores Marlow's divided loyalties in the novel.

Secondly, by dramatizing a character's past experience as a tale told to an audience, Conrad can reveal purposes, motivations, and resolutions immediately, as they form in the speaker's mind. In "The Lagoon," of course, the main focus is on the adventure story as a sequence of events, but we are aware of the rhetorical framework each time Arsat speaks directly to the white man, or shifts (rather too obviously) from an "even, low voice" to an "intense whisper," or evokes one of the listener's replies. In fact, we rely on this framework to interpret Arsat's intentions in telling the tale because we are not given his thoughts or feelings directly by the narrator. Moving from omniscient analysis to a mode that invites interpretation by the reader allowed Conrad to present character in *Lord Jim* as it actually is—opaque, ambiguous, and subject to the limitations of each observer's understanding. Virginia Woolf's playful use of the calendar in her remark that "in or about December, 1910, human character changed" reminds us that Conrad's early experiments anticipate the impressionist search for techniques to involve the reader in this concept of human nature. Incidentally, one of the first reviews of *Tales of Unrest* when it was published in 1898 referred to Conrad as an "impressionist realist."[10]

As I have indicated, the implications of Arsat's tragedy are explored indirectly through the anonymous white man and the narrator of the story. The latter describes the setting and offers vaguely philosophical comments. In the first section of "The Lagoon" the scenic descriptions create an impression of immobility that fits the mood of retrospection and the theme of arrested action. Conrad's rhetoric, however, is so insistent that it becomes "self-generating"—to borrow Barthes's term for language that calls attention to itself over and above what it suggests or refers to. To convey the immobility of a land "from which the very memory of motion had forever departed," Conrad repeats grammatical constructions—

especially prepositional phrases—and individual words in almost every sentence.[11] Similarly, the idiosyncratic postpositioning of adjectives, which emphasizes the impression of arrested motion, is so obtrusive that it tends to distance us from the scene. The following passage occurs at the beginning of the description:

> The forests, sombre and dull, stood motionless and silent on each side of the broad stream. At the foot of big, towering trees, trunkless nipa palms rose from the mud of the bank, in bunches of leaves enormous and heavy, that hung unstirring over the brown swirl of eddies. In the stillness of the air every tree, every leaf, every bough, every tendril of creeper and every petal of minute blossoms seemed to have been bewitched into an immobility perfect and final. (189)

At the end of the description, we have this sentence: "Darkness oozed out from between the trees, through the tangled maze of leaves; the darkness mysterious and invincible; the darkness scented and poisonous of impenetrable forests" (189).

The narrator's most suggestive commentary is contained in the thematically interesting passage that is partly an extension of the white man's thoughts:

> The fear and fascination, the inspiration and the wonder of death—of death near, unavoidable, and unseen, soothed the unrest of his race and stirred the most indistinct, the most intimate of his thoughts. The ever-ready suspicion of evil, the gnawing suspicion that lurks in our hearts, flowed out into the stillness round him—into the stillness profound and dumb, and made it appear untrustworthy and infamous, like the placid and impenetrable mask of an unjustifiable violence. In that fleeting and powerful disturbance of his being the earth enfolded in the starlight peace became a shadowy country of inhuman strife, a battle-field of phantoms terrible and charming, august or ignoble, struggling ardently for the possession of our helpless hearts. (193-94)

The repetitions, antitheses and parallels overstress the idea that "there is nothing" (as the white man later assures Arsat) in the world except the "phantoms" men themselves create. In *Lord Jim* Marlow develops similar thoughts about the illusory quality of existence, and relates them to his attempts to understand Jim. In its effort to suggest the significance of an individual's conduct indirectly and tentatively, "The Lagoon" anticipates the novel. Indeed, if the above commentary were voiced by the white man and linked to Arsat's plight, we would have a first-person narrator with the potential for complex interpretation.

As it is, "The Lagoon" is inconclusive enough to convince some readers, though not others, that despite Arsat's decision to return he cannot pay for his crime against his brother with heroic action, and remains, instead, immobilized in a world of his own illusions. The critical discussion of this point, in fact, resembles a much-simplified version of the ongoing debate over the ending of *Lord Jim*.[12] Looking at the narrative structure of the short story, we can see that some ambiguity is inherent in its form. Thus, the central tale of Diamelen's abduction is a romantic adventure story celebrating the chivalric ideals of loyalty and courage. Arsat's brother, for instance, performs prodigious feats to prove his fidelity to the hero, and he longs to issue a ritual challenge to his enemies. To this tale, however, Conrad opposes interpretive comments by the white listener and the framing narrator that create a wider universal context in which the chivalric code is questioned. To Arsat's expression of grief for Diamelen, "I can see nothing," the white man replies: "There is nothing" (203). Similarly, the narrator's conclusion after the Malay announces his intention to issue his brother's challenge for him and strike the retaliatory blow seems pessimistic: "Arsat had not moved. He stood lonely in the searching sunshine; and he looked beyond the great light of a cloudless day into the darkness of a world of illusions" (204). In other words, Conrad appears to set up a dichotomy between romantic action and ironic reflection.

Revisions to the last sentence from the serial to the book version, however, make this opposition somewhat less forbidding than in the original.[13] In *The Cornhill* the conclusion reads: "In the searching clearness of crude sunshine he was still standing before the house, he was still looking through the great light of a cloudless day into the hopeless darkness of the world." By changing the verb forms from continuous past to the simple past, and eliminating the repeated "still," Conrad makes Arsat seem less likely to remain motionless for longer than the "little while" he plans to mourn Diamelen. Moreover, altering "the hopeless darkness of the world" to "the darkness of a world of illusions" introduces the possibility of ideals that can function in the world as "illusions" instead of disintegrating into nihilistic hopelessness. That is, the narrator implies that Arsat's affirmation of solidarity with his brother ("In a little while I shall see clear enough to strike") is as much an illusion as his dream of escaping death, but it allows him to act purposefully. Looking back across a widening space of water, the white man seems to see his friend's figure, sunlit against the darkness, as symbolic in its loneliness and steadfastness. The imagery anticipates Marlow's last view of Jim as "only a speck, a tiny white speck, that seemed to catch all the light left in a darkening world." Indeed, this final suggestion of Arsat's unwavering idealism isolated in a chaotic, "dumb" natural world and viewed by a reflective, sceptical intelligence is a fragmentary sketch for the central issue of personal honour in *Lord Jim*.

With the exception of Albert Guerard, critics have shown little interest in this story as a serious attempt, despite its shortcomings, to develop important formal and thematic concerns.[14] David Thorburn, for example, claims that in both "The Lagoon" and "Karain" Conrad "is at one with the conventional writers of exotic adventure stories, and the clearest evidence of this is his use of the exotic setting for mere novelty and his reliance on the shallowest clichés of the adventure partnership."[15] I have tried to show that in the narrative mode of "The Lagoon" Conrad was experimenting with an interpretive framework for the "adventure story," and that the essential aspect of this framework is the relationship between the central figure and the listener, who becomes involved with the character through the story. In "Karain," in fact, the listener evolves into a teller himself, looking forward more obviously to Marlow as the narrator of *Lord Jim*. The formal proportions of "The Lagoon" illustrate the writer's preoccupation with this feature, for well over half of the 5,700 words are devoted to the framing commentary rather than to Arsat's narration. And yet, Conrad wrote the piece for *The*

Cornhill, which had solicited on June 3, 1896 a short story of from 6,000 to 8,000 words,[16] and which favoured adventure narratives that submerged the reader as quickly as possible in the action.

The issue of the magazine in which "The Lagoon" appeared (January 1897) contains an unintentionally amusing example of this type. The narrator of "Never the Lotus Closes," by E. and H. Heron, introduces the main sequence of events abruptly: "I concluded he had a tale to tell, and I felt it was my duty to make him tell it." By establishing a rhetorical context for the action which delays the story, builds suspense, and involves us in moral considerations such as the white man's meditation on evil while he waits for Arsat to reappear, Conrad was transforming the "told-tale" convention of the standard nineteenth-century adventure story. Thus, in "Heart of Darkness" Marlow postpones telling his listeners about his meeting with Kurtz by drawing them into his reflections on the central moral issues of the story. The promised "adventures," therefore—Marlow's struggle for Kurtz's soul in the wilderness and his meeting with the Intended—satisfy our expectations as fully realized, dramatic actions because they have been anticipated and partially investigated by the digressions, but our focus continues to be the moment-by-moment associations of Marlow's exploring mind. In *Lord Jim,* because of the more obvious parallel between the white man who shares Arsat's, or Karain's, act of betrayal and Marlow, who shares Jim's, we can see the development from short story to the later narrative strategy more clearly.

Our curiosity about Jim's version of the *Patna* affair is aroused by the disruption in chronological order between chapters 3 and 4, when the omniscient narrator leaps directly from the collision to the trial and Jim's doubt that he can ever express "the true horror" of a sequence of events unknown to us. When Marlow assumes the role of investigator, he increases both our suspense and our involvement in the deciphering of meaning by relating episodes connected to the case such as the chief engineer's admission to the hospital and Brierly's suicide, which comment indirectly on Jim's tale at the same time as they delay it.[17] Of course, the form of any story is largely determined by the convention Marlow dramatizes here; as Roy Pascal says, "At all stages, a story must awaken expectations, hold them in suspense, cheat them temporarily, before it leads to some satisfactory conclusion."[18] In Conrad's fiction, withholding the protagonist's story—Karain's or Jim's—increases the reader's involvement with the narrator who listens and interprets. Twenty-seven thousand words, one-fifth of the text of *Lord Jim,* must be read before Jim begins his story and, as Ian Watt points out, Marlow's digressions prepare us to take "a more sympathetic and understanding view of Jim's predicament" as well as to interpret the outward signs of speech and gesture as symbols of inner meaning.[19] We approach the central narrative at the Malabar Hotel, therefore, with the expectation of discovering the truth—the story Jim could not tell in court—and we have learned to rely on an interpretive framework, a narrator whose observations and emotions mediate between Jim's view of the actual happening and our moral evaluation of his stand.

The story of the desertion of the *Patna,* the longest block of narrative in *Lord Jim* except for the Patusan sections, is the dramatic action most essential to the meaning of the novel as a whole. Jacques Berthoud shows how Jim's actions in Patusan systematically reenact and reverse the events comprising the *Patna* episode. Even Jim's "magnificent fidelity to the natives of Patusan" is "the converse of his betrayal of the pilgrims of the *Patna.*"[20] Conrad immerses the reader in Jim's version of the event, and Marlow's account gains its effectiveness because his narrative voice modulates successfully between interpretive commentary in the fictive present and a dramatic enactment of the past episode. A passage from Jim's horrified vision of the sinking ship illustrates this control and flexibility:

> He saw here and there a head lifted off a mat, a vague form uprise in sitting posture, listen sleepily for a moment, sink down again into the billowy confusion of boxes, steam-winches, ventilators. He was aware all these people did not know enough to take intelligent notice of that strange noise. The ship of iron, the men with white faces, all the sights, all the sounds, everything on board to that ignorant and pious multitude was strange alike, and as trustworthy as it would for ever remain incomprehensible. It occurred to him that the fact was fortunate. The idea of it was simply terrible.
>
> You must remember he believed, as any other man would have done in his place, that the ship would go down at any moment; the bulging, rust-eaten plates that kept back the ocean, fatally must give way, all at once like an undermined dam, and let in a sudden and overwhelming flood. He stood still looking at these recumbent bodies, a doomed man aware of his fate, surveying the silent company of the dead. They *were* dead! Nothing could save them! There were boats enough for half of them perhaps, but there was no time. No time! No time! It did not seem worth while to open his lips, to stir hand or foot. Before he could shout three words, or make three steps, he would be floundering in a sea whitened awfully by the desperate struggles of human beings, clamorous with the distress of cries for help. There was no help. He imagined what would happen perfectly; he went through it all motionless by the hatchway with the lamp in his hand—he went through it to the very last harrowing detail. I think he went through it again while he was telling me these things he could not tell the court. (85-86)

Through Marlow, we share Jim's experience of the scene. Just before this passage, the sound of steam exhaling from the engines is finely expressed in a simile that conveys Jim's conviction of imminent doom—a mighty note is struck in the air: "Its deep rumble made the whole night vibrate like a bass string. The ship trembled to it." His visual impressions are restricted to fragmentary glimpses of individual sleepers as they separate themselves from the mass, and the rising and falling movement of live, stirring bodies is suggested by the verbs of action, "lifted," "uprise," "sink down," and the verbal adjective, "billowy." Marlow also shows us Jim's hyperactive imagination as he recreates the scene through the eyes of the pilgrims, to whom all objects and sounds are strange: "the ship of iron, the men with white faces, all the sights, all the sounds, everything on board. . . ." This insight gives the young man the "terrible," paralyzing apprehension of the pilgrims' complete trust in the doomed world on board the *Patna.*

In his simultaneous interpretive commentary, Marlow involves his listeners in Jim's plight with the sentence beginning "You must remember. . . ." They are urged to consider the particular circumstances of Jim's case and put themselves in his place. A little later Conrad repeats this strategy when Marlow challenges his listeners to imagine their own death by drowning:

> Nothing in the world moved before his eyes, and he could depict to himself without hindrance the sudden swing upwards of the dark sky-line, the sudden tilt up of the vast plain of the sea, the swift still rise, the brutal fling, the grasp of the abyss, the struggle without hope, the starlight closing over his head for ever like the vault of a tomb—the revolt of his young life—the black end. He could! *By Jove! who couldn't?* And you must remember he was a finished artist in that peculiar way, he was a gifted poor devil with the faculty of swift and forestalling vision. (96; my italics)

In the earlier passage we are considering, Marlow modulates from his summary of Jim's feelings ("he believed . . . that the ship would go down at any moment"; he was "a doomed man aware of his fate") to narrated monologue, in which Jim's actual thoughts are reported. Expressive features such as the exclamations and the emphatic "they were" convey the sincerity and horror of the protagonist's conviction, as well as the urgency of the situation. Marlow's sympathetic self-identification with the younger man extends to the concrete description of the sea "whitened awfully" by bodies, which reproduces Jim's mental vision in the narrator's language. Clearly, Jim is not the only one to "go through it all again" in the telling; Conrad implies a repeated reenactment of the experience on an imaginative level from Marlow to listener and reader.

The intimacy implied by Marlow's faithful, unironic reenactment of Jim's perceptions, thoughts, and feelings[21] becomes possible when the listener remembers and recreates what he has heard. Arsat and Karain tell their stories in direct discourse; their listeners can respond but they do not share, in as subtle a manner, "the true horror" of the event. To the extent that Marlow does, he proves indirectly, despite his claims to be unimaginative, his readiness to be imaginatively "swayed" by Jim. At the same time, Conrad insists that no listener, no matter how sensitive or skilled, can fully understand or reproduce the effect of a critical experience on the character directly involved. Marlow admits that Jim remains incomprehensible in "the mystery of his attitude." However, the simultaneity of times and places created by this narrative mode allows considerable freedom of interpretation. While he retells the *Patna* episode, Marlow also recreates the scene at the Malabar Hotel, giving us Jim's direct discourse, facial expressions, and physical movements; the chatter of the hotel guests; and his own responses, spoken and unspoken. We see that, like Arsat, Jim tries to justify his actions by drawing the listener into his story, imputing hypothetical actions and motives to him and appealing to his specialized knowledge of life at sea in order to emphasize the desperateness of his situation.

Conrad uses the narrator's commentary to emphasize this point. Marlow states that Jim required "an ally, a helper, an accomplice," and he stresses the difficulty of remaining objective: "I felt the risk I ran of being circumvented, blinded, decoyed, bullied, perhaps, into taking a definite part in a dispute impossible of decision if one had to be fair to all the phantoms in possession—to the reputable that had its claims and to the disreputable that had its exigencies'' (93). Marlow's problem is compounded by his own indecision. Accordingly, his responses during Jim's narration range from "pitiless," "merciless," and "vicious" to at least one expression of unreserved commitment: "I was moved to make a solemn declaration of my readiness to believe implicitly anything he thought fit to tell me" (127). Marlow's interpretive commentary to his listeners is similarly ambivalent. On the one hand, he is acutely aware that Jim has betrayed a fixed code of conduct, which, because it has no "sovereign power," must be obeyed in order to preserve "the fellowship of the craft." He tells his listeners repeatedly that Jim's mistake is irretrievable: "He had indeed jumped into an everlasting deep hole," he says. "He had tumbled from a height he could never scale again" (112). At the end of Jim's confession, Marlow passes judgment: "He was guilty—as I had told myself repeatedly, guilty and done for" (152).

On the other hand, the narrator makes a confession of his own that reveals his divided loyalties. "What wonder that when some heavy prod gets home the bond is found to be close; that besides the fellowship of the craft there is felt the strength of a wider feeling—the feeling that binds a man to a child" (129). Thus, Conrad controls our response to Jim's "breach of faith with the community of mankind" by stressing the listener-narrator's contradictory reactions: Marlow's attempts to uphold "the solidarity of the craft" conflict with his expressions of personal loyalty to the individual. The interpretation of the protagonist's story by an engaged narrator, therefore, intensifies the ambiguity hinted at in "The Lagoon" and anticipated, as we shall see, by "Karain: A Memory."

At the same time, Conrad uses the "told-tale" device in Lord Jim to dramatize the process of understanding by the listener, in a development of the technique he had first tested in "The Lagoon." Marlow learns during the course of Jim's story that the illusions of his own youth are still alive in this "very young brother"; in fact, he realizes that this is the source of Jim's appeal. Moreover, the presence of an audience allows Marlow to stress the universality of Jim's idealism, and to plead for the reader's understanding: "Hadn't we all commenced," he says, "with the same desire, ended with the same knowledge, carried the memory of the same cherished glamour through the sordid days of imprecation?" Even his explicit condemnation of Jim's conduct is also a paradoxical expression of the bond shared by two romantics: "I was aggrieved against him, as though he had cheated me—me!—of a splendid opportunity to keep up the illusion of my beginnings, as though he had robbed our common life of the last spark of its glamour" (131). Like the white man when Arsat's story is ended, Marlow searches for a practical way to help Jim, although his scepticism makes him tragically aware that "this was one of those cases which no solemn deception can palliate, which no man can help." For another version of the listener who becomes an "ally" and a "helper" while remaining a sceptic, however, we should consider the narrator of "Karain" as an important link between "The Lagoon" and Lord Jim.

In "Karain: A Memory" Conrad returns to the study of an individual who seeks personal redemption for a "breach of faith with the human community." Completed two months after *The Nigger of the "Narcissus,"* which celebrates the solidarity of a ship's crew, this story takes for its hero an extraordinary leader, a figure who "sum[s] up his race, his country, the elemental force of ardent life, or tropical nature," an exile who walks through a landscape peopled with human admirers but can tell no one of his secret. The resemblance to Jim in Patusan is obvious, but also important is the identification Conrad makes between the land itself and his protagonist: "he had its luxuriant strength, its fascination; and, like it, he carried the seed of peril within." As a representative of the East and its passionate, barbaric mysticism, Karain is the polar opposite of Western materialism and the commercial attitudes revealed by motifs in the story such as the Jubilee sixpence and the bankers who finance the schooner's trading expeditions. Conrad had struggled unsuccessfully with this conflict in *The Sisters,* the narration from Stephen's point of view tending toward melodramatic expressions of romantic sensibility and crudely overt criticism of the rational, European world view. The indirect narrative perspective of the short story, however, creates a distance that permits a playfully ironic treatment of the relationship between imaginative feeling and scepticism. There are moments of gaiety in "Karain," and sympathy for the hero is mixed with amusement.

The narrator who is partially responsible for this tone is the immediate forerunner of Marlow, although he is considerably more prosaic, less subjective, and less digressive than the narrator of "Youth." As in the stories of Edgar Allan Poe and Hoffman, the credibility of an eye-witness lends some authority to the incomprehensible and extraordinary.[22] In "Karain," for example, the narrator testifies to the protagonist's superhuman battle with the ghost by describing his physical aspect: "Of course it had been a long swim off to the schooner; but his face showed another kind of fatigue, the tormented weariness, the anger and the fear of a struggle against a thought, an idea—against something that cannot be grappled, that never rests—a shadow, a nothing, unconquerable and immortal, that preys upon life" (23).

More important, however, is his function as a listener who remembers and interprets the experience of his "very good friend." In this respect, he can provide a richer context for the central story of betrayal than the combination of listener and framing narrator in "The Lagoon." Even the opening descriptions of Karain, which are presented as the narrator's memories of an old friend, are calculated to appeal to the reader's understanding and sympathy. Thus, the narrator uses a simple analogy to make Karain's ludicrous yet splendid "show" comprehensible to Western minds. He compares the chieftain's rule over his land and people to an actor's mastery of his stage and audience: "He was treated with a solemn respect accorded in the irreverent West only to the monarchs of the stage, and he accepted the profound homage with a sustained dignity seen nowhere else but behind the footlights and in the condensed falseness of some grossly tragic situation" (6–7).

A dichotomy between East and West emerges in the narrator's remark that the sceptical West reveres only "monarchs of the stage," a comment which should be compared with Karain's "chivalrous respect" for the British Queen. To Western minds, therefore, the chieftain's exceptional hold over the imaginations of his followers and onlookers can be explained most effectively by the theatrical metaphor. In fact, in "Karain" we have the first example of Conrad's use of a dramatized narrator as a mediator between contrasting views of the world. As we shall see in subsequent chapters of this study, mediation becomes increasingly more complex as Conrad develops the role of the dramatized narrator.

By his gestures and stage presence, Karain is able to persuade other men that his domain is infinite:

> From the deck of our schooner, anchored in the middle of the bay, he indicated by a theatrical sweep of his arm along the jagged outline of the hills the whole of his domain; and the ample movement seemed to drive back its limits, augmenting it suddenly into something so immense and vague that for a moment it appeared to be bounded only by the sky. . . . Karain swept his hand over it. "All mine!" He struck the deck with his long staff; the gold head flashed like a falling star. (4–5)

Describing the Malayan landscape, the narrator stresses the impression it gives of being an imaginary world created by Karain's "accomplished acting":

> In many successive visits we came to know his stage well—the purple semi-circle of hills, the slim trees leaning over houses, the yellow sands, the streaming green of ravines. All that had the crude and blended colouring, the appropriateness almost excessive, the suspicious immobility of a painted scene; and it enclosed so perfectly the accomplished acting of his amazing pretences that the rest of the world seemed shut out forever from the gorgeous spectacle. There could be nothing outside. It was as if the earth had gone on spinning, and had left that crumb of its surface alone in space. (7)

As an audience to Karain's performance, the sceptical narrator testifies to its almost complete triumph over reality: "As to Karain, nothing could happen to him unless what happens to all—failure and death; but his quality was to appear clothed in the illusion of unavoidable success" (7). In all of these theatrical images, the narrator balances an appreciation of the power of the illusion with a sceptical awareness of paint and costumes, gestures and rhetoric. By representing both Eastern and Western perceptions of Karain, Conrad makes his readers more understanding of his protagonist's strange plight.

The theatrical analogy also contributes to the plot movement because it allows the narrator to hint at a dark side to Karain's "illusion of unavoidable success." The character who is "aggressively disguised" as an actor has an inner life which he hides from the audience. Conrad exploits this aspect of the metaphor to maintain the reader's expectations of hearing Karain's "real" story "in the wings, so to speak, and with the lights out."

Like Arsat's and Jim's tales, the story is one of betrayal. As a youth, Karain had dedicated his life to a friend's mission to find and kill a dishonoured sister and her Dutch lover. Having become obsessed during the hunt with an imaginary image of the girl, Karain shot Pata Matara, his friend, instead of the Dutchman and is now haunted mercilessly by the ghost of his dead comrade. The sword bearer who always attends the chieftain keeps the phantom at bay with whispered incantations, and Karain's belief in the old man's supernatural powers gives him the confidence to sustain his "amazing pretenses." At the beginning of the story the narrator suggests this interrelationship when he juxtaposes the two figures standing on the schooner's deck. The sword bearer "was there on duty, but without curiosity, and seemed weary, not with age, but with the possession of a burdensome secret of existence. Karain, heavy and proud, had a lofty pose and breathed calmly" (5).

Like the narrative structure of "The Lagoon," the opening descriptive section of "Karain" is as long as the central story of betrayal, which it both anticipates and enriches with interpretive commentary. As he does in *Lord Jim*, Conrad establishes a strikingly visual first impression of Karain regally posed on the schooner's deck and refers to a hidden mystery, which he then withholds. While the reader is expecting its disclosure, the narrator's impressionistic arrangement of memories presents the character in a series of vividly coloured pictures, suggesting certain traits and attitudes without penetrating Karain's inner life—to this limited extent, the explorative opening section anticipates Marlow's assembling of separate episodes and impressions to illuminate different aspects of Jim's conduct. In the short story the reader is involved in the narrator's relatively long reflection about the central character before the sequence of events begins with the white traders' last visit to Karain's bay. In the developing form of Conrad's fiction from "The Lagoon," "Karain," and "Heart of Darkness" to *Lord Jim* the emphasis falls increasingly on the process of this involvement and the nature of the attitude taken toward a "straggler" from the ranks of the human community.

Although Conrad does not include a dramatized audience in the framework of his stories until "Youth," the narrator's opening commentary seems to be addressed to the friends of his adventurous past, perhaps Jackson and Hollis, who have been long exposed to "the smoky atmosphere" and "befogged respectability" of English life:

> We knew him in those unprotected days when we were content to hold in our hand our lives and our property. None of us, I believe, has any property now, and I hear that many, negligently, have lost their lives; but I am sure that the few who survive are not yet so dim-eyed as to miss in the befogged respectability of their newspapers the intelligence of various native risings in the Eastern Archipelago . . . the printed words scent the smoky atmosphere of today faintly, with the subtle and penetrating perfume as of land breezes breathing through the starlight of bygone nights. (3)

The playfully ironic tone of this passage is directed at "respectable" Western readers in general, who (like the capitalists in countinghouses who decide that the risks are too great for the schooner to continue its trips) must have their adventures secondhand. When Karain's belief in the supernatural powers of a Queen Victoria Jubilee sixpence allows him to recreate his "illusion of unavoidable success," the narrator speaks to his readers directly: "I wondered what they thought; what he thought; . . . what the reader thinks?"

The multiple ironies of the situation sustain the comic tone of Conrad's attempt to involve us imaginatively in the opposition between the mystical East and the sceptical West, and the technique succeeds in drawing our attention to this central idea. Moreover, the question "I wonder what the reader thinks?" looks forward to Marlow's use of dramatized listeners for rhetorical purposes. Here, for example, Marlow deliberately provokes his "respectable" readers in order to gain sympathy for Jim:

> Frankly, it is not my words that I mistrust but your minds. I could be eloquent were I not afraid you fellows had starved your imaginations to feed your bodies. I do not mean to be offensive; it is respectable to have no illusions—and safe—and profitable—and dull. Yet you, too, in your time must have known the intensity of life, that light of glamour created in the shock of trifles, as amazing as the glow of sparks struck from a cold stone—and as short-lived, alas! (225)

The reader of "Karain" is also urged to sympathize with the chieftain's illusory dreams and phantoms by a series of contrasts at the end of the story, when the narrator jumps forward in time to "some years afterwards" in London. In the midst of "innumerable eyes star[ing] straight in front," "blank faces" and the "headlong shuffle" of the people in the Strand, he meets Jackson, one of the adventurers who had heard Karain's tale. Not only does Jackson, with his head "high above the crowd" and his "inspiring" vitality, emphasize by contrast the spiritless anonymity of the crowds, but the "current of humanity" itself, with its "sombre and ceaseless stir," is set against the narrator's last visual impression of Karain, as he is welcomed back into the community of his people—an idyllic scene in which human life blends with animals, green pasture, and fruit trees. Are the sorceries and staged illusions of this culture as "real" as the parade of life passing on the Strand?

Conrad dramatizes this question in the exchange between Jackson and the narrator, when Jackson wonders about Karain's story: "'. . . I mean, whether the thing was so, you know . . . whether it really happened to him. . . . What do you think?' 'My dear chap,' I cried, 'you have been too long away from home. What a question to ask! Only look at all this'" (54). Here, the narrator describes the busy London scene in a series of concrete details and images. Finally, Jackson replies: "'Yes; I see it,' said Jackson, slowly. 'It is there; it pants, it runs, it rolls; it is strong and alive; it would smash you if you didn't look out; but I'll be hanged if it is yet as real to me as . . . as the other thing . . . say, Karain's story.' I think that, decidedly, he had been too long away from home" (55). Like the theatrical analogy that controls our impression of Karain, the narrator's scepticism draws our attention to the paradoxical nature of the illusion.

Despite the comic insouciance of this ending, the two different responses to Karain's experience demonstrate an early attempt by Conrad to explore a complex issue by indirection and multiple perceptions. As Lawrence Graver points out, the story anticipates "Heart of Darkness" in this respect,[23] and one can also see the origin of Marlow's narrative practice in *Lord Jim*. In the novel the narrator juxtaposes the views expressed by characters of different backgrounds and loyalties (such as the French lieutenant and Stein) in order to create a richly paradoxical and ambiguous context for Jim's tragedy. In "Karain" the voices of Jackson (who affirms his individual vision against the conventional view of reality) and the narrator (who doubts what he cannot see) are similarly opposed. The unresolved question keeps Karain and his story in our minds—a much simplified version of the resonance created by the differing interpretations of Jim's conduct in the novel.

Similarly, the responses of the narrator and his friends during Karain's storytelling provide an interpretive framework that extends and universalizes the themes of the story. The death of Karain's sword bearer has left the chieftain at the mercy of the unseen—Pata Matara's ghost. In desperation Karain turns to his "unbelieving" friends from the West for help, and tells his story not only to persuade them to take him away but also because, like Arsat and Jim, he has no one to share his guilt: "And I can tell no one. No one. *There is no one here faithful enough and wise enough to know*" (25; my italics). The role of the listener is more clearly defined here than in "The Lagoon," drawing our attention to the relationship between teller and audience and adding suspense to the outcome of the story. How will these listeners fulfill Karain's expectations? One of the reasons for the interrogative and retrospective aspects of Marlow's narration in *Lord Jim* is the duty imposed upon him by Jim to "understand," and the more Marlow demonstrates his struggle to comprehend, the more clearly the reader perceives his commitment. Thus, Marlow tells us that "I cannot say I had ever seen him distinctly—not even to this day, after I had my last view of him; but it seemed to me that the less I understood the more I was bound to him in the name of that doubt which is the inseparable part of our knowledge." In "Karain" Conrad anticipates Marlow's struggle to understand and communicate. Thus, the narrator refers to the impossibility of conveying "the effect of [Karain's] story," of making it "clear to another mind."

The problems of apprehending another human being clearly are usually increased when the two are of different races, yet the narrator minimizes this fact in his affirmation of the conditions that make communication possible: "No man will speak to his master; but to a wanderer and a friend, to him who does not come to teach or to rule, to him who asks for nothing and accepts all things, words are spoken by the camp-fires, in the shared solitude of the sea, in riverside villages, in resting-places surrounded by forests—words are spoken that take no account of race or colour. One heart speaks—another one listens . . ." (26). Here, Conrad condemns the paternalistic aspects of colonialism, as they are illustrated, for example, by Lingard, Kayerts and Carlier, and Kurtz. Except for the narrator's remark that he is paid "like a banker" by Karain (a simile that links the adventurer to the men in countinghouses at home) Conrad emphasizes the idealistic, individualistic nature of the white man's relationship with the native.

Some aspects of the chivalric friendship between Jim and Dain Waris can be found in this story—particularly in Karain's appeal for sanctuary: "Karain spoke to me. 'You know us. You have lived with us. Why?—we cannot know; but you understand our sorrows and our thoughts. You have lived with my people, and you understand our desires and our fears. With you I will go'" (44). The rhythmic cadence, repetitions, and formal inversion make this statement resemble a ritual oath of loyalty. Moreover, the appeal reflects the tone of Karain's story—a tale of intense feeling heightened by the supernatural which, as Andrzej Busza has shown, can be traced to Conrad's familiarity with Polish romantic literature in general and Adam Mickiewicz's ballad "The Ambush" in particular.[24] In their response to this tale of irrational, folkloric belief the men from the sceptical "irreverent" West dramatize the symbolic aspect of the oral mode in this story. As the narrator has said, the bond between teller and listener represents essential human ties "that take no account of race or colour."

Conrad continues to insist upon the cultural differences between Karain and his friends because, paradoxically, it is the "unbelievers" who are most committed to the troubled chief. This idea develops the suggestion in "The Lagoon" that racial differences often coexist with profound understanding between individuals. "You went away from my country," says Arsat to the white man with whom he shares his guilt, "in the pursuit of your desires, which we, men of the islands, cannot understand." Karain's own people are limited by their dependence on the leader's "illusion of unavoidable success"; in Marlow's words describing Jim, they see only "the side turned perpetually to the light of day." Like Jim, however, Karain has another side "which, like the other hemisphere of the moon, exists stealthily in perpetual darkness," and he shows these secret feelings to his Western friends. This concept becomes more complex when Conrad includes differences in moral outlook which seem to involve a subtle, if tentative, understanding. In "Heart of Darkness," for example, he explores Marlow's loyalty to Kurtz in the wilderness and afterwards, and in *Lord Jim* the narrator's ambivalent feelings about Jim's romantic idealism are investigated.

The role of Hollis, the brash young sailor whose ingenuity rescues the chieftain, illustrates this paradoxical truth with a comic irreverence that fits the mood of the story. In contrast to Jackson and the narrator, Hollis affects indifference to Karain's arrival, but his immediate reactions to the story are imaginative and practically sound. He recognizes that Karain requires something to believe in, rather than the "respectable" received ideas of the West. "You won't soothe him with your platitudes," he tells the narrator. Moreover, he foresees the consequences of the white men's failure to help their friend: "the end of this shall be, that some day he will run amuck amongst his faithful subjects and send *ad patres* ever so many of them before they make up their minds to the disloyalty of knocking him on the head." The narrator agrees with this prediction, which anticipates Marlow's fear for Jim, that if he continues unaided in his struggle against "the ghost of a fact" he will be defeated by drink and despair. Both men need imaginative scope to assert their ideals through redemptive action. Like Marlow, the narrator of "Karain" emphasizes the listener's personal responsibility for the teller who has revealed his "dark" side: "He had given himself up to us; he had thrust into our hands his errors and his torment, his life and his peace."

Hollis's success in helping Karain to maintain his illusions (a performance, incidentally, that echoes the narrator's theatrical analogy, with its depiction of a truth revealed through appearances which are all too obvious to the onlooker) has led some critics to consider him as a "proto-Stein."[25] Although Bruce Johnson, who is the most convincing, makes a good case for the comparison, to define Hollis as "Stein" and the narrator as "Marlow" is to lose some of the humour in the scene as well as to overlook details such as Hollis's command to the others, "Can't you lie a little . . . for a friend!" which looks forward to Marlow's lie to the Intended. Hollis's affirming act is at least partially comic. Unlike Stein, who has followed the dream himself, the young sailor mocks the spiritual and unseen in a parody of the sword bearer's magic that emphasizes the great distance between East and West:

> [H]e talked to us ironically, but his face became as grave as though he were pronouncing a powerful incantation over the things inside.
> "Every one of us," he said, with pauses that somehow were more offensive than his words— "every one of us, you'll admit, has been haunted by some woman. . . . And . . . as to friends . . . dropped by the way. . . . Well! . . . ask yourselves. . . ."
> He paused. Karain stared. A deep rumble was heard high up under the deck. Jackson spoke seriously—
> "Don't be so beastly cynical."
> "Ah! You are without guile," said Hollis sadly. "You will learn . . . meantime this Malay has been our friend. . . ."
> He repeated several times thoughtfully, "Friend . . . Malay. Friend, Malay," as though weighing the words against one another. (47)

Here, the two terms "Friend" and "Malay," sceptic and believer, are in symbolic (and comic) opposition. When Hollis and the others enact the ritual of placing the Queen Victoria sixpence about Karain's neck, the cultural differences are ironically implied, complicating their gesture of solidarity.

In the narrator's response during the story, however, Conrad dramatizes the listener's imaginative, unironic involvement. For example, when Karain first appears in the ship's cabin, he looks to the objects around him for protection against the unseen. Conrad uses the ship's chronometers to suggest "the strong life of white men, which rolls on irresistible and hard on the edge of outer darkness." Thus, the narrator juxtaposes the haunted aspect of his friend and the corresponding fury of the elements outside with the predictable empiricism of "the two chronometers in my cabin ticking along with unflagging speed against one another." When

Karain pauses in his tale, the narrator has become so moved by the story that he seems to share his friend's fear and awe. Just as Karain did earlier, he looks toward the safety of Western order (Greenwich time) for protection—cultural differences between the two have all but disappeared.

Moreover, in this passage, which recalls Conrad's words in the preface to *The Nigger of the "Narcissus"* about the "solidarity in dreams," the narrator communicates a sense of fellowship with all men who have been faithful to their illusions:

> And I looked on, surprised and moved; I looked at that man, loyal to a vision, betrayed by his dream, spurned by his illusion, and coming to us unbelievers for help—against a thought. The silence was profound; but it seemed full of noiseless phantoms, of things sorrowful, shadowy, and mute, in whose invisible presence the firm, pulsating beat of the two ship's chronometers ticking off steadily the seconds of Greenwich Time seemed to me a protection and a relief. Karain stared stonily; and looking at his rigid figure, I thought of his wanderings, of that obscure Odyssey of revenge, of all the men that wander amongst illusions; of the illusions that give joy, that give sorrow, that give pain, that give peace; of the invincible illusions that can make life and death appear serene, inspiring, tormented, or ignoble. (40)

Once again, the commentary emphasizes the personal responsibility of the "unbelievers" to Karain, but the narrator's chain of associations also leads him to affirm the power of beliefs themselves. The "noiseless phantoms" return when Hollis opens his box of "charms," and they are defined as "all the ghosts driven out of the unbelieving West by men who pretend to be wise and alone and at peace—all the homeless ghosts of an unbelieving world . . . all the cast-out and reproachful ghosts of friends admired, trusted, traduced, betrayed, left dead by the way—they all seemed to come from the inhospitable regions of the earth to crowd into the gloomy cabin, as though it had been a refuge and, in all the unbelieving world, the only place of avenging belief."[26] The narrator's repetition of the phrase "the unbelieving West" (or, "the [an] unbelieving world") creates a refrain that underlines the essential dichotomy in "Karain." In these passages Conrad persuades us of the human necessity for illusions and also, of the vitality of the past. In this way, he prepares us for the narrative irony at the end of the story.

The important thematic parallel between "Karain" and *Lord Jim* is not, as Bruce Johnson has written, that both men expect their "guilt" to become manageable at some sort of cultural barrier.[27] The conflict between East and West is indeed central to the short story, as I have shown, but Karain sustains his "illusion of unavoidable success" very well without the help of the white men for the first half of the story because his belief in the sword bearer's magic gives him the imaginative freedom to create an image of himself as ruler. As for Jim, one can argue (as Marlow, in fact, does) that "of all mankind [he] had no dealings but with himself," and that Jim is not as concerned with managing his guilt as with salvaging his "exalted egoism." In both the story and the novel, therefore, the protagonist is first crippled and then redeemed by his imagination, and it is the dual nature of this faculty "of swift and forestalling vision" that "Karain" tests, in preparation for *Lord Jim*. The phantom of Karain's remorse has the same origin as his splendidly absurd dignity; both of these "fantasies" are juxtaposed with the soulless materialism of bankers and "respectable" men. Karain's ability to sway others is intimately connected to his secret knowledge of the avenging spirit over his shoulder. In this respect, he is the prototype of Jim, who "had the gift of finding a special meaning in everything that happened to him," whether on the *Patna* or in Patusan.

Imagination leads Karain, like Jim, into betraying an oath of loyalty and then haunts him remorselessly with "the ghost of a fact." Like Jim also, but more unequivocally, he is rescued by an idealistic belief that allows him to act out his role on "a conquered foothold on the earth"—a role to which he must prove faithful because, as Jim says of his reign in Patusan, "nothing less will do." The native "risings" in the newspaper that prompt the narrator's memory, therefore, are testimony "in black and white" of Karain's loyalty to his beliefs, because before the sword bearer's death, the chieftain had been planning a tribal war "with patience, with foresight—with a fidelity to his purpose and with a steadfastness" that his friend is not accustomed to find in Malays.

At the end of the story Jackson returns to the subject of Karain's activities ("He will make it hot for the caballeros") and the details of the setting are carefully chosen. He is contemplating a row of guns in a shop window, "dark and polished tubes that can cure so many illusions." Stein tells us, in *Lord Jim*, that "one thing alone can us from being ourselves cure" and the problem for Jim is not "how to get cured" but "how to be." As the narrator thinks about death, and Jackson wishes Karain luck in his enterprise, the firearms reflected in the glass together with Jackson's bearded face take on a Flaubertian suggestiveness; that is, they seem to epitomize Conrad's meaning in the story. In the past, Karain betrayed his friend with "a sure shot" from the gun given him by Pata Matara. Now, the "dark and polished tubes"—destructive, concrete objects provided by his Western friends—are made to serve an illusory ideal of conduct.

Conrad explores the imaginative idealism of Jim and Karain indirectly, through the perceptions of a first-person narrator who becomes sympathetically involved—first, as a listener to the other's tale and later, as a teller who remembers. In "Karain" the narration is merely a primitive sketch for the later Marlow tales, but features such as the impressionistic montage of the first section and the spirited, playfully ambiguous coda succeed in engaging the reader; to a limited extent, we are encouraged to discover the meaning of the story ourselves. Also important is the narrator's persuasive presentation of the protagonist's experience. In this story Conrad locates the point of view within an individual personality with patriotic loyalties[28] and a taste for adventure who can control and persuade the reader, extending the implications of Karain's story to include men of other cultures and times. Attempting to gain our sympathy for the protagonist, Conrad begins to explore the rhetorical possibilities of a dramatized narrator. At the same time, although the former gunrunner who tells this story lacks Marlow's moral commitment to a code, his response to Karain's theatrical performance is not unmixed with irony and scepticism, and his tone modulates from concern to comic disengagement. These intimations of ambiguity anticipate Conrad's complex treatment of Kurtz and Jim.

"The Lagoon" and "Karain: A Memory" are experimental stories. At every level of the discourse, from individual words and phrases to the controlling metaphors and narrative structure, Conrad tests different methods of fusing form and content. Here, for example, in the passage introducing Karain's narration, he experiments with mimetic aural effects: "His words sounded low, in a sad murmur as of running water; at times they rang loud like the clash of a war-gong—or trailed slowly like weary travellers—or rushed forward with the speed of fear." On a symbolic level, the "told-tale" device that controls the structure of the stories reveals meaning and significance through its form. In each case, an exile communicates his "adventure" to the reader through an interpreter, a listener who mediates, sympathizes, and explores. The listener's response universalizes the experience, and the outcast becomes "one of us." In these stories and in *Lord Jim* the framing convention has the opposite effect from the "intense compositional rigor," the *"limitation"* that Dorothy Van Ghent finds characteristic of the "told-tale" device in *Wuthering Heights.*[29] Conrad's narrative framework extends the "adventure" (or central story) instead of limiting it, emphasizing the communal aspect of the mode as well as its potential for ironic contrast. In this respect, the teller and listener relationship reflects an impulse toward integration that is emphatically denied in the narrative soliloquies created by such postmodern writers as Beckett, Céline, and John Hawkes.

4
"Youth," "Heart of Darkness," and *Lord Jim*

Although we do not know exactly when Conrad began to write "Youth: A Narrative," the last page of the manuscript contains the date of its completion: "May, 1898."[1] Below this notation and in the lower right corner is inscribed the note, "for B'woods." In an indirect way, the Edinburgh magazine can be related to the creation of Marlow as the narrator of this story, for although Conrad occasionally criticized *Blackwood's* for its narrow-mindedness,[2] he welcomed a reading audience that comprised "a good sort of public." Writing for men who had experiences and professions in common ("There isn't a single club and messroom and man-of-war in the British Seas and Dominions which hasn't its copy of Maga," he commented in a letter to J. B. Pinker),[3] Conrad developed an English seaman persona whose habits of speech and patriotic sentiments would appeal to the reader. One of Marlow's most important functions in "Youth," as Conrad's revisions to the story indicate,[4] is to clarify the opening premise that "this could have occurred nowhere but in England" by introducing substantial commentary about the national character.

The date inscribed on the last page of the manuscript can also be related to aspects of Conrad's technique in "Youth," for it suggests that the first draft of the story was written even more quickly than has previously been thought. Because we can assume that Conrad began the fragment "Tuan Jim" in April,[5] completing some 4,000 words before starting "Youth," the latter story may have taken him only about two or three weeks to write. The manuscript supports this deduction, for it contains many signs of having been composed at considerable speed. Particularly in the first thirty pages of text, and throughout the entire eighty-three, Conrad leaves out words, and even phrases in the rough draft. The following sentence (from the scene in which the crew of the *Judea* struggles to right the ship by shovelling wet sand from one side of the hold to the other) is one of many that seem to indicate fluency and rapidity of composition. The original version reads: "One of the ship impressed by the gloom of the scene wept as if his heart would break" (MS 10a); Conrad amended this, and added an explanatory note: "One of the ship's boys (we had two) impressed by the gloom of the scene wept as if his heart would break.'' Further evidence that Conrad was writing relatively easily and quickly can be found in the blocks of narrative that required very little revision.[6] Moreover, a comparison of the "Youth" manuscript with either the first draft of "An Outpost of Progress" or the almost contemporaneous "Tuan Jim" fragment shows that he had fewer problems with Marlow's subjective analyses than with the passages of omniscient commentary in the earlier works.

Using Marlow as a storyteller helped Conrad to emerge from a period of self-doubt and creative impasse, which had begun during his difficulties with "The Return" in September 1897. As we can see from the colloquial phrasing of the sentence quoted above, generated partly by the expression "wept as if his heart would break" and partly by the aside, many features of Marlow's speech are calculated to imitate the pace and tone of an authentic oral performance in an informal setting. By adding a carefully delineated audience of ex-seamen, Conrad created a dramatic context which allowed him to indulge his natural tendency toward rhetorical amplification. When the advantages of telling a story from a specifically English point of view and the attractive stylistic features of oral discourse are combined with the fact that Conrad's subject matter comprised "a record of experience," which (as he wrote in the preface to the book edition) "in its inwardness and in its outward colouring, begins and ends in myself," the explanation for his relative ease in writing "Youth" seems clear.

According to Zdzisław Najder,[7] there is a close relationship between this short story and Conrad's essay on Captain Marryat and James Fenimore Cooper, entitled "Tales of the Sea" and published in June 1898. Conrad's comments about the American writer are particularly interesting because they anticipate Marlow's claim in "Youth" that national character can be determined by nature, or the sea. For Cooper, he writes, "nature was not the framework, it was an essential part of existence." In his fiction, "the sea inter-penetrates with life; it is in a subtle way a factor in the problem of existence, and, for all its greatness, it is always in touch with the men, who, bound on errands of war or gain, traverse its immense solitudes."[8] Conrad develops this thought in the next few sentences, using parallel phrases to emphasize the interrelationship of men and the elements, and the effect of this association on the men. Speaking of Cooper's descriptions, he tells us that they include "the great loneliness of the waters, the stillness of watchful coasts, and the alert readiness which marks men who live face to face with the promise and the menace of the sea." Finally, Conrad points out that the realistic portrayal of this "inter-penetration" tends to involve the writer's patriotic feelings: "If he pitches upon episodes redounding to the glory of the young republic, surely England has glory enough to forgive him, for the sake of his excellence, the patriotic bias at her expense. The interest of his tales is convincing and unflagging; and there runs through his work a steady vein of friendliness for the old country which the succeeding generations of his compatriots have replaced by a less definite sentiment" (56).

In "Youth" Conrad dramatizes these ideas, using Marlow to explore the values of commitment and patriotism. As Polish critics have shown, Conrad's respect for these virtues derives from the tutelary figures of his childhood and the romantic poets of his cultural background. "Youth" demonstrates a loyalty to England that is also found in some of the letters written at about this time, especially those in which he seeks confirmation of his place among native Englishmen. Writing to Ted Sanderson on March 26, 1897, for instance, Conrad creates an anecdote in which two different pieces of paper are artfully arranged in order to symbolize his acceptance by the country where he lives and works:

> Only the other day I've re-read Miss Helen's letter—*the letter* to me. It is laid away with some of my very particular papers. It is so unaffectedly, so irresistibly charming—and profound too. One seems almost to touch the ideal conception of what's best in life. And—personally—those eight pages of Her writing are to me like a high assurance of being accepted, admitted within, the people and the land of my choice. And side by side with the letter I found the printed paper signed by the Secretary of State. The form of nationalisation and its reality—the voice of what is best in the heart of peoples.[9]

As we shall see, in this story Conrad's development of the first-person narrative method he had used in "Karain" and his selection and arrangement of material seem to be motivated partly by a desire to identify "what is best" in his adopted country and establish Marlow's solidarity with his English listeners. Throughout the different stages of composition, many of his revisions reveal the consistency of this purpose.

For example, the central episode of "Youth" (in which the *Judea*'s coal cargo catches fire and explodes, forcing the crew to abandon the burning ship) underwent considerable rewriting to make Marlow's impressions more concrete and immediate. However, another effect created by the changes and additions is rhetorical. To persuade the reader of the sailors' tenacity and solidarity despite the essential futility of their tasks, Conrad takes special pains with the remarks directed by Marlow to his audience of ex-seamen. In the following excerpt from the manuscript the italics indicate an interlined sentence, which uses repetition to draw the point to the reader's attention: "But that crew of Liverpool hard cases had the right stuff in them. *They had it.* It is the sea that gives it, the vastness the loneliness surrounding their dark *stolid* lives" (*MS,* 12b). For the serial and book versions Conrad added a sentence and rewrote the interlined passage to give Marlow's praise even more authority by referring to the narrator's experience at sea: "But they all worked. That crew of Liverpool hard cases had in them the right stuff. It's my experience they always have. It is the sea that gives it—the vastness, the loneliness surrounding their dark stolid souls" (25). By moving the idiomatic phrase "the right stuff" to the end of the sentence, Conrad emphasizes Marlow's Englishness, as well as his moral approval. In addition, the substitution of "souls" for "lives" gives the vital relationship between men and the sea a quality of inwardness that develops the first narrator's claim: "This could have happened nowhere but in England, where men and sea inter-penetrate...."

Conrad's use of Marlow to endorse this premise becomes more apparent in his revisions to the subsequent action involving the crew. As the smouldering *Judea* is being towed behind the steamer *Somerville,* the men are ordered aloft to furl the sails. Like trimming the yards after the deck has been reduced to splinters, this work has no practical value. In the manuscript Marlow suggests this idea indirectly in his image of the sailors aloft, absorbed in their ritual task while completely cut off from the ship herself: "From the yards we could not see the ship for smoke; and the men worked carefully passing the gaskets with even turns" (MS 15b). In the serial and book versions, however, the futility of the men's attention to detail in this situation[10] is underlined by a question directed to Marlow's listeners: "We coughed on the yards, and were careful about the bunts. Do you see the lot of us there, putting a neat furl on the sails of that ship doomed to arrive nowhere? There was not a man who didn't think that at any moment the masts would topple over. From aloft we could not see the ship for smoke and they worked carefully, passing the gaskets with even turns" (28). Conrad also added the narrator's tribute to the men's courage; because they are conscious of the danger, their performance is all the more remarkable.

At this point in the text Marlow interrupts his story to explore the significance of the crew's obedience. In the manuscript he says:

> These were men with no drilled in habit of obedience. They had no professional reputation to lose, no examples, no praise. They all knew well enough how to dodge and laze—when they had a mind to—and mostly they had. They didn't think their pay half good enough; but there was something inborn in them, not to be equalled by a French or German crew; a principle, a masterful instinct, the racial difference which shapes the fate of nations. (MS 16b)

When Conrad revised this passage for *Blackwood's* he cancelled the reference to the superiority of the English sailors ("'not to be equalled by a French or German crew"), stressing instead the essential *difference* between the cultures.[11] At the same time he introduced rhetorical questions and answers to involve the audience, and transformed Marlow's direct statement into an investigation of this "racial difference":

> What made them do it—what made them obey me when I, thinking consciously how fine it was, made them drop the bunt of the foresail twice to try and do it better? What? They had no professional reputation—no examples, no praise. It wasn't a sense of duty; they all knew well enough how to shirk, and laze, and dodge—when they had a mind to it—and mostly they had. Was it the two pounds ten a-month that sent them there? They didn't think their pay half good enough. No; it was something in them, something inborn and subtle and everlasting. I don't say positively that the crew of a vulgar French or German merchantman wouldn't have done it, but I doubt it. And it wouldn't have been done in the same way. There was a completeness in it, something solid like a principle, and masterful like an instinct—a disclosure of something secret—of that hidden something, that gift of good or evil that makes racial difference, that shapes the fate of nations. (*B* 323)

Revising this passage yet again for the book edition, Conrad cancelled the coloured adjective "vulgar" and changed "but I doubt it" to read "but I doubt whether it would have been done in the same way." This mitigates even further the suggestion of racial superiority.

In this excerpt the use of Marlow to investigate a moral issue anticipates "Heart of Darkness" and *Lord Jim,* but with an important difference that illustrates Conrad's desire to establish Marlow's national solidarity with his audience in "Youth." First, let us consider a passage from "Heart of Darkness," very similar in technique to the excerpt above, in which the narrator engages his listeners in the process of speculation and resolution. When Marlow realizes that his native crewmen are cannibals, he explores the meaning of their remarkable self-control during the river journey to the Inner Station. He begins by drawing attention to the issue with a grotesque manipulation of the colloquial expression, "a good tuck-in": "Why in the name of all the gnawing devils of hunger they didn't go for us—they were thirty to five—and have a good tuck-in for once, amazes me now when I think of it" (104). In "Youth" Conrad uses colloquialisms to establish the cohesiveness of the group to which Marlow belongs, whereas in "Heart of Darkness" he often takes idioms or clichés out of their conventional contexts in order to expose the manner in which we use language to mask our basic instincts of survival. Thus, the phrase "a good tuck-in" euphemizes human hunger, and the commentary which follows develops some of the implications of this revelation.

Having shocked his audience by the incongruous choice of an expression associated with rituals such as teatime, Marlow continues by appealing to reason in a manner similar to the passage from "Youth." The pattern of his argument is highly rhetorical, emphasizing his discovery of the cannibals' innate integrity:

> Restraint! What possible restraint? Was it superstition, disgust, patience, fear—or some kind of primitive honour? No fear can stand up to hunger, no patience can wear it out, disgust simply does not exist where hunger is; and as to superstition, beliefs, and what you may call principles, they are less than chaff in a breeze. Don't you know the devilry of lingering starvation, its exasperating torment, its black thoughts, its sombre and brooding ferocity? Well, I do. It takes a man all his inborn strength to fight hunger properly. (105)

The third and fourth sentences contain two rhetorical schemes: counter-inference, in which the speaker answers his own questions and meets his own objections, and *enumeratio,* a pattern created by repeating the sentence in inverse order. By these means, the narrator emphatically rejects conventional wisdom; that is, the arguments his listeners would be most likely to provide in order to explain and reduce this "unfathomable enigma." Instead, he stresses the moral validity of the cannibals' self-control, and invites his audience to examine their own "inborn strength." Similar rhetorical devices pervade Marlow's discourse in "Youth" and *Lord Jim,* helping to guide the reader through the ambiguities created by the fiction. Because Conrad presents Marlow's perceptions with point and urgency, we are more likely to be persuaded of the virtues of restraint, work, and solidarity than if the narrator were unreliable or detached from events. That is, the indirectness of the narrative mode allows the writer to insist upon the individual's moral responsibility while maintaining, at the same time, a strict artistic objectivity.

In his letter to the *New York Times Saturday Book Review* (August 2, 1901) Conrad defends *The Inheritors,* a novel written "in collaboration with" Ford Madox Heuffer, against the charge of proselytism. "The business of a work striving to be art is not to teach or to prophesy," he says, adding that "fiction . . . demands from the writer a spirit of scrupulous abnegation." Conrad continues, in words that recall both Maupassant's praise of objective representation in "Le Roman" and his own preface to *The Nigger of the "Narcissus,"* to speak of the writer's "self-forgetful fidelity to his sensations" as the means to "fundamental truth."[12] By creating a dramatized narrator (whether he is the Marlow of "Youth" or the Marlow of *Lord Jim*) who can imitate an authentic oral performance and occupy a concrete, physical space in time, the author appeals to our senses. By giving this narrator a cultural identity that differs in some respects from his own, he achieves impersonality, although (as we have seen in the passages quoted above) Marlow's rhetoric draws us in and persuades us of the "right" answers. Moreover, Conrad uses the relationship between the narrator and his dramatized audience to qualify or reinforce these ethical statements.

In "Youth," Marlow's analysis of the crew's service to its ship supports the first speaker's claim that in England, nature and man have "interpenetrated" to create a particular type of sailor. Like Conrad's careful managing of colloquial terms and diction in this story, the corresponding points of view sustain the solidarity between Marlow and his listeners around the mahogany table. In contrast, the author consistently uses his storyteller in "Heart of Darkness" to undermine the famous opening commentary, which culminates in a stirring reference to the "sacred fire" carried into unknown lands by civilized colonizers. Thus, Marlow continues his investigation of the cannibals' restraint (quoted above) by comparing it with the white manager's unscrupulous manipulation of Kurtz's rescue in order to exploit the Africans more successfully himself: "He was just the kind of man who would wish to preserve appearances. That was his restraint" (106). A little later, we discover that Kurtz, who professes to bring moral enlightenment to the natives and who has been educated partly in England, has responded to the wilderness with unrestrained, primitive savagery.

In fact, as Marlow explores the various reactions of individuals tested by hunger, isolation, or illness the categories of "civilized" and "savage" tend to dissolve. We learn that Marlow, like the cannibals, has "inborn strength," and that the native helmsman, who is killed when he abandons his post at the wheel, is like Kurtz: "He had no restraint, no restraint—just like Kurtz—a tree swayed by the wind" (119). In contrast to the first speaker (the listener on board the *Nellie* who alludes with confidence to the "torch" borne by "the messengers of the might within the land") Marlow becomes increasingly concerned with the disjunction between ideals and reality. Moreover, while the first speaker historicizes the Thames and invests the present with "the august light of abiding memories," Marlow's narrative begins by conflating times and places to reveal the unchanging truths of human experience. And when Marlow's last words are spoken and the listener resumes his narration, a chiasmic pattern is created by the differing perspectives of these two speakers.

Marlow's tale ends in the drawing room of the Intended, where he makes a gesture of affirmation by deciding not to betray the girl's trust in the ideal Kurtz, a trust he describes as "that great and saving illusion that shone with an unearthly glow in the darkness, in the triumphant darkness from which I could not have defended her—from which I could not even defend myself" (159). Marlow's lie preserves the illusion that man is essentially good, but Conrad does not end "Heart of Darkness" with this difficult and complex act of solidarity. In contrast to the story's opening, in the closing paragraph it is the anonymous listener who conflates times and places, putting Marlow's commentary within a broader and more sceptical context: "The offing was barred by a black bank of clouds, and the tranquil waterway leading to the uttermost ends of the earth flowed sombre under an overcast sky—seemed to lead into the heart of an immense darkness." The symbolism of this concluding sentence contradicts the impression created by Marlow's last words ("I could not tell her. It would have been too dark—too dark altogether. . . .") of a darkness kept at bay by the light of the Intended's idealism. Moreover, by returning to the viewpoint of the listener, who has learned some disturbing truths which he seems to be analyzing and developing after the end of Marlow's tale, Conrad draws our attention to the universal human need to "plot" one's own life. That is, for Marlow, the scene in the girl's drawing room, with its symbolic oppositions to Kurtz and the wilderness,[13] helps to resolve an unbearable disjunction between idealism and reality, but for the listener who looks into the future, the shape of experience is still evolving, and the darkness is "immense."

In "Heart of Darkness," then, Conrad opposes his narrative points of view at the beginning and end in order to reflect the ongoing process of moral discovery and disillusionment suggested by Marlow's interaction with his audience throughout the tale. In contrast, the ending of "Youth" reinforces the narrator's idealism, since there is no gap between Marlow's perspective and that of his audience. Like "Heart of Darkness," "Youth" combines a climactic episode (Marlow's lyrical vision of the East) with a return to the fictive present and the listener who concludes the story. Conrad did not alter this form for the book edition, despite his apparent agreement with H. G. Wells's criticism shortly after "Youth" appeared in *Blackwood's:* "Yes. The story should have been ended where you say or perhaps at the next paragraph describing the men sleeping in the boats."[14] Wells seems to have felt that the more effective ending would have been the moment when young Marlow opens his eyes on the East, but Conrad chose to retain the narrator's emotional summary and the listeners' response.

Therefore, because it emphasizes the storyteller's close relationship with an audience, "Youth" gives us a dramatic illustration of the artist's function as it is described in the preface to *The Nigger of the "Narcissus":* "He speaks . . . to the latent feeling of fellowship with all creation—and to the subtle but invincible conviction of solidarity that knits together the loneliness of innumerable hearts." This bond is suggested in the last scene, when Marlow's listeners acknowledge the storyteller's appeal to a fundamental human experience—the death of youthful illusions:

> And we all nodded at him: the man of finance, the man of accounts, the man of law, we all nodded at him over the polished table that like a still sheet of brown water reflected our faces, lined, wrinkled; our faces marked by toil, by deceptions, by success, by love; our weary eyes looking still, looking always, looking anxiously for something out of life, that while it is expected is already gone—has passed unseen, in a sigh, in a flash—together with the youth, with the strength, with the romance of illusions. (42)

Moreover, the coda allows Conrad to restate the theme of the story, through Marlow's rhetorical appeal to his listeners. The interrelationship of nature and man is identified as one of the conditions of knowing "the best" in life; the other, of course, is youth itself: "But you here—you all had something out of life: money, love—whatever one gets on shore—and, tell me, wasn't that the best time, that time when we were young at sea; young and had nothing, on the sea that gives nothing, except hard knocks—and sometimes a chance to feel your strength—that only—what you all regret?" (42). Marlow's phrase, "that time when we were young at sea," makes these two conditions interdependent. To find romance in nature's absurd tests of the *Judea* and her crew, one must be young and "have nothing"; conversely, youthful idealism requires the circumstances of life at sea in order to realize its true strength. If we compare this use of the coda to summarize thematic material with earlier examples in *The Nigger of the "Narcissus"* and "Karain," we find that in each case Conrad assigns the expository function to a first-person narrator, but that Marlow's commentary at the end of "Youth" clarifies the writer's intentions most fully because it involves a dramatized audience that reinforces the narrator's final statement.

Marlow's experiences and perceptions in "Youth" differ markedly from those in "Heart of Darkness" or *Lord Jim,* and the differences are reflected in the complex endings of the later works. In "Heart of Darkness," as we have seen, the narrator's tentative resolution of a moral problem is subtly modified by the coda, dramatizing the inconclusive nature of Marlow's experience. In *Lord Jim* Marlow's attempt to sum up, to speak "the last words about Jim," reveals an inability to decide whether the experience of Patusan has redeemed that of the *Patna.* In contrast to "Youth," the first-person narrator's statement is sceptical, and his audience, the silent reader who receives Marlow's letter, does not reappear to answer the question "Who knows? He is gone, inscrutable at heart. . . ." In both "Heart of Darkness" and *Lord Jim* the techniques that Conrad uses to recapitulate the moral ideas of "Youth" (Marlow's summary and the listeners' response) create ambiguity and involve the reader in conflicting interpretations. Common to all three narratives, however, is one of the essential characteristics of the oral tradition Conrad is imitating; that is, the storyteller's assumption that his audience shares certain values and experiences.[15] On the deck of the *Nellie* Marlow can appeal to "the fellowship of the craft" and patriotic emotions in order to involve his listeners in the tale. Similarly, Marlow's refrain, "He was one of us," which helps give *Lord Jim* thematic and structural coherence, invokes standards of conduct which are accepted without question by the dinner guests and, indirectly, the reader. In both works, therefore, Conrad is able to test the validity of public attitudes toward efficient labour, patriotism, and professional ethics because Marlow's communication with his listeners depends, to some degree, on these very "norms."

In contrast, the narrator's appeal to group solidarity in "Youth" is unqualified; as we have seen, Conrad makes cultural homogeneity a theme in the story. Moreover, the revisions at the manuscript stage and before serial publication show that his desire to explore the "racial difference" of an English crew governed his selection of material. "Youth" is one of the writer's most autobiographical works, although G. Jean-Aubry's description of the story as "precisely in every detail the story of the barque *Palestine*"[16] is, of course, an overstatement. In his pioneering study of Conrad's sources and methods, John D. Gordan points out that the value of identifying the historical events that have inspired the fiction lies in an understanding of how the writer used his raw materials.[17] A pertinent example can be found in the discrepancy between the fictional crew of "Liverpool hard cases" and the men who actually sailed from Falmouth for Bangkok. Najder tells us that "in fact there was not a single Liverpudlian on the *Palestine*. Five men came from Cornwall, one from Ireland, and the remainder were foreigners—an Australian, a Negro from the Antilles, a Dutchman, and a Norwegian."[18]

A fascinating case of transformation from fact to fiction is revealed in the revisions. At the point in the manuscript when the ship prepares to leave Newcastle with her cargo, Conrad introduces a modified description of the historical crew:

> They loaded us at last. We shipped a crew. (I don't remember that lot well) Eight able seamen and two boys. There were amongst them a big Irishman called Sullivan, of course, *and* an East Coast chap with a kind of apostle face, *You know* big swimming eyes a serene expression and rather long fair hair. These were in my watch together with a fat *smoothfaced* Dutchman who spoke in a warbling tone and another man—a little lean *choleric* chap with black eyes—a Welshman. (MS 12a–13a)

Notice that, although Conrad originally has Marlow admit to a faulty memory of the crew's composition, the completed description is concrete and detailed. Whether partly by invention or partly by recollection of shipmates from different ships as well as from the *Palestine,* Conrad creates an impression of national heterogeneity similar to the composition of the actual crew. However, by having this crew leave from Newcastle rather than Falmouth (because the men disband when the ship puts back into port to be stripped and caulked) Conrad is able to introduce the "Liverpool hard cases" at the crucial point when the *Judea* sails from Falmouth on her last, doomed attempt to reach Bangkok.[19]

Moreover, his desire to emphasize the new crew from Liverpool probably led to a substantial revision before the serial publication, when he cancelled his description of the men who sail from Newcastle, in the passage quoted above. In both the *Blackwood's* version and the book edition the text reads: "They loaded us at last. We shipped a crew. Eight able seamen and two boys. We hauled off one evening to the buoys at the dock-gates" (7). The elimination of descriptive detail from Marlow's reference focusses attention on the crew from Liverpool, with its impressive discipline and spirit. When the reader recalls the events of the story, he is able to visualize only one group of men—the black-faced, bandaged "scarecrows" who trim the yards of the wreck. And, as we have seen, part of Conrad's narrative strategy involves emphasizing the heroic aspect of this crew's performance.

"Youth" carries on the affirmative view of solidarity through collaborative labour expressed in the last few pages of *The Nigger of the "Narcissus"* without documenting the lapses and exceptions that give the novel its moral realism. Because the romantic egocentricity of young Marlow is repeatedly and passionately invoked by the middle-aged narrator, critics have tended to either minimize the theme of solidarity or overlook it entirely.[20] Yet, as we have seen in the coda, Marlow suggests that the idealism of youth is fully realized only through the conditions of life at sea. One of these conditions, communal labour in the service of the ship, is dramatized frequently in the story: "Everyone took his turn, captain included. There was equality, and if not exactly fraternity, then a deal of good feeling. Sometimes a man, as he dashed a bucketful of water down the hatchway, would yell out, 'Hurrah for Bankok!' and the rest laughed" (21). Even Mrs. Beard, by preparing the "outfits" for the captain and his second mate, contributes in an indirect way to the sailing of the *Judea*.

Relating the episodes in which the men's endurance is tested to the fullest, Conrad shifts the narrative perspective to the first-person plural, recalling the technique he had used to make the crew the hero of *The Nigger of the "Narcissus"*:

> There was for us no sky, there were for us no stars, no sun, no universe—nothing but angry clouds and an infuriated sea. We pumped watch and watch, for dear life; and it seemed to last for months, for years, for all eternity, as though we had been dead and gone to a hell for sailors. We forgot the day of the week, the name of the month, what year it was, and whether we had ever been ashore . . . we turned, we turned incessantly, with the water to our waists, to our necks, over our heads. It was all one. We had forgotten how it felt to be dry.
>
> And there was somewhere in me the thought: By Jove! this is the deuce of an adventure—something you read about; and it is my first voyage as second mate—and I am only twenty—and here I am lasting it out as well as any of these men, and keeping my chaps up to the mark. (11–12)

Then, in the movement from first-person plural in the first paragraph to first-person singular in the second, and the corresponding stylistic change from heavy *anaphora* (imitating the repeated, laboured turns of the pump) to Marlow's free association, his thoughts loosely joined by coordinate conjunctions and dashes, the narrator shows us the spontaneous egoism of youth as well as its ironic dependence on the context of communal effort. Although the twenty-year-old mate is unaware that he owes much of his buoyant spirit to this effort, Marlow at forty-two makes the grinding, unimaginative labour a necessary condition for the "moments of exaltation" experienced by youth. In contrast, the adventurous young Russian sailor in "Heart of Darkness" becomes Kurtz's disciple because the wilderness offers him no alternative form of service that can direct his "unreflecting audacity."

Moreover, as a source of humour, young Marlow's idealism unites the teller and his listeners, although with an essentially sympathetic irony different from any of Conrad's other works. The narrator juxtaposes his "heroic" descent into the burning hold with the undignified fishing expedition that rescues him, and his proud "first command" with the "cockleshell" he actually steers, but these comic discrepancies do not significantly reduce the hero's stature. In the revisions of "Youth" Conrad carefully controls Marlow's tone in order to capitalize on the mildly ironic nature of the humour without disturbing the reader's sympathy for the protagonist. For example, the familiar account of young Marlow's rescue from the hold loses much of its energy in the manuscript version because the metaphor ("to fish one out of his trouble") is not sufficiently developed: "Then I leaped down to show how it [sic] easily it could be done. They fished me out with a chain hook" (MS 6-7b). For the serial publication Conrad added visual detail and a wry commentary, dramatizing the figure of speech more clearly: "Then I leaped down to show how easily it could be done. They had learned wisdom by that time, and contented themselves by fishing for me with a chain-hook tied to a broom-handle, I believe" (21). Notice how the revision emphasizes the narrator's tone of genial irony. Once again, the crew's concerted action supports youth's absurdly romantic gesture.

In "Heart of Darkness" Conrad also dramatizes puns and figures of speech, communicating moral concepts and values to the reader through the sardonic humour of the wordplay. For example, when Marlow meets the agent, or "brickmaker," at the Central Station, and this official reveals the mean, self-seeking motives for inviting Marlow into his room, the latter comments, "He talked precipitately, and I did not try to stop him. I had my shoulders against the wreck of my steamer, hauled up on the slope like a carcass of some big river animal" (83). The agent's talk centers on the influential friends Marlow is supposed to have in Europe—the "gang of virtue" that connects him with Kurtz in the minds of the colonial officials. "I let him run on," says Marlow, "and think what he pleased about the powers that were behind me. I did! And there was nothing behind me! There was nothing but that wretched, old, mangled steamboat I was leaning against, while he talked fluently about 'the necessity for every man to get on'" (83). After the two men separate for the night, Conrad develops the irony of Marlow's situation, and introduces an explicit statement of the value of work:

> It was a great comfort to turn from that chap to my influential friend, the battered, twisted, ruined, tin-pot steamboat. . . . I had expended enough hard work on her to make me love her. No

> influential friend would have served me better. She had given me a chance to come out a bit—to find out what I could do. No, I don't like work. I had rather laze about and think of all the fine things that can be done. I don't like work—no man does—but I like what is in the work,—the chance to find yourself. Your own reality—for yourself, not for others—what no other man can ever know. (85)

The virtues Marlow ascribes to work are linked to the pun on "the powers that were behind me." Thus, the steamboat's solid "influence," which stands "behind" Marlow, provides him with an active project (requiring real rivets and a purpose) that opposes the agent's "Mephistophelean" pretenses and, paradoxically, causes Marlow to lie for Kurtz by silently feigning the type of influence he does not have. Work also prompts the individual to explore "his own reality" or inner self; the idle "brickmaker" has "nothing inside but a little loose dirt." Moreover, the "influence" exerted by the ruined old boat gives Marlow solidarity with another good worker, the boilermaker at the station who joins him on the iron deck in a symbolic dance of defiance against the wilderness and its white colonizers. In this example, then, the wordplay on the powers that stand "behind" Marlow is used to explore serious ideas, both by the force of the comparison and by the narrator's shift in tone from sardonic to reflective.

While "Heart of Darkness" demonstrates Conrad's dramatic use of puns and colloquialisms as vehicles for moral ideas, with humour playing a subordinate role, "Youth" focusses on the comic situation. But as we have already seen, Conrad is careful to control the ironic tone of the narration so that neither young Marlow nor his shipmates and senior officers are ridiculed. In his revisions to the episode containing Captain Beard's ludicrously hasty rescue of his wife during the collision in Newcastle harbour, for example, Conrad adds the critical word "heroically" to Marlow's exclamation: "Just imagine that old fellow saving heroically in his arms that old woman—the woman of his life" (9). The geniality of the humour in "Youth" acts as a solid bridge between the narrator and his audience, a bridge which helps Marlow to appeal to common values and traditions.[21]

Why was Conrad so concerned to emphasize solidarity in the themes and techniques of this short story? As I have indicated, "Youth" was his first piece of overtly autobiographical fiction, and it appears to have been motivated by the conventional autobiographical impulse to record an important change in the direction of one's life.[22] In Conrad's case this impulse was complicated by feelings of cultural dislocation. As Najder says when he describes this period of transition in the writer's life: "Now after so many years, the lonely man and wanderer settled down and established a family; the sailor dropped anchor in a quiet village; the marine officer changed, with difficulty, into a man of letters; and the exile tried to take root in an alien country."[23] Perhaps one of the effects of Conrad's sense of "living amongst strangers" (as he wrote to Wincenty Lutoslawski on June 9, 1897)[24] was to compensate for his foreignness by emphasizing English place names and colloquial expressions in "Youth."

In the first part of the story the geography of England is so carefully reproduced that the reader has little difficulty tracing the sea route of the *Judea* from London to Newcastle, or imagining the environs of Falmouth, where young Marlow waits impatiently to set sail for Bangkok. In contrast to the specificity of the Western setting, the East of Marlow's dreams is evoked through suggestion and allusion. In the following sentence, for example, Conrad revised his first draft to include colourful historical allusions: "And I thought of men of old who centuries ago went that road, in ships that sailed no better, to the land of palms, *and spices* and yellow sands, and brown nations ruled by kings more (rich and) cruel *than Nero the Roman and more* splendid than (words can express) Solomon the Jew" (MS 40a). As a symbol of the romantic illusions of youth (which include the glamour of the unknown) the East is described in evocative terms such as "magic" and "blessed," rather than located precisely, as if on a map. Conrad's next story, "Heart of Darkness," follows the same pattern, taking the reader from a specific location to an increasingly less defined and more symbolic inner world.

Similarly, Marlow's fondness for proverbial or colloquial expressions tells us much about Conrad's desire to reach a specific cultural audience. Comparison of Marlow's discourse with that of the narrator in "Karain" suggests that the informal framework of storyteller and audience in "Youth" freed the writer to exploit colloquialisms, idioms, and informal diction, creating an impression of group solidarity. Another factor which probably contributed to Marlow's informality was Conrad's increased experience with this aspect of the English language. One of the significant categories of his revisions consists of additions to the stock of common expressions in the story, for in most cases these changes illustrate Conrad's control of the narrative tone at times when he wanted to reinforce Marlow's intimate relationship with the listening audience. For example, he revised "put her into a third class carriage" (describing young Marlow's attentions to Mrs. Beard) to "put her all comfy into a third class carriage" (MS 18a), and he emphasized Marlow's anxiety about the small boats alongside the burning ship by adding a colloquialism: "the boats would not keep astern where they were safe but persisted *in a pigheaded way boats have* in getting under the counter and then swinging alongside" (MS 41b). A. J. Lord, a scholar and historian of the oral narrative, stresses the importance of terms and expressions known to all speakers in the community to the themes and repertory of the individual artist.[25] Because he was imitating an oral performance in "Youth," "Heart of Darkness," and *Lord Jim,* Conrad could use this language to explore, through his persona, a national temperament which was in many ways alien to his own cultural background.

Moreover, by representing in concrete terms a group of listeners to Marlow's tale Conrad brings the "real" world into the microcosm of the fiction. In his influential essay on the novel Ortega y Gasset writes that, in his judgment, "no writer can be called a novelist unless he possesses the gift of forgetting, and thereby making us forget, the reality beyond the walls of his novel. Let him be as realistic as can be; that is to say, let the microcosm of his novel consist of unquestionably true-to-life elements—he will have lost out if he cannot keep us from remembering that there exists an extramural world.''[26] As the reader's surrogates, the dramatized listeners represent the ''extramural world'' while remaining, at the same time, creatures belonging to Conrad's fiction. Through Marlow's appeals to the audience the writer can remind us of our moral and political lives in the real world, and encourage us to relate them to the story he tells. Therefore, in ''Youth'' Conrad experiments with a narrative structure which enables him to enlarge the scope of his fiction by incorporating the reader's most fundamental values and concerns.

Other short story writers with whom Conrad was familiar, such as Turgenev and Henry James, create ''framing'' situations which derive from the oral narrative. Turgenev's tale, ''A Lear of the Steppes,'' for instance, begins with a party of six gathered together one winter evening at the home of an old college friend, whose reminiscences of his childhood gradually evolve into the story of Harlov, the protagonist. The narrator involves his listeners in a limited way by asking them to picture or imagine characters and events for themselves, a technique Conrad uses repeatedly in his Marlow stories. In other respects, however, Conrad developed the ''framing'' situation well beyond its traditional function of establishing an atmosphere of authenticity and ''tellability'' at the beginning of the story. Especially in ''Heart of Darkness'' Marlow's listeners play a crucial role in challenging the reader and extending the thematic implications of the narrative.[27] Moreover, Conrad's careful delineation of the speaker and his audience, which anticipates Faulkner's work three and four decades later, is also related to his use of repetition, colloquialisms, and rhythmic patterns to give Marlow's speech the pace and tone of an authentic oral performance.

For Conrad, the dreamlike quality of life renders all experience ultimately impossible to grasp or communicate, but one of the writer's best hopes is to be found in the concrete representation of reality. As he wrote to Fisher Unwin in August 1896, ''Inevitableness is the only certitude; it is the very essence of life—as it is of dreams. A picture of life is saved from failure by the merciless vividness of detail.''[28] Although Conrad's use of the word ''picture'' seems to limit fiction to visual impressions, aural immediacy forms part of his strategy to communicate experience to the reader. Similarly, the dramatized listeners provide a realistic focal point for Marlow's voice, objectifying the audience the artist struggles to reach. In a letter to A. Quiller-Couch Conrad compares the writer's isolation to that of a sailor when at sea:

> Writing in a solitude almost as great as that of the ship at sea the great living crowd outside is somehow forgotten; just as on a long, long passage the existence of continents peopled by men seems to pass out of the domain of facts and becomes, so to speak, a theoretical belief. Only a small group of human beings—a few friends, relations—remain to the seaman always distinct, indubitable, the only ones who matter. And so to the solitary writer.[29]

The oral mode allowed Conrad to focus not only on Marlow's experience of "inevitable" reality in the past, but on the active transmission and reception of that experience in the fictive present, employing visual and aural sense impressions in an attempt to pin down the essential nature of communication.

In the manuscript revisions of "Youth" as well as the additions to the story before serial publication both the listeners and their physical setting are rendered more concretely and suggestively than in the first rough draft. In the manuscript Conrad increases the number of the group from four to five, adding the solicitor who had served on the historic, square-rigged ships of England's most famous merchant line. The thematic reason for the lawyer's inclusion emerges at the end of the story, when each man is characterized by his professional role ("And we all nodded at him: the man of finance, the man of accounts, the man of law") in order to stress the value of romantic idealism and imagination as opposed to material wealth and position. The few descriptive details of the setting also appear to have been added to the rough draft during the process of composition: "There were (four) five of us (in the room) round a mahogany table that reflected the bottle, the glasses and our faces as we leaned on our elbows" (MS 1a). Here, Conrad apparently decided to substitute the dramatic motif of passing the claret bottle—so that the reader is continually reminded of the gap between past and present times—for the conventional static opening in which the group is simply assembled "in a room." In the last paragraph of the story the addition of colour to the polished table that mirrors the faces "like a still sheet of *brown* water" (MS 41b) contrasts with the bright azure of the sea in Marlow's memory of his youth.

These intimations of Conrad's interest in making the narrative frame more suggestive anticipate the poetic effects achieved seven months later in "Heart of Darkness." As Marlow tells his story the sky darkens perceptibly around the *Nellie,* and the first narrator comments, "It had become so pitch dark that we listeners could hardly see one another" (83). The gathering darkness and heaviness of the night air echo the impression Conrad creates in the opening paragraph of the Earth's sun moving inexorably toward cold extinction: "And at last, in its curved and imperceptible fall, the sun sank low, and from glowing white changed to a dull red without rays and without heat, as if about to go out suddenly, stricken to death by the touch of that gloom brooding over a crowd of men" (46). Against this apocalyptic image, which suggests the end of human life, the traffic of the city goes on. As Marlow speaks, the "lights of ships moved in the fairway—a great stir of lights going up and going down." This visual impression of commercial activity is contrasted to the imagined darkness of pre-civilized England as Marlow stretches time in the opposite direction: "Light came out of this river since—you say Knights? Yes; but it is like a running blaze on a plain, like a flash of lightning in the clouds. We live in the flicker—may it last as long as the old earth keeps rolling! But darkness was here yesterday" (49). That "great stir of lights" (a comforting sight to an accountant, lawyer or director of companies) is metaphorically reduced to less than a "flicker" of civilization in an abyss of past and future time; in fact, as Marlow takes his audience deeper and deeper into "the night of first ages" in his narrative, a "faint uneasiness" conquers at least one of the listeners, and the tiny flames crossing and recrossing each other on the river are completely extinguished in our last, sombre view of the waterway.

As we saw earlier in the contrasting perspectives of Marlow and the first speaker, the relationship between the two levels of narrative develops and interprets themes instead of restating them. The present "reality"—that which is seen and heard by the listeners, and their response—is so closely integrated with the main story that, like the haze surrounding the glow in Conrad's metaphor, it suggests more meanings than the events themselves can encompass. However, when Conrad adapts this narrative mode to a longer form, it loses some of its suggestiveness. In *Lord Jim* Marlow's interactions with his audience and the references to the storyteller's physical surroundings are less frequent, and the reader cannot rely upon the same concentration of images, motifs, and wordplay. Moreover, although the narrator of the novel involves his listeners by questioning their capacity for imaginative sympathy, he does not challenge their ideological stance as directly and completely as Marlow in "Heart of Darkness."

Many critics have analyzed the dynamic engagement of Marlow's audience in the narrative process throughout "Heart of Darkness," and have pointed to its evolution from the simple frame of "Youth." In the revisions to the story before serial publication Conrad added several rhetorical phrases and questions, which contribute to the aural immediacy of Marlow's narration. Reminders of the audience such as "You'll admit that . . . ," "I need not tell you," and "Would you believe it?" reproduce the natural speech rhythms at the same time as they emphasize important points in the story. As J. Wilkes Berry and Marion C. Michael have shown in their examination of the typescript of "Heart of Darkness," Conrad subjected that story to a similarly rigorous reworking in order to stress its oral framework.[30] In both tales the bond of friendship among the five ex-seamen is emphasized by the explicit appeal to common nautical experiences and memories of the past; incidentally, the sentence "We all began life in the merchant service" was added to the opening paragraph of "Youth" before it went to *Blackwood's*. However, in the revisions to the earlier story there is no evidence that Conrad was exploring the possibility of presenting Marlow in a more ambivalent light.

Not until "Heart of Darkness" does he show a narrator struggling to give expression to his thoughts. In the later story Marlow hesitates before he begins his tale, and his silence parallels the moment of "startled pause" before undertaking a journey to "the centre of the earth." As the moral implications of his past experience disturb the course of Marlow's narration, yielding periods of silence, reflection, and self-contradiction, he discovers the inadequacy and ambiguity of the words he must use. The memory of "one immense jabber" haunts the storyteller and paralyzes his speech:

"A voice. He was very little more than a voice. And I heard—him—it—this voice—other voices—all of them were so little more than voices—and the memory of that time itself lingers around me, impalpable, like a dying vibration of one immense jabber, silly, atrocious, sordid, savage, or simply mean, without any kind of sense. Voices, voices—even the girl herself—now—"
He was silent for a long time.
"I laid the ghost of his gifts at last with a lie," he began, suddenly. (115)

At this point in the story Marlow's silence has the dramatic effect of delaying the introduction of Kurtz's Intended, but more important, it reminds us that the narrator himself has a voice which, despite its capacity for truth-telling, can never reproduce the shape of experience as it actually is or was. In this passage (and in the three other expressive pauses in Marlow's tale) Conrad invites the reader to interpret the narrator's silence. He juxtaposes the Intended's "lies" or illusions with Kurtz's egoistic abuse of language and the self-seeking lies of the other Europeans. The long silence implies the equivocal nature of Marlow's lie in this context, and the uneasy compromises it represents.

By making the reader account for pauses in the narration Conrad demonstrates the truth of Marlow's declaration to his listeners that "you fellows see more than I could then" (83). Similarly, the allusive and ambiguous nature of words leads the narrator to make statements that are open to various interpretations by the reader. Consider, for example, his affirmation of "an unselfish belief in the idea—something you can set up, and bow down before, and offer a sacrifice to," which suggests Kurtz's perversion of idealism as well as the Intended's purity. The ambiguity of words and their shifting contexts prompts Marlow's realization that "it is impossible to convey the life-sensation of any given epoch of one's existence—that which makes its truth, its meaning—its subtle and penetrating essence" (82). Behind the narrator's repeated beginnings as he "stops and starts" in his attempt to make sense of human conduct lies the image of a disjunction between language and reality, "one immense jabber . . . without any kind of sense." Because Marlow sustains his contract with an audience despite this forbidding truth, Conrad affirms the ethical and epistemological functions of the storyteller's or writer's task. "We live, as we dream—alone," says the narrator, but he seeks, nevertheless, to build a community of morally involved listeners. Moreover, through the vividness of aural and visual impressions he can explore a significant part of reality, even if he does not grasp the whole.

The largest category of substantial revisions to the story reveals the importance of this aspect of Marlow's narration in "Youth." About one-seventh of the cancellations and additions that appear in the manuscript are devoted to sharpening the focus of visual sense impressions. In many cases, Conrad added a concrete detail, a modifier, a verbal or a figure of speech that renders colours, shapes or gestures more accurately. Sometimes, as in the following excerpt from the episode in which the crew shovels sand-ballast in the midst of a storm, the addition suggests the "unreal" quality of the experience as well as the concrete immediacy of the scene:

"And there we were in that hold; (the gale howled,) gloomy like a cavern, the tallow-dips *stuck and* flickering on the beams, the gale howling *above* the ship tossing about *like mad* on her side" (MS 10a). The revision transforms the ship's hold into a solid rock or earthen cave grotesquely in motion, and prepares us for the subsequent comparison of the shovelling to "that gravediggers work."

After the manuscript stage Conrad's revisions were less numerous, but much more substantial. Many sequential sentences were added, as well as paragraphs and even an episode. In fact, the range and precision of the additions and cancellations testify to a determination to make the *Blackwood's* text as close to the writer's ideal conception of the story as possible, which disproves Richard Curle's statement that Conrad "was not much concerned about perfecting his text for serial publication."[31] Conrad's reworking of the story for *Blackwood's* transforms some scenes dramatically, introducing incongruous images, descriptive detail or direct speech. For example, when we compare the different versions of Marlow's impression of the *Judea*'s deck after the explosion we find that Conrad intensifies the visual appearance of the scene considerably by emphasizing its strangeness and lack of logic.

The manuscript reads: "Then we retreated aft. The deck was a tangle of planks on edge, on end, of splinters, of ruined woodwork. Here and there a piece of timber *stuck* upright resembled a post. A portion of the deck protruded over the rail, like a gang-way leading upon nothing, to the deep sea, to death—inviting us to walk the plank and end our ridiculous troubles. And all the time the air the sky—a ghost, was hailing the ship" (MS 12b–13b). In the revised serial version Conrad's forest metaphor gives the scene a hallucinatory vividness:

> Then we retreated aft and looked about us. The deck was a tangle of planks on edge, of planks on end, of splinters, of ruined woodwork. The masts rose from that chaos like big trees above a matted undergrowth. The interstices of that mass of wreckage were full of something whitish, sluggish, stirring—of something that was like a greasy fog. The smoke of the invisible fire was coming up again, was trailing, like a poisonous thick mist in some valley choked with dead wood. Already lazy wisps were beginning to curl upwards amongst the mass of splinters. Here and there a piece of timber, stuck upright, resembled a post. Half of a fife-rail had been shot through the foresail, and the sky made a patch of glorious blue in the ignobly soiled canvas. A portion of several boards holding together had fallen across the rail, and one end protruded overboard, like a gangway leading upon nothing, like a gangway leading over the deep sea, leading to death— as if inviting us to walk the plank at once and thus end the poignant comedy of that voyage. And still the air, the sky—a ghost, something invisible was hailing the ship. (*B*, 321)

Like the comparison of the ship's hold to a cavern in the earth, the forest metaphor relies upon the suggestion of grotesque incongruity for its effectiveness. Moreover, the reader is involved in the dreamlike scene because Conrad withholds the logical explanation for the presence of "something whitish, sluggish, stirring" until the initial impression of fog shrouding a dead forest has been strongly established in our minds. The addition of visual details emphasizing colour contrast and geometric shapes heightens the sensuous impact of the description, while the juxtaposition of the concrete facts and "something invisible" which seems to haunt the doomed ship contributes to our sense of absurd unreality.[32]

Ian Watt has used the term "delayed decoding" to describe one of Conrad's techniques for rendering visual impressions directly. Discussing Marlow's narration of the explosion on board the *Judea,* he says: "Conrad presented the protagonist's immediate sensations, and thus made the reader aware of the gap between impression and understanding; the delay in bridging the gap enacts the disjunction between the event and the observer's trailing understanding of it."[33] In the rough draft we find that the moment of the explosion is presented largely as it appears in the serial and book versions (an indication, perhaps, of the writer's natural tendency to "see" events in this way) and that the revisions to this scene are chiefly concentrated on intensifying the disjunctive effect of the "delayed decoding." To alert the reader without revealing the subsequent action, Conrad added the captain's remark, "It's wonderful how that smell hangs about the cabin," and modifiers were carefully chosen to reflect comically upon young Marlow's ignorance only *after* the episode had been decoded. On a first reading we share the protagonist's irritation: "And then I perceived *with annoyance* the fool was trying to tilt the bench. I said *curtly* 'Don't Chips'" (MS, 9b). The narrator continues to record young Marlow's momentary sensations, and documents his thoughts in the order they occur until the cause of the mystery is revealed.[34]

To heighten Marlow's impression of living "an absurd dream," Conrad made some important revisions before the serial publication. In the manuscript there is nothing exceptional about Marlow's first meeting with Captain Beard after the explosion because the effect of the disaster on the older man is described in the past tense rather than presented dramatically, in scenic form. The narrator says: "Presently I saw the I saw the [*sic*] captain. The old chap it seems was in his (cabin) berth winding up the chronometers when the shock sent him spinning. At once it occurred to him that the ship had (hit) something. He ran (out of the room) into the cabin. There he saw that the cabin table had vanished somewhere. Where we had our breakfast that morning there was a hole in the floor. This impressed him so immensely that what he saw and heard (afterwards) after he got on deck were *mere trifles in comparison*" (MS 10–11b).

Revising the episode for the serial version, Conrad retained this commentary (with some additions) but prefaced it with the direct presentation of the captain's irrational behaviour. This order results in yet another form of "delayed decoding," for Marlow gives us the story of Beard's experience only after the following scene, which culminates in an absurd Dickensian exchange:

> Presently I saw the captain—and he was mad. He asked me eagerly, "Where's the cabin-table?" and to hear such a question was a frightful shock. I had just been blown up, you understand, and vibrated with that experience,—I wasn't quite sure whether I was alive. Mahon began to stamp with both feet and yelled at him, "Good God! don't you see the deck's blown out of her?" I found my voice, and stammered out as if conscious of some gross neglect of duty, "I don't know where the cabin-table is." It was like an absurd dream.

> Do you know what he wanted next? Well, he wanted to trim the yards. Very placidly, and as if lost in thought, he insisted on having the foreyard squared. "I don't know if there's anybody alive," said Mahon, almost tearfully. "Surely," he said, gently, "there will be enough left to square the foreyard." (24)

The direct discourse, descriptive inquit, and dramatic action involve the reader in Marlow's comic predicament, and the initial question "Where's the cabin-table?" is as inexplicable and surprising to us as it is to the protagonist.

Conrad's impressionistic presentation of the dreamlike or hallucinatory nature of existence fulfills the aesthetic principle outlined in his letter to Fisher Unwin on August 22, 1896, quoted earlier. Conrad writes: "A picture of life is saved from failure by the merciless vividness of detail." He then goes on to explain that "like a dream it must be startling, undeniable, absurd and appalling. Like a dream it may be ludicrous or tragic and like a dream pitiless and inevitable; a thing monstrous or sweet from which You cannot escape. Our captivity within the incomprehensible logic of accident is the only fact of the universe." In his revisions of "Youth" Conrad seeks to render more suggestively the fluid and contingent qualities of human experience, the "raw stuff" that appears dreamlike because it refuses to be ordered. Another major category of these revisions, which includes the writer's syntactical alterations for the sake of emphasis, clarity, or rhythm, cannot be easily separated from his techniques to make sense impressions more vivid and arresting.

For example, let us look at another excerpt from the explosion scene, immediately after young Marlow picks himself up and "bolts" towards the poop-ladder. The manuscript reads: "The first person I saw was Mahon. His eyes were like saucers, his white hair (stood like halo) *standing on end* made a silver halo for his head. The sight of the main deck heaving up before his eyes had petrified him on the top step" (MS 10b). Conrad's addition to the first draft, "standing on end," makes the description more precise, but in his revisions before the serial publication the syntax emphasizes the visual impression: "The first person I saw was Mahon, with eyes like saucers, his mouth open, and the long white hair standing straight on end round his head like a silver halo. He was just about to go down when the sight of the main-deck stirring, heaving up, and changing into splinters before his eyes, petrified him on the top step" (23). Conrad makes us see Mahon more clearly by concentrating our attention on the circle shape: the round eyes, mouth, and head are described in a series of parallel phrases. Syntactically, the first sentence combines two shorter ones in the manuscript, so that greater emphasis falls on the last word of the series, "halo." The repetition of "like" avoids the much weaker manuscript ending, "a halo for his head," thus emphasizing Mahon's strange transformation. Here and elsewhere in the revisions the addition of concrete details, modifiers, or figures of speech is accompanied by syntactical rearrangement to sharpen the sense impression.

In passing, we should notice Conrad's expansion of the sentence describing Mahon's view of the deck during the explosion. By adding the verbals "stirring" and "changing" [into splinters], he compresses the entire dramatic action into a few seconds of reading time, imitating the "infinitesimal fraction of a second" that actually passed between the first tilt of the carpenter's bench to Marlow's landing full-length on the cargo. In contrast, when we experience the same action from young Marlow's point of view, that "fraction of a second" is stretched to correspond to the protagonist's "lived" time. In this way, Conrad presents two views of the explosion—an external, objective perspective that follows almost immediately after the internal, subjective impression.

For the sake of ready comprehension, I have limited my examples of Conrad's impressionism to the scene in which the *Judea*'s cargo explodes, but "Youth" is composed of a whole series of episodes seen in this startling and immediate way. First, a red gleam flashes mysteriously in the darkness of Newcastle harbour as the *Judea* prepares to begin her voyage, with young Marlow alone on deck. The light vanishes and reappears before he can associate it with the fore-end of the steamer that rams his ship. The next catastrophe is also apprehended through the senses before it can be decoded:

> One night when tied to the mast, as I explained, we were pumping on, deafened with the wind, and without spirit enough in us to wish ourselves dead, a heavy sea crashed aboard and swept clean over us. As soon as I got my breath I shouted, as in duty bound, "Keep on, boys!" when suddenly I felt something hard floating on deck strike the calf of my leg. I made a grab at it and missed. It was so dark we could not see each other's faces within a foot—you understand.
>
> After that thump the ship kept quiet for a while, and the thing, whatever it was, struck my leg again. This time I caught it—and it was a saucepan. At first, being stupid with fatigue and thinking of nothing but the pumps, I did not understand what I had in my hand. Suddenly it dawned upon me, and I shouted, "Boys, the house on deck is gone. Leave this, and let's look for the cook." (12–13)

In order to describe the sensation more precisely, Conrad added a modifier ("hard") and a specific detail ("the calf of my leg") to the manuscript version, which reads, ". . . I felt something floating on deck strike my leg" (MS, 25b,26a). Even after we have discovered the immediate cause of this sensation, we may not understand the significance of the event until Marlow's announcement to the crew. In this way, the reader (like young Marlow) experiences the main episodes of the story directly, and participates in the search for meaning.

The impressionist techniques of "Youth" anticipate those in "Heart of Darkness," which is perhaps the most intensely visualized of Conrad's works. As in "Youth," we first experience Marlow's physical surroundings through the senses, but the length of time between the initial impression and its revealed meanings is often much longer. As Marlow climbs the path to the Outer Station, for example, he sees that "to the left, a clump of trees made a shady spot, where dark things seemed to stir feebly" (64). The dying victims of European greed are first perceived in this disturbingly vague, yet sensuous image. Against the "blinding sunlight" the patch of darkness is clearly defined, but the modifying phrase, "where dark things seemed to stir feebly," is evocative without being concrete, and suggests subhuman forms of life. After he registers this brief but troubling impression Marlow moves on, with no intention of investigating the "shady spot." The sights he encounters—a meaningless explosion, an "artificial" hole in the slope, and a chain-gang comprising six natives and their black overseer—are apparently unrelated to his initial impression, as is the sudden memory he has of "that ship of war . . . firing into a continent."

The progress toward the clump of trees is interrupted and oblique, allowing the images of folly, impotence, and tyranny to accumulate in the reader's mind before Marlow finally identifies the "dark things" and perceives their connection with the other discoveries made during his walk to the station: "Black shapes crouched, lay, sat between the trees leaning against the trunks, clinging to the earth, half coming out, half effaced within the dim light, in all the attitudes of pain, abandonment, and despair. Another mine on the cliff went off, followed by a slight shudder of the soil under my feet. The work was going on. The work! And this was the place where some of the helpers had withdrawn to die" (66). As Marlow's view of the native workers becomes more and more sharply focussed, he realizes that the "things" are not simply "helpers" in "the great cause," but individual human beings: "I began to distinguish the gleam of the eyes under the trees. Then, glancing down, I saw a face near my hand. The black bones reclined at full length with one shoulder against the tree, and slowly the eyelids rose and the sunken eyes looked up at me, enormous and vacant, a kind of blind, white flicker in the depths of the orbs, which died out slowly. The man seemed young—" (66-67). Marlow's acute visual perception of the body lying at his feet gives rise to his compassion for the man's desperate condition, the offer of a ship's biscuit being the dramatic expression of an inner response to suffering. Here, as when the narrator discovers, through a "nearer view" with his binoculars, that the round, carved balls decorating the posts at Kurtz's station are human heads impaled on stakes, the powerful clarity of Marlow's physical sensations yields a deeper imaginative understanding of the moral issue.

In the latter case the detailed examination of one of the human heads is associated with the narrator's first sustained insight into the nature of Kurtz:

> I want you clearly to understand that there was nothing exactly profitable in these heads being there. They only showed that Mr. Kurtz lacked restraint in the gratification of his various lusts, that there was something wanting in him—some small matter which, when the pressing need arose, could not be found under his magnificent eloquence. Whether he knew of this deficiency himself I can't say. I think the knowledge came to him at last—only at the very last. But the wilderness had found him out early, and had taken on him a terrible vengeance for the fantastic invasion. I think it had whispered to him things about himself which he did not know, things of which he had no conception till he took counsel with his great solitude—and the whisper had proved irresistibly fascinating. It echoed loudly within him because he was hollow at the core. . . . I put down the glass, and the head that had appeared near enough to be spoken to seemed at once to have leaped away from me into inaccessible distance. (131)

By emphasizing the relationship between visual perception and the imaginative awareness of other individuals, Conrad implies an ethical as well as an epistemological value in Marlow's careful, close study of his surroundings. In this respect, the narrator of "Heart of Darkness" resembles the imaginative artist described in *A Personal Record*, for whom the sole moral justification for a "spectacular" world is to be found in man's "unwearied self-forgetful attention to every phase of the living universe reflected in our consciousness," the task being "to bear true testimony" actively and without despair.[35]

While Marlow distinguishes the native victims of colonization lying beneath the trees gradually, the reader is not compelled to keep pace with his process of understanding. As in "Youth," when young Marlow seems slow to grasp the meaning of a floating saucepan, Conrad urges us to make our own associations between the initial sense impression (the "dark things") and the black men in chains, the smashed drainage-pipes, the decaying machinery and the rusty rails—all abandoned tools of the Europeans' brutal assault on the wilderness. In fact, the full ironic impact of this scene depends on the reader's having made these connections before Marlow reaches the grove of trees, for, as he tells us, his "purpose" was "to stroll into the shade for a moment." Similarly, the passage describing Marlow's view of the severed head on a pole at the Inner Station is dramatically effective because of the narrator's reluctance to disclose the details of a sight for which both his own preamble and the conversation with the young Russian have fully prepared us. Thus, all the information the reader requires to decipher the curious fact of ornamental posts in the midst of a primitive trading station is contained in Marlow's hints and the Russian's brief history of Kurtz's career. By making associations we participate in the narrator's investigation of human nature tested by the "great solitude" of the wilderness. In contrast, because our involvement in Marlow's "decoding" of his impressions in "Youth" is limited to the physical circumstances surrounding an immediate event, the relationship between visual perception and moral awareness is not established. As a result, "Youth" lacks the complexity and comprehensiveness of the longer story.

In "Heart of Darkness," gaps between the narrator's first impressions and his coherent interpretation of the signs occur just as frequently on the conceptual as on the perceptual level. Comments such as the chief accountant's judgment of Kurtz ("He is a very remarkable person") and the Central Station manager's appraisal of the time required to repair the steamboat ("That ought to do the affair") imply more than they seem to signify in their immediate context. As Marlow realizes in retrospect, the steamboat affair "was too stupid . . . to be altogether natural." However, although a plot against Kurtz seems obvious after Conrad has given us clues such as the manager's conversation with his uncle and the testimony of the Russian trader, the narrator's lingering doubts frustrate the reader's attempt to find an absolute solution to the mystery: "I did not see the real significance of that wreck at once. I fancy I see it now, but I am not sure—not at all" (72). Similarly, the accountant's description of Kurtz's achievements "in the true ivory-country, at 'the very bottom of there'" (69) creates an impression of exceptional determination and imagination, which draws Marlow into the wilderness like a magnet. Although Conrad is deliberately ambiguous about whether Kurtz's "methods" were well-known throughout the district, the accountant's expressive gestures and conspiratorial remarks are signals to Marlow and the reader that the mission to relieve Kurtz might uncover more serious concerns than large percentages and professional competitiveness. Only after Marlow has involved himself deeply in Kurtz's affairs, however, can he attempt to identify or explain the sense in which the agent is "remarkable."

Although the revelation of events and characters through Marlow's gradual discovery of their complexity is not a feature of "Youth," Conrad's representation of commonplace happenings as "mysteries" to be solved immediately and easily is a comic version of the technique. In the cabin-table episode, as we have seen, revisions to the manuscript are calculated to involve the reader in young Marlow's bewilderment by withholding the logical explanation for Captain Beard's strange behaviour. Similarly, Conrad made some minor changes to the first draft of the collision scene in order to keep us inside young Marlow's perceptions until the narrator reveals the circumstances behind the captain's being adrift in a lifeboat at the time of the accident. The manuscript reads:

> "This means another month in this beastly hole" said Mahon to me, as we peered with lamps about the splintered bulwarks and broken braces. "But where's the captain?"
> We had not heard or seen him all that time. We went *aft* to look. A doleful voice was heard hailing somewhere in the middle of the dock. "Judea ahoy!" How the devil did he get there? "*Hallo!*" *we shouted.*—"I am adrift in our boat without the oars" he cried. A *belated* waterman offered his services and Mahon *struck a* bargain with him for half-a-crown (and) He towed (the) our skipper alongside. Mrs. Bears came up the ladder first: they had been floating about the dock in that mizzly cold rain for an hour. (It) *I was never so surprised in my life.*
> It appears, when he heard my shout "Come up" he understood at once what was the matter, (and ran up) caught up his wife, ran up on deck and across and down the boat fast by the ladder. (MS 15a–16a)

Like Captain Beard's question ("Where's the cabin-table?") after the explosion, Mahon's "But where's the captain?" presents young Marlow with a seemingly inexplicable puzzle. The evidence of his senses—the voice heard across the water, the captain's words, and the unexpected appearance of Mrs. Beard—does not solve the mystery of how the skipper arrived in the middle of the dock. Moreover, Conrad's addition to the manuscript, "I was never so surprised in my life," emphasizes the protagonist's limited point of view. The comic aspect of young Marlow's reaction becomes evident when the narrative perspective immediately shifts to the older and wiser Marlow, who "demystifies" the ludicrous event. In contrast, in "Heart of Darkness" and Lord Jim the narrator involves us in problems which refuse to be solved: the implications of his experience with Kurtz are "not very clear" to the storyteller, and Jim is "inscrutable" to the end.

Despite the comic distance between Marlow as narrator and Marlow as protagonist of "Youth," many critics claim that Conrad takes an ironic attitude toward his narrator in order to criticize sentimental romanticism. Some "symbolic" interpretations of the story even argue that in Marlow's sympathetic account of the voyage Conrad satirizes all religious quests for salvation.[36] To impose a systematic religious or historical pattern on a work whose so-called Biblical imagery consists largely of the substitution of the fictional name *Judea* for the actual *Palestine* is surely to distort the author's intention. Moreover, Conrad gives us no alternative reason to suppose that the middle-aged Marlow is mistaken in praising youth's imagination and resilience. In the course of her otherwise convincing interpretation of the story, "Conrad's 'Three Ages of Man': The 'Youth' Volume," Juliet McLauchlan assumes a gap between what Marlow says and what Conrad means. She concludes that "even more subtle in this supposedly simple tale is the way the young Marlow's virtual unawareness of the reality of old age and failure is carried over into the forty-two-year-old Marlow's facile rhetorical comments on the sadness of the passing of time and loss of youth. These do not ring true and are not intended to do so."[37]

If Marlow's comments about youthful illusions seem overly mannered or rhetorical we should not assume that Conrad meant to be ironic. On the contrary, the writer's revisions to the story indicate that he consistently sought to emphasize Marlow's solidarity with his listeners, the psychological contrast of youth and age, and the affirmation of youthful idealism. In his first use of Marlow as a persona Conrad was experimenting with the rhetorical possibilities of the mode (the discussion of "racial difference" is a pertinent example) but there is less distance between Conrad and the narrator in "Youth" than in "Heart of Darkness" or *Lord Jim,* as the lack of contrasting viewpoints or suggestive ambiguities would tend to indicate. The temptation to become sentimental about the experiences of one's past is kept under control, for the most part, by the older Marlow's mildly ironic tone and retrospective point of view. Later, in *Lord Jim,* Conrad develops this aspect of his narrative strategy by using Marlow's testiness to regulate the reader's response to Jim's plight.

Nevertheless, in his article assessing the use of Marlow from "Youth" to *Lord Jim* Murray Krieger criticizes Conrad's mixture of the absurd and the heroic in "Youth":

> There is not objective ground sufficient to sustain young Marlow's fervor, so that there is difficulty in our taking him seriously throughout the tale any more than we can take seriously his "first command," his captaincy of the lifeboat at the end. To be sure, this may be as the older Marlow meant it to be and why he is patronizing and ironic toward the memory of his younger self. Still, in his tribute to the glories of youth implied throughout the story and stated explicitly at the end, our narrator *is* being serious, perhaps more serious than the earlier situation has allowed for.[38]

"Patronizing" is perhaps too strong a term for the narrator's tone, but it is true that irony coexists with idealistic affirmation throughout Marlow's account. In fact, in his revisions of the first draft Conrad took care that his ironic juxtapositions did not undercut the narrator's lyricism too seriously. Thus, he cancelled a grotesque figure of speech in the following passage: "O! Youth! *The strenght* [sic] *of it, the faith of it. The imagination of it.* To me she was not an old rattle-trap carting a lot of coal (in her belly) for a freight; to me she was the endeavour, the test, the trial of life" (MS 25a–26a). Moreover, as we can see in the interlined addition to this excision, Marlow does not emphasize the heroic *deeds* of his protagonist (the "objective ground" referred to by Krieger). Instead, he praises the romantic imagination of youth, which transforms and orders the unheroic facts of life, making the illusory appear real. If this affirmation were unqualified by a keen appraisal of the absurd, the story would resemble pure romance. As it is, Conrad's realistic treatment of imagination and its ironic dependence on ordinary events and human beings anticipates his more complex exploration of the theme in *Lord Jim*.

The modulations in the narrator's tone in "Youth," and the shifts in perspective from a direct, impressionistic rendering of events to general commentary are signals of Marlow's potential flexibility and subtlety as a storyteller. In "Heart of Darkness" and the first half of *Lord Jim* Conrad controls the reader's moral involvement by alternating passages of reflection with those of direct presentation. As we have seen, the narrator's philosophical comments to his audience in "Youth" underline certain humanistic values, such as patriotism and solidarity.

Moreover, even commentary which appears to be unrelated to moral issues can illuminate Conrad's central concerns when examined closely. For example, an interesting revision to the manuscript expands Marlow's appraisal of Jermyn, the melancholy North Sea pilot who attends the *Judea en route* to Newcastle: "He mistrusted my youth and my seamanship and made a point of showing it in a hundred little ways. (I hate him to this day) I daresay he was right. It seems to me I knew very little then and know not much more now, but (I hate that man to) I cherish a hate for that Jermyn to this day" (MS 8a,7b). Before the serial version Conrad made Jermyn's criticism of young Marlow even more emphatic, saying "He mistrusted my youth, my common-sense, and my seamanship. . . ." It is this rigid intolerance that the author evaluates indirectly in his revisions by clarifying Marlow's grounds for continuing to resent the pilot's attitude. That is, even if Jermyn had been justified in his assessment of the young mate's abilities his lack of solidarity threatened the good order and harmony of the ship. Marlow's memory of this man, therefore, contrasts tellingly with his memories of the captain, Mrs. Beard, and Mahon, each of whom had displayed generosity and tolerance toward the youth's weaknesses.

Marlow's ability to develop thematic material in the course of telling "a good story" is closely related to his function as the reader's guide to formal aspects of the work. For the ostensible benefit of his listeners, the narrator emphasizes symbols, correspondences, and impressionistic techniques which help to reveal the author's meaning. Similarly, the oral framework allows Conrad to draw the reader's attention to Marlow's artistry by dramatizing the listeners' response. In

"Heart of Darkness," for instance, the first narrator on board the *Nellie* comments on the storyteller's inconclusiveness, the impressionist and symbolic modes of his narrative, and (not without a trace of irony) his moral function: "'Mind,' he began again, lifting one arm from the elbow, the palm of his hand outwards, so that, with his legs folded before him, he had the pose of a Buddha preaching in European clothes and without a lotus-flower" (50). Conrad experiments with this indirect method of critical analysis when, at the beginning of "Youth," the first narrator tells us that Marlow's tale is actually a "chronicle": "Marlow (at least I think that is how he spelt his name) told the story, or rather the chronicle, of a voyage" (3). The term "chronicle" suggests that the listeners have been impressed by the authenticity or "historical" character of the tale, and also by the narrator's concern for pacing and the order of events.

Young Marlow's anticipation of each new adventure on the way to Bangkok emphasizes the teleological aspect of the story and the importance of chronological sequence. At some points in the action one event seems to be the signal for another to appear on the horizon: "The captain had surrendered the wheel, and apart, elbow on rail and chin in hand, gazed at the sea wistfully. We asked ourselves, What next? I thought, Now, this is something like. This is great. I wonder what will happen. O youth! Suddenly Mahon sighted a steamer far astern" (26). The first of these sentences, added before the serial publication, juxtaposes the aging captain's response to the explosion at sea with young Marlow's eagerness for "something to happen." Another addition, "This is great," emphasizes youth's love of adventure for its own sake—that "absolutely pure" spirit that governs the young Russian sailor in "Heart of Darkness." Conrad made a third revision to this passage before the story went to *Blackwood's,* expanding Marlow's commentary by two highly rhetorical sentences which he subsequently cancelled for the book edition. The serial reads, "I wonder what will happen. I exulted as if after a triumph. O youth! And are we not all descendents [*sic*] of Don Quixote, all the wise, all the simple—all of us in the quixotism of our youth?" (*B,* 322). By deciding to limit the narrator's comment to "O youth!" Conrad preserved the balance of irony and nostalgia in Marlow's tone, and also kept the story line in the foreground.

As one situation seems to generate another, each is more perilous than the last. The cargo ignites because of overhandling while the leaks were being caulked, the steamer that comes to the aid of the *Judea* merely fans the flames of the fire by towing her, and so on. Like parodies of the adventures young Marlow describes as "something you read about," the ludicrous mishaps that haunt the ship have a strong cumulative impact on the reader, who is programmed to expect the worst. In a good story, as E. M. Forster says, we all want to know what happens next, and the swift pacing, as well as the stress on events created by young Marlow's buoyant enthusiasm, appeals to this "primeval curiosity."[39] However, while the stories of James Fenimore Cooper, Captain Marryat and the early Robert Louis Stevenson evoke a sense of "casting off"[40] by immersing the reader completely in the plot, "Youth" combines narrative progression with rhetorical commentary. Moreover, as we have seen, Marlow's relationship with his audience is partly based on an ironic view of the disjunction between romance and reality that causes us to identify more closely with the teller of the tale than with the protagonist. Nevertheless, the term "chronicle" points to a formal aspect of the work that emphasizes novelty, spontaneity, and directness, and that prepares the reader for a lack of complexity in the subject matter and treatment.

Similarly, Conrad uses Marlow's commentary on his own performance to indicate the manner in which the story should be read. When Marlow describes his "first command" in a few brief impressions he asks his audience to imagine the episode for themselves: "I need not tell you what it is to be knocking about in an open boat," he says (36). The reader understands that the narrator's memories are greatly condensed and that, as in the two-hundred-mile tramp to the Central Station in "Heart of Darkness," the passage of time is implied impressionistically, by repetition and selective detail. In the following excerpt from the latter story Marlow summarizes his experience in a manner similar to the "first command" episode in "Youth": "No use telling you much about that. Paths, paths, everywhere; a stamped-in network of paths spreading over the empty land, through long grass, through burnt grass, through thickets, down and up chilly ravines, up and down stony hills ablaze with heat; and a solitude, a solitude, nobody, not a hut" (70). Like the narrator's account of young Marlow's endurance test on the Indian Ocean, the description of this trek through an African wasteland invites the reader's creative participation in piecing together fragmentary impressions. Moreover, by unexpectedly shifting the setting to England Marlow challenges his audience to imagine not only his own sense of dislocation, but also the natives' reaction to the European invasion: "Well, if a lot of mysterious niggers armed with all kinds of fearful weapons suddenly took to travelling on the road between Deal and Gravesend, catching the yokels right and left to carry heavy loads for them, I fancy every farm and cottage thereabouts would get empty very soon" (70).

In passages such as this one Conrad extends Marlow's involvement of the reader from a limited perspective to a more comprehensive view of the whole situation. Narrative perspectives multiply in *Lord Jim,* where the writer asks us to reconstruct a character—first, from the impressions Jim makes on Marlow and then, by comparing Marlow's views with those of the French lieutenant, Stein, Jewel, and others. As in the earlier stories, Conrad uses Marlow to direct the reader toward this method of interpretation: "He existed for me, and after all it is only through me that he exists for you. I've led him out by the hand; I have paraded him before you. Were my commonplace fears unjust? I won't say—not even now. You may be able to tell better, since the proverb has it that the onlookers see most of the game" (224). While to Marlow, Jim plays a "symbolic" role, to Stein, he is a romantic; to Jewel, a false lover; and to the French lieutenant, a professional man who has lost his honour. Only in the reader's imagination do all truths about Jim coexist and from them, each reader must create his own pattern.

A similar evolution can be traced in Conrad's use of Marlow to point out the symbolic meaning inherent in realistic events. In "Youth" the central theme of the story is underlined for the reader in the narrator's opening comment: "You fellows know there are those voyages that seem ordered for the illustration of life, that might stand for a symbol of existence" (3-4). Incidentally, Conrad rewrote this sentence before the serial publication, adding the critical phrase "a symbol of existence" to stress the universality of the *Judea*'s quest. Throughout the story Marlow develops this archetypal symbol, indicating (for example) the similarity between the old ship and the middle-aged ex-seamen: " 'Her youth was where mine is—where yours is—you fellows who listen to this year' " (17). The *Judea*'s death at sea suggests the defeat of man's heroic resistance to the random misfortunes of life; the flames of the fire, "leaping audaciously to the sky," are compared with the glamorous illusions of youth; and the fabled East, with the fulfilment of romantic dreams. Conrad's desire to impress the reader with these wider implications yields an intense concentration of metaphor and simile at climactic points in the narrative; in his study of Conrad's figurative language, Donald Yelton estimates that episodes such as the sinking of the *Judea* are "more prolific of metaphors than any comparable tract of prose in the entire range of his work."[41]

Yelton's survey of the frequency of simile and metaphor in Conrad's prose indicates a significant increase (particularly in the case of "interior imagery") beginning with the first Marlow story and culminating in *Lord Jim*. In his conclusion about the influence of Marlow as a narrative device on Conrad's use of figurative language, he writes: "Marlow has, like his creator, an eye for external appearances, and he produces his share of sensory images; but his characteristic role is either that of reflection and comment upon the inwardness of the events he describes (akin to the role of the Greek chorus), or else it is that of psychopomp or guide through an inner landscape (his own or another's) and delineator of its features" (127). Keeping in mind the difficulty of making precise distinctions between some metaphors and similes that focus on the "inwardness of events" or "inner landscape" and those that emphasize physical impressions, the reader of "Youth" cannot fail to notice Marlow's tendency to rely upon the former type of comparison to clarify the symbolism of his story for the audience. When the decision is made to "see the last of" the *Judea* rather than take passage to Singapore on the steamship *Somerville,* for example, the narrator conveys the psychological reaction of his youthful self through the image of the ship's fire: "Oh, the glamour of youth! Oh, the fire of it, more dazzling than the flames of the burning ship, throwing a magic light on the wide earth, leaping audaciously to the sky, presently to be quenched by time, more cruel, more pitiless, more bitter than the sea—and like the flames of the burning ship surrounded by an impenetrable night" (30).

Like most other purely rhetorical comments in "Youth," this passage received very little revision. In contrast, revealing meaning through concrete images in the manner of Flaubert required painstaking alterations, as we can see in an excerpt from the manuscript version of Marlow's description of the burning ship:

(And) Between the darkness of (sky and) earth and (the sky) heaven she (flamed gloriously upon) was burning fiercely upon a disc of purple sea (with a purple disc shot by red gleams darkened by the water) shot by the play of red gleams upon a disc of water glittering and sinister. (The immense flame floated on the water) A high *clear* flame an immense and lonely flame ascended from the ocean and from its summit the *black* smoke poured continuously at the sky. She burned (magnificently) furiously, mournful and imposing like a funeral pile kindled in the night, (Surrounded) surrounded by the sea, watched over by the stars. (MS 33b)

Conrad substitutes the more evocative "heaven" for "sky" to frame the *Judea*, and cancels some inexact terms ("gloriously" and "magnificently"). Moreover, by combining regal and funereal colours (purple, red, and black) with a monumental shape (the pillar of fire towering over a flat horizon) he appeals to our senses in order to suggest heroism indirectly.[42] The simile "like a funeral pile" is more explicit, and Marlow continues to develop this image in his next comment: "A magnificent death had come like a grace, like a gift, like a reward to that old ship at the end of her laborious days. The surrender of her weary ghost to the keeping of stars and sea was stirring like the sight of a glorious triumph" (35). In this and similar figures of speech the use of Marlow as a narrative device allows Conrad to elaborate the wider relevance of events in the story. Unlike Flaubert, whose narrator is disengaged from the scenes he describes, Conrad uses Marlow's immediate response to develop symbolic implications. In this way, he can emphasize the meaning suggested by the sensory details.

Moreover, the symbolic elements in "Youth" comprise an unambiguous explication of the ways in which the voyage of the *Judea* can be regarded as a general representation of the life of man. Compared with the searching complexity that is the hallmark of Marlow's storytelling in "Heart of Darkness" and *Lord Jim*, this method of conveying meaning seems simple and allegorical in nature. "Youth" should be considered as a preliminary trial of Marlow's ability to suggest and develop significant correspondences. Later, as the first narrator in "Heart of Darkness" tells us, the method evolved so that the meaning of a narrative "was not inside like a kernel but outside, enveloping the tale which brought it out only as a glow brings out a haze, in the likeness of one of these misty halos that sometimes are made visible by the spectral illumination of moonshine" (48). As in "Youth," at the very beginning of "Heart of Darkness" Marlow alerts his listeners to the symbolic level of the story by indicating that the journey represents an inner moral and psychological quest for knowledge. He tells us that the Inner Station was "the farthest point of navigation and the culminating point of my experience. It seemed somehow to throw a kind of light on everything about me—and into my thoughts" (51). However, he also suggests that the journey's significance will not be easily perceived. Echoing the first narrator's comparison of meaning with a haze, or a misty halo, Marlow says that his experience is "not very clear" to him, and yet, he repeats that "it seemed to throw a kind of light."

As he does in "Youth," Conrad uses Marlow's response to his surroundings, often expressed through figures of speech, to elaborate symbolic meaning; in this story, however, the narrator passes through different stages of perception, which involve shifting versions of "the inner truth." For example, Marlow's subjective impression of the wilderness surrounding him at the Central Station follows the basic pattern of the narrator's response to the burning ship in "Youth," for sense impressions are almost immediately transformed into metaphors that reflect inner feelings. Thus, Marlow personifies the wilderness, identifying it with a power, or "thing," whose motives are beyond man's comprehension. Unlike "Youth," however, "Heart of Darkness" explores more than one symbolic meaning for the setting, and suggests a fundamental ambivalence that stems partly from Marlow's discovery of an "appeal" in the savage heart of the wilderness.

By the time Marlow reaches the Inner Station he has learned to make a distinction between the forms of primitive energy surrounding him and the evil resulting from Kurtz's corruption. The wilderness has two faces: the open, "ugly" expression of violent savagery and the still, dark mask that broods over "an inscrutable intention." The narrator's ability to respond to the former and recognize his "kinship" with the natives while understanding, at the same time, the terrible consequences of complicity with primitive forces sets him apart from all other characters in the story, with the exception of Kurtz on his deathbed. In Marlow's meeting with the Intended, Conrad develops this aspect of the theme. Marlow links Kurtz's African mistress, who embodies the dark, passionate soul of the wilderness in a way that recalls the "pure, uncomplicated savagery" of the tribal rites, with the idealistic Belgian girl, who is innocent in a different way. At the same time, the perverted force of the wilderness is represented by Marlow's vision of Kurtz on the stretcher, his mouth open "as if to devour all the earth with all its mankind," and the "triumphant" darkness that seems to enter the house with him.

Conrad's gradual, indirect revelation of meaning through Marlow's metaphoric elaboration of a concrete natural setting evolved from his first use of a dramatized narrator to clarify the themes of "Youth" by pointing out symbolic correspondences. Although Marlow's figures of speech reflect his inner feelings at a particular time and place, they also form a pattern (which in "Heart of Darkness" resembles an intricate web stretching over the entire narrative) through repetition and associative links. Even in "Youth" the comparison of the burning *Judea* with the funeral pile of a dead hero develops the narrator's earlier identification of youthful idealism with the leaping flames soon to be extinguished by the surrounding sea. Although Conrad's patterns are created by the protagonist's subjective response to events rather than by the report of a detached, omniscient narrator, their communication to a carefully delineated audience makes the symbolic meaning seem universal rather than personal or solipsistic. Thus, in "Heart of Darkness" the first narrator contributes to the general implications of Conrad's theme when he repeats the central metaphor in his concluding sentence.

Eventually, the reader can understand the "inner truth" that is "not very clear" to the narrator, although, as Cedric Watts points out in his analysis of the "janiform" aspects of "Heart of Darkness" (*Conrad's "Heart of Darkness": A*

Critical and Contextual Discussion), the text is complicated by inconsistencies. In contrast, in *Lord Jim* the patterning of metaphors, similes, and "symbolic" images is systematically ambiguous.[43] Again, the narrator uses the term "not clear" to describe a lack of resolution, but in the novel he is more emphatic: "He was not—if I may say so—clear to me. He was not clear. And there is a suspicion he was not clear to himself either." In this statement Marlow speaks for Conrad, who refuses to reveal his judgment of events or characters in the manner of "Youth" and (less completely) in "Heart of Darkness." Comparison indicates that the author's meaning becomes more ambiguous as the form becomes longer partly because Marlow is allowed more scope to explore the significance of his experience—through "interior imagery," for example. In the novel the narrator's repeated attempts to describe Jim metaphorically (he is habitually seen "under a cloud" or "in a mist") reveal the increasing ambivalence of his feelings, and contrast ironically with the first view of the protagonist in bright sunshine, when Marlow's judgment is swift and unequivocal: "looking at him, knowing all he knew and a little more too, I was as angry as though I had detected him trying to get something out of me by false pretences."

Finally, while Conrad's revisions to "Youth" show a concern with narrative perspective, impressionist techniques, and symbolism that anticipates his subsequent work in "Heart of Darkness" and *Lord Jim,* his most substantial addition before the serial publication involves a complication of the story line itself. In the manuscript young Marlow's voyage ends with his triumphant entry into the Eastern port three hours ahead of Captain Beard's flagship, and his captivation by the romance of his surroundings: "And I sat weary beyond expression (triumphant) exulting like a conqueror, sleepless and entranced as if before a profound, a fateful enigma" (MS, 26b). The captain arrives, broken and dispirited by his ordeal, and the two men finally fall asleep after exchanging information: "We conversed in low whispers as if afraid to wake up the land. Guns, thunder, earthquakes would not have awakened the men just then. Our voices died out. He dozed off and then I too went to sleep at last, in the great silence of the East. And when I opened my eyes this silence was as complete as if it had never been broken" (MS 25b,24b).

Revising the story for *Blackwood's,* Conrad added young Marlow's encounter with the captain of the *Celestial,* beginning after the second sentence above and ending at the climactic point when he opens his eyes on a radiant, new world. As a result, the meaning of Marlow's reference to the breaking of a "great silence" is substantially altered from the manuscript to the serial version. In the former the silence is broken by the whispered conversation of the captain and his second mate; in the latter, by the torrent of abuse from the steamer's captain, whom young Marlow visits at Beard's request to ask for a passage and who mistakes the little boat for the caretaker's vessel. Let us consider the thematic implications of this alteration.

First, the *Celestial* episode develops the motif already suggested by Conrad's juxtaposition of an exhausted Captain Beard with the jubilant protagonist; that is, the transfer of power. The *Celestial's* disruptive entry into port, the "metallic hollow clangs" of her engine-room, her captain's shouts and curses, and the aggressive assertion of commercial values dramatize the ascendancy of steam over sail power.[44] Marlow's chronicling of this transition has social and cultural implications which, although not comprising an important theme in the story, contribute to the solidarity he establishes with his listeners, who remember "the good old days." Moreover, the addition of this episode undercuts young Marlow's romantic first impression of the East, when the land surrounding him in the night appeared "perfumed like a flower, silent like death, dark like a grave." It is this seductive illusion that is shattered by the comic fury of the captain, and the last two sentences of the addition to the manuscript version underline the disjunction between appearance and reality: "I had faced the silence of the East. I had heard some of its language" (40). Similarly, the ship's name, *Celestial,* was clearly selected for its ironic impact on the reader; unlike *Judea,* it is not a version of an actual name. The steamer that took Conrad from Muntak to Singapore was called the *Sissie*.[45]

Evidence of the trouble Conrad took to maintain narrative continuity when he made a substantial revision such as this can be found in another addition to the manuscript version. To provide a credible background for the new episode, he rewrote Marlow's arrival in port. In the manuscript there is a reference to a navigation light on the wharf, but no indication that it is fading: "We had made out a red light in that bay and steered for it guessing it must mark some small coasting port. We passed two vessels outlandish and high-sterned sleeping at anchor, and ran the nose of the boat against the end of the wharf" (MS 26b). When he included the *Celestial* episode Conrad altered the earlier part of the narrative, providing factual evidence to support the captain's claim that the caretaker was endangering his ship. Notice also the addition of the modifier "jutting," which suggests that an element of risk may have been involved: "We passed two vessels, outlandish and high-sterned, sleeping at anchor, and, approaching the light, now very dim, ran the boat's nose against the end of a jutting wharf" (37). Many more of Conrad's revisions add to the realism of the story. These include the adjustment of time periods to correspond with the action, the addition or alteration of nautical terms and details,[46] and clarification of the action.[47]

The addition of the *Celestial* episode, then, gives an ironic twist to the simple plot line, a development that may be related to the fact that Conrad made the revision only three or four months before beginning "Heart of Darkness." Perhaps the latter story, with its ironic structure of the romantic quest, was already in his mind. Paradoxically, young Marlow's encounter with the steamship captain contributes to the affirmative view of idealism taken by Conrad in "Youth," because it is followed by a vision of the East in which the imagination of youth transforms reality for the last time in Marlow's story. Compared with the passage describing the burning *Judea,* this long paragraph is remarkably free from manuscript revisions or later alterations. In fact, the only substantial addition locates the old skipper more precisely; in the serial version, he is "leaning back in the stern of the longboat." In spite of this Conrad's writing is polished, and the paragraph structure effectively integrates East and West, and past and present:

> And then I saw the men of the East—they were (gazing) looking at me. The *whole length* jetty [*sic*] was full of people. I saw brown, bronze, yellow faces—the black eyes, the glitter, the colour of an Eastern crowd. All these beings stared without a murmur, without a sigh, without a movement. They stared down at the boats, at the sleeping men who at night had come from the sea. Nothing (stirred) moved. The fronds of palms stood still against the sky. Not a branch stirred along the shore, and *brown* roofs of hidden houses peeped through the folliage of big leaves that hung shining and still like leaves *forged* (of metal) of heavy metal. This was the East of the ancient navigators, so old, so mysterious and sombre, living and unchanged, full of danger and promise. And these were the men! I sat up suddenly. A wave passed (along) through the crowd from end to end, passed along the heads, swayed the bodies, ran along the jetty like a ripple on the water, like a breath of wind on a field—and all was still again. I see it now. The wide sweep of the bay, the wealth of green infinite and varied, the glittering sands, the sea blue like the sea of a dream, the crowd of attentive faces, the blaze of vivid colour—the water reflecting it all, the curve of the shore, the jetty, the high-sterned outlandish craft floating still—and the three boats with the tired men of the west sleeping unconscious of the land and the people and the violence of sunshine. They (lay) slept thrown across the thwarts, curled on bottom boards in the careless attitudes of death. The head of the old skipper had fallen on his breast and he looked as though he would never wake. Further out Mahon's face was upturned to the sky, the long white beard spread out on his breast as though he had been shot where he sat at the tiller; and a fellow all in a heap in the bows of the boat slept with both his arms embracing the (gunwale) stem-head *and with* his cheek resting on the gunwale. The East looked at them without a sound. (MS 24b–22b)

The cadence of this passage (which owes much to Flaubert), the shift in verb tense, and the repetition from first to last sentence of the motif (East looking at West) contribute to the overall impression of harmony. Juxtaposed with the *Celestial* episode, Marlow's vision contains and counteracts the comic disillusionment of the youth's earlier experience. Unlike *Sentimental Education* or *Great Expectations,* Conrad's story celebrates human illusions by demonstrating their "truth" in the face of reality (in the form of the steamship captain) and in spite of time (the memory still inspires the middle-aged narrator). Moreover, although the older Marlow testifies, in the coda, to the failure of his dreams, we are not shown the painful process of his disillusionment.

In summary, various thematic and formal elements link "Youth" to the earlier "Karain," and anticipate Conrad's next works, "Heart of Darkness" and *Lord Jim.* The invention of the Marlow persona appears to be connected to the "autobiographical impulse" that distinguishes this story from "Karain," and that probably motivated Conrad to make full use of techniques common to the oral narrative. In this respect, the development of a dramatized audience is critical, for comparison of "Youth" with "Heart of Darkness" and *Lord Jim* reveals that the same features that establish Marlow's solidarity with his listeners in the earlier story allow the writer to challenge conventional ideas in the later works. In "Heart of Darkness" and *Lord Jim* the theme of national solidarity, or patriotism, receives very different treatment from its unqualified affirmation in "Youth." However, when Conrad opposes materialism to idealistic values in "Youth" he exploits Marlow's relationship with "the man of finance, the man of accounts and the man of law," and this more ambivalent function of the dramatized audience anticipates the complex rhetoric of the later stories.

Many of Conrad's revisions to "Youth" are concentrated on the various impressionist techniques he was exploring at this time. Again, comparison with "Karain" indicates that the more personal matter of "Youth" is related to an intensification of visual impressions, in the manner of *The Nigger of the "Narcissus,"* but limited to Marlow's point of view. Anticipating "Heart of Darkness," Conrad experiments with narrative "mysteries" and involves the reader in revising first impressions. Moreover, from "Youth" to "Heart of Darkness" and *Lord Jim,* we can trace an evolution from the depiction of outward, physical impressions to the exploration of inner, moral ideas and concerns. And as Conrad modifies the formal aspects of his work (such as codas, the multiplication of narrative perspectives, and patterns of motifs and images), we perceive a corresponding movement toward ambiguity.

5
"Heart of Darkness" and *Lord Jim*

In the last chapter we saw how Conrad's revisions to "Youth" anticipate significant formal and thematic aspects of "Heart of Darkness" and *Lord Jim*. In this chapter I shall focus on the links between the latter two works, concentrating on Kurtz and Jim as complementary illustrations of imaginative egoists. Conrad implied a close relationship between the story and the novel when he wrote to Meldrum that, despite the decision to publish *Lord Jim* as a novel, the work was "not . . . planned to stand alone. *H of D* was meant in my mind as a foil, and *Youth* was supposed to give the note."[1] Although the word "foil" emphasizes the dialectical aspect of the connection between the two works, it also suggests thematic correspondences and similarities of technique. In this chapter we shall see how Conrad repeats certain basic narrative situations and motifs from "Heart of Darkness" in *Lord Jim* as he explores the essential difference between "demonic" and "exalted" egoism.

How does the term "egoism" apply to Jim? At the end of the novel Conrad describes his hero as "an obscure conqueror of fame, tearing himself out of the arms of a jealous love at the sign, at the call of his exalted egoism" (416). Here, the modifier ("exalted") does not accord very well with the conventional meaning of "egoism," which stresses self-interest as the foundation of morality and the guiding principle of action. Even in the first four chapters of the novel, when he portrays Jim with considerable irony, Conrad does not imply that he acts (or wishes to act) with regard to his own self-interest. In the Patusan section he suggests that Jim's lofty, idealistic concept of himself allows him to work for the benefit of the entire community. In fact, Marlow makes the statement that "he seemed to love the land and the people with a sort of fierce egoism" (248) in the context of Jim's gratitude for "that work which had given him the certitude of rehabilitation." "Egoism" as it applies to Jim suggests "self-idealization" rather than self-interest.

To understand the crucial relationship between "Heart of Darkness" and *Lord Jim*, we must reassess Conrad's earliest, pre-Kurtz portrayal of Jim, in the fragment "Tuan Jim: A Sketch."[2] In contrast to Eloise Knapp Hay's argument that Conrad did not decide to make his hero a romantic idealist until he rewrote the opening of the story for *Blackwood's*,[3] my reading of the fragment indicates that

Conrad imagined Jim as a romantic egoist when he first began the story. More important, it suggests that he originally intended to condemn Jim's egoism unequivocally.

At first glance, "Tuan Jim" appears to support Hay's thesis. As she says, "The Harvard manuscript gives us nothing of Jim's tendency to cast himself in the role of hero—a tendency which, in the serial version as in all editions of the book, was already fully developed in the first chapter, when Jim, as a boy aboard a training ship, met his first emergency situation, and failed in it."[4] However, a close examination of the sketch yields several hints that the training ship episode, as well as the background information about Jim's youthful dreams of heroism, were actually written at this time although they are not included in the manuscript at Harvard. First, the word count that Conrad was making in the margin of the notebook skips from 1300 to 3300 in the second chapter, just before the celebrated description of the embarking pilgrims. Because the revised serial version follows the manuscript at this point, we can assume that Conrad wrote about 2,000 words on separate pages in order to develop an earlier part of the story, probably in the first chapter.[5] Two facts suggest that the missing passages are the same ones that appear in the novel, which are used by Hay to support her claim that Conrad did not decide to make Jim a romantic egoist until he returned to the story.

As in the revised serial and book versions, chapter 2 of the fragment opens with a brief history of Jim's career at sea, and the incident in which he is crippled by a falling spar during a storm. This episode begins with the following sentence: "Only once in that time he had again the glimpse of the earnestness in the anger of the sea." As in the published versions, the word "again" provides an explicit link with the training ship episode in the first chapter, when Jim's opportunity to become the hero he imagines himself to be is lost because he perceives "a fierce purpose in the gale, a furious earnestness in the screech of the wind, in the brutal tumult of earth and sky, that seemed directed at him, and made him hold his breath in awe" (5). Moreover, the length of the missing passages is roughly 2,000 words, comprising the description of Jim's parsonage background and the "light holiday" reading of adventure stories, his dreams of personal glory, and his failure on the training ship. In fact, without these passages chapter 1 of the fragment consists of barely forty words, which break off in the midst of a cancelled description of Jim's duties as a ship-chandler's salesman. This suggests that Conrad continued the passage on another page, and filled in his character's background at the same time.

If these pages had survived, the first draft of the opening chapters would presumably have the same narrative line as the revised version—a visual impression of Jim and references to a mysterious event in his past, followed by a summary of the protagonist's history such as we find in the earlier *Almayer's Folly, An Outcast of the Islands,* and "An Outpost of Progress."[6] Like the final version, the fragment uses a critical, detached narrator and anticipates Jim's failure on the *Patna,* a result of his romantic imagination ("the enemy of man"). Moreover, because the second paragraph of the sketch looks forward to the protagonist's retreat from "the haunts of white men" to a Malayan village where he is called "Tuan Jim," the projected ending would very likely have emphasized the ironic disjunction between his "lordly" ideals and reality.[7] Thus, a careful study of the existing first draft contradicts Hay's thesis that Conrad "added to the sketch of 'Tuan Jim' the halo and curse of Jim's romantic egoism"[8] when he revised the fragment. Rather, it suggests that Conrad planned his character's self-idealization from the initial stages of the work, that he intended the Patusan ending as an ironic commentary on the folly of trying to uphold a lost illusion, and that he probably abandoned the concept because of its limited possibilities for character or plot development. After he had explored Kurtz's destructive egoism in "Heart of Darkness," however, Conrad was more interested in the redemptive aspects of Jim's imaginative self-idealization.

Perhaps Conrad originally thought of Jim's egoism as a complementary (and less attractive) version of Tom Lingard's self-centered idealism in *The Rescue*. Lingard's "proud conviction that of all the men in the world, in his world, he alone had the means and the pluck 'to lift up the big end' of such an adventure"[9] closely resembles Jim's belief that "when all men flinched, then—he felt sure—he alone would know how to deal with the spurious menace of wind and seas" (7). We know that Conrad was working on the first stages of Lingard's inner conflict between his commitment to the Malayan "adventure" and his feelings of solidarity with the European intruders just before he drafted the "Tuan Jim" sketch.[10] Conrad's tendency to develop his ideas obliquely from one work to another is illustrated in the different treatments of the two Englishmen, each of whom betrays his ideal conception of himself. Whereas Jim's heroic illusions are mocked by the ironic mode of the fragment, Lingard's conflict is heightened and romanticized by the "theatre" images and character stereotyping in *The Rescue*. In neither case, however, did Conrad develop a method flexible enough to express his complex ideas about human egoism.

In his public and private statements about the relative virtues of egoism Conrad appeared to accept the necessity for an aggressive self-interest, but with reservations. Perhaps his strongest affirmation of the individual *contra* the community is contained in a well-known letter to Cunninghame Graham, dated February 8, 1899, in which he writes, "Fraternity means nothing unless the Cain-Abel business. Thats your true fraternity. Assez. L'homme est an animal méchant. Sa méchanceté doit être organisée. La société est essentialment criminelle—ou elle n'existerait pas. C'est l'égoisme qui sauve tout—absolument tout—tout ce que nous abhorrons tout ce que nous aimons."[11] Graham's invitation to a political meeting of pacifists who wished to promote the programs of international socialists (including Russians and Germans) was no doubt responsible for Conrad's bitter scepticism and consequently, his rather extravagant praise of egoism on this occasion. In an earlier letter to the same friend, he described individualism and solidarity as equally desirable, but of little ameliorative value because of man's tragic alienation from nature: "Yes. Egoism is good, and altruism is good, and fidelity to nature would be the best of all, and systems could be built, and rules could be made—if we could only get rid of consciousness."[12]

On another occasion Conrad explained the equation implied in the first part of this last statement. In a letter to the *New York Times Saturday Book Review* (August 2, 1901) he claimed that individualism performs an important social function, but only if it coexists with the recognition of communal values: "Egoism, which is the moving force of the world, and altruism, which is its morality, these two cannot serve us unless in the incomprehensible alliance of their irreconcilable antagonism."[13] Writing about Kurtz taught Conrad how to explore the complex implications of this view. Through Marlow's relationship with Kurtz and then Jim, Conrad criticizes egoism if it is unrestrained by the altruistic principles affirmed by the narrator; but he also uses Marlow as a mediator who can bridge the gap between the safe, "respectable" community and the outcast whose imagination has led him to put his self-image about the interests of the social group. More important, using Kurtz as an illustration of the negative or destructive aspects of egoism seems to have led him to emphasize the positive, though problematic, nature of Jim's self-idealization.

The most obvious way in which Kurtz prefigures Jim is in the influence he assumes over primitive peoples. In his study of Conrad's politics Avrom Fleishman has shown how the myth of Sir James Brooke, "the white Rajah of Sarawak," provided Conrad with the example of an individualistic, benevolent colonizer, and how Kurtz is a grotesque parody of this ideal. Jim is "a higher development of Kurtz" because he exploits his "charismatic power" in order to improve the lot of the native community. Fleishman argues that the significant difference between Kurtz and Jim is political: "Jim learns to employ his power in reordering the structure of the community, rather than, like Kurtz, accepting and exploiting the community's worst potentialities. Like Kurtz, Jim is an energetic worker, but he turns to economic pursuits only after stabilizing the political situation and distributing social justice. . . . Kurtz seeks to drain rather than develop the land; his primary concern is acquiring ivory."[14] As if to emphasize this difference, in *Lord Jim* Conrad repeats the Kurtzian motif of the white man who comes into the midst of the natives like a god, but with some important changes.

Describing Kurtz's arrival at the Inner Station in a metaphor that suggests Jupiter or Zeus, the Russian trader tells Marlow that "he came to them [the natives] with thunder and lightning" (128). First and foremost, Kurtz's charismatic authority is based on his use of firearms, the means by which he raids the country and enslaves the primitive mind. In contrast, Jim gains his influence over the Malays gradually, by his imaginative, constructive actions, his willingness to listen before judging,[15] and his trustworthiness, although he too appears "like a creature not only of another kind but of another essence." In fact, Marlow tells us that "had [the natives] not seen him come up in a canoe they might have thought he had descended upon them from the clouds" (229). However, Conrad stresses the fact that Jim comes to Patusan with an unloaded revolver, and he transforms weapon bearing into a comic affair when Marlow describes his friend's departure:

> Looking out of the stern-port I saw the boat rounding under the counter. He sat in her leaning forward, exciting his men with voice and gestures; and as he had kept the revolver in his hand and seemed to be presenting it at their heads, I shall never forget the scared faces of the four Javanese, and the frantic swing of their stroke which snatched that vision from under my eyes. Then turning away, the first thing I saw were the two boxes of cartridges on the cuddy-table. He had forgotten to take them. (238)

Although Jim's physical appearance accounts for a considerable part of his appeal to the natives, he becomes their leader only by inspiring them with his inner qualities. In his description of Jim's conduct during the assault on Sherif Ali's camp, for example, Conrad seems to offer us an "exalted" or creative counterpart to Kurtz's armed raids.

Patusan gives Jim the chance to exalt his own best instincts in order to create an illusion of personal "impeccability." Like Conrad's essay about Lord Nelson (written five years after this novel), *Lord Jim* interprets leadership as the expression of a heroic personality.[16] Moreover, although Fleishman is right when he says that Jim "discovers himself" within the context of the community, Conrad also emphasizes the hero's inevitable isolation, and makes it a condition of his achievement. Marlow says: "I know, of course, he was in every sense alone of his kind there, but the unsuspected qualities of his nature had brought him in such close touch with his surroundings that this isolation seemed only the effect of his power. His loneliness added to his stature" (272). In fact, at no time does Jim appear "greater and more pitiful in the loneliness of his soul" than when his moral leadership is unequivocally affirmed by the native council debating Brown's fate (393). In contrast, Kurtz is dominated and absorbed by his surroundings; in his lust for power, his egoism paradoxically leads to the loss of a coherent personal identity or character. As Marlow points out: "The thing was to know what he belonged to, how many powers of darkness claimed him for their own" (116). In the Patusan section of *Lord Jim* one can see most clearly how Conrad repeated specific motifs—from weapon bearing to the fundamental situation of being "alone of one's kind" in a setting almost completely cut off from civilized contacts—as if to illustrate the differences between demonic and exalted egoism. For example, Jim's tragic fulfilment of his pledge to the people of Patusan ("He hath taken it upon his own head") can be seen as a positive alternative to the ironic disjunction between Kurtz's words and actions. But this dialectical exploration of egoism is not limited to the repetition of thematic motifs: it is also reflected in the different ways Conrad portrays the characters of the egoists, Kurtz and Jim.

In "Heart of Darkness" Conrad's characterization of Kurtz becomes less realistic and more abstract as the story unfolds. This movement from realistic character portrayal to symbolism corresponds with Marlow's discovery that, lacking the crucial trait of restraint, Kurtz has abandoned his personal identity—the complex "character" that expresses itself through choice. In contrast, after the first four chapters of *Lord Jim* Conrad's conception of the hero's egoism becomes increasingly more ambiguous and complex. Marlow's gradual discovery of unsuspected traits in Jim's character reverses the technique used in "Heart of Darkness," where Kurtz's "real" nature is revealed to be more limited than Marlow's first impressions suggest.

Because the reader, like the narrator, becomes actively involved in a realistic reconstruction of Kurtz's character before Marlow reaches the Inner Station, the discovery of his true nature, which is grotesquely unrealistic and symbolic, emphasizes Conrad's point about demonic egoism. This effect is carefully planned. Thus, in the first section of the story Marlow tries to ensure his listeners' participation in the project to "see" Kurtz in the conventional way—that is, by inferring realistic character traits from the reports of various people on the journey up-river. For example, in the chief accountant's opinion Kurtz is resourceful, ambitious, and industrious; the Manager of the Central Station and his first-class agent (the "brickmaker") confirm his report by their resentment of these abilities, and the brickmaker adds two further traits: creative imagination and idealism. Marlow asks his listeners to imagine the character for themselves, in the same way that they would evaluate a human being in the real world. At one point, he says: "I had a notion it [the "lie" to the "brickmaker" on Kurtz's behalf] somehow would be of help to that Kurtz whom at the time I did not see—you understand. He was just a word for me. I did not see the man in the name any more than you do. *Do you see him?*" (82; my italics).

In fact, Marlow's limited perspective and the fragmentary nature of the information about Kurtz force us to participate in the reconstruction of a realistic character even more actively than we usually do in fiction. The air of mystery created by the extravagant praise of Kurtz from both the chief accountant and the Manager's agent, and the lack of direct evidence to support their claims, keeps us acutely aware that we, like Marlow, must form an impression of the man that is based on hearsay information. While we remain on our guard against false leads, we are continually discovering new traits that seem to prove the complexity of Kurtz's personality. Like Marlow, we may even anticipate areas of conflict between some of the characteristics, such as idealism and ambition: "I wasn't very interested in him. No. Still, I was curious to see whether this man, who had come out equipped with moral ideas of some sort, would climb to the top after all and how he would set about his work when there" (88). However, when Marlow eventually meets this mysterious figure, Conrad's method of characterization shifts dramatically, to reflect the fact that Kurtz's essential nature is no longer capable of growth or change.

Unlike the usual portrayal of character in fiction, which becomes more complex and open-ended as the plot unfolds, Marlow's impressions of Kurtz in the latter part of the story preclude our discovery of new, unsuspected traits or suggestive discrepancies. References to Kurtz as a "Shade," an "initiated wraith from the back of Nowhere," a "disinterred body," "an animated image of death carved out of old ivory," and so on, describe a single, unifying image instead of contributing to an evolving "character." This image—a lifeless or insubstantial outer form—illustrates the true nature of demonic egoism, for Kurtz's destructive greed has consumed all other personal characteristics in its determination to seize and maintain power. Not until the epilogue does Conrad return to a conventional portrayal of Kurtz, in which the impressions of the Company's official, the journalist, Kurtz's cousin, and the Intended parody Marlow's initial characterization on the journey up-river. The cousin even repeats the phrase, "He was a universal genius," used by the "brickmaker" at the Central Station to describe Kurtz.

In *Lord Jim* the movement from ambiguity to irony is reversed. When Conrad developed the fragment "Tuan Jim" into the first four chapters of the novel after writing "Heart of Darkness," he maintained its limited, ironic view of the egoist. From chapter 5 to the Patusan section, however, the characterization of Jim becomes progressively more ambiguous. Like the shift in mode from realistic character portrayal to irony and symbolism in "Heart of Darkness," the stylistic change in the novel has important thematic implications, for it tends to emphasize the positive aspects of Jim's self-idealization. To appreciate the dialectical nature of Conrad's investigation, though, we must look a little more closely at Marlow's function in "Heart of Darkness."

One of the most effective techniques that Conrad adapted from "Heart of Darkness" to *Lord Jim* is the use of Marlow to mediate between the "civilized" community and the egoistic outsider. In the shorter fiction Marlow tries to make his listeners aware of the "slave mentality" as a fundamental aspect of human nature, an "inner truth" which one can resist only by affirming the values of an active "surface" existence. The significance of Marlow's function is apparent when we compare Conrad's insights into the slave's willing abandonment of his own identity in "Heart of Darkness" with his insistence in "Autocracy and War" (1905) that the mass political slavery that exists under Russian despotism is completely foreign to Western perception.[17] The demonic egoism that binds Kurtz to "the powers of darkness" and the African natives to their white god becomes, through Marlow's narration, an essentially human condition.

Some of the specific ways in which Conrad involves the reader in Kurtz's situation have a more positive effect when he explores Jim's exalted egoism in the novel. For example, Marlow's descriptions of strange events and emotions are calculated to involve his audience as directly as possible while maintaining, at the same time, an epistemologically sceptical outlook. Thus, Marlow can describe for his listeners his moral and emotional response to "The horror!" but he cannot penetrate the mystery behind Kurtz's last cry. Nowhere are the narrator's vague generalizations more strategically employed than in his speculations about "some image," "some vision," or "that supreme moment of complete knowledge" as he scrutinizes the dying man's face. In a similar way, Marlow interprets the expression on Jim's face at Malabar House, and his own response to it, while he emphasizes that the nature of the vision cannot be verified or communicated:

> He was very far away from me who watched him across three feet of space. With every instant he was penetrating deeper into the impossible world of romantic achievements. He got to the heart of it at last! A strange look of beatitude overspread his features, his eyes sparkled in the light of the candle burning between us; he positively smiled! He had penetrated to the very heart—to the very heart. It was an ecstatic smile that your faces—or mine either—will never wear, my dear boys. (83-84)

The contrast of vague generalization ("the impossible world of romantic achievements") with Marlow's concrete impressions is a technique Conrad repeated from the description of Kurtz on his deathbed. Unhampered by the egoist's imaginative absolutism, the narrator analyzes the meaning of outward appearances and actions, and finds that there is no "last word." In his comparison of Conrad and Henry James, Ian Watt points out that the use of Marlow allowed Conrad to "let his protagonist muddle out the meaning of his own experiences as best he can" without implying authorial control or intervention.[18] As we shall see later, in *Lord Jim* Marlow's scepticism seems to have freed Conrad to explore the virtues of imaginative self-idealization without affirming it uncritically.

Marlow's deliberate provocation of his listeners ("It was an ecstatic smile that your faces—or mine either—will never wear, my dear boys") illustrates another technique that Conrad used to involve the reader in the egoist's plight. One of the most celebrated passages in "Heart of Darkness" takes the form of a passionate and challenging outburst to the "civilized" listeners who rely on outward forms of restraint rather than "innate strength" and "capacity for faithfulness to an obscure, back-breaking business." Because readers tend to identify with a dramatized audience, Marlow's description of the average European in a modern state, restrained by conventions, "stepping delicately between the butcher and the policeman, in the holy terror of scandal and gallows and lunatic asylums" (116) is, like the rest of Conrad's rhetoric in this passage, skilfully devised to expose our false or pretentious conceptions of civilization. In a similar but more affirmative way, Conrad reminds his readers in *Lord Jim* of their own youthful illusions each time that Marlow alludes to the past, when "we all . . . carried the memory of the same cherished glamour" (129).

Finally, Marlow's partial self-identification with the young Russian trader in "Heart of Darkness" is a good example of the way that Conrad mediates between the egoist and the community in both works. In the shorter fiction, however, the narrator's sense of solidarity (with the Russian trader, and later, with Kurtz) serves to clarify Conrad's moral position on the issues of self-restraint and self-definition. Thus, Marlow criticizes the signs of idolatry in the youth's intense loyalty: "I did not envy him his devotion to Kurtz, though. He had not meditated over it. It came to him, and he accepted it with a sort of eager fatalism. I must say that to me it appeared about the most dangerous thing in every way he had come upon so far" (127). The lack of self-consciousness that seems so attractive in the younger man is discovered, on closer examination, to be an ominous foreshadowing of Kurtz's hollowness. That is, without inner resources or a "deliberate belief," the Russian trader has been invaded by Kurtz in the same way that Kurtz has been "consumed" by the wilderness. Marlow tells us that "the man filled his life, occupied his thoughts, swayed his emotions" (128).

Marlow's role as a mediator between his listeners and the young Russian makes his criticism of demonic egoism less severe, but not ambiguous. The narrator feels "something like admiration—like envy" for the youth's "unreflecting audacity" because he too has been ruled by the glamour of adventure.[19] When he was young, he had a "passion" for maps, and would "lose [him]self in all the glories of exploration"; at the outset of this expedition, he was "charmed" by a snake-like river, and in his arrangements to secure an appointment as quickly as possible, he acted from impulse rather than reflection: "I felt somehow I must get there by hook or by crook" (53). But although Marlow's partly equivocal attitude toward the younger man springs from a sympathetic instinct to "lose himself" in an adventure, his strong criticism reveals how much he has learned since the journey's beginning. Conrad manipulates the gap between story time and discourse time to communicate the narrator's changed perceptions to the reader. Because of Marlow's proleptic description of the real Kurtz and his "ideas," which immediately precedes his meeting with the young trader, we are alert to the full irony of the latter's claims for Kurtz. For the same reason, we can see that even before he is told about Kurtz's excesses, Marlow correctly diagnoses a "master-slave" relationship between the two men, and he realizes that the youth's idealism is absurdly at odds with reality. Therefore, although the reader's knowledge about Kurtz involves some dramatic irony at Marlow's expense (when he suggests that Kurtz may have been simply "exploring" on his forays into the wilderness) its chief effect is to emphasize the narrator's moral insight and judgment, which triumph over the primal impulse to "lose" oneself.

In a more complex way, Marlow's partial self-identification with Kurtz also involves the "civilized" reader while expressing, at the same time, a clearly defined moral point of view. Albert Guerard argues that Marlow's feelings of solidarity with Kurtz suggest a deep, psychological identification.[20] On two separate occasions in "Heart of Darkness" the narrator confesses to an instinctual, irrational loyalty to Kurtz; for example, when he brings the dying agent back from the forest: "I was anxious to deal with this shadow by myself alone,—and to this day I don't know why I was so jealous of sharing with anyone the peculiar blackness of that experience" (141–42). However, Marlow also has an altruistic or ethical motive for rescuing Kurtz, and so his action cannot be interpreted solely as a symbolic confrontation with the anarchic impulse in his own nature. His sense of personal commitment to a cause—even to a "nightmare" and even after Kurtz is discovered to be spiritually "lost" despite the effort to rescue him[21]—is evident in his use of the word "choice" as well as his wry recognition of the "destiny" to which the decision commits him: "I did not betray Mr. Kurtz—*it was ordered* I should never betray him—*it was written* I should be loyal to the nightmare of my choice" (141; my italics). Having chosen to ally himself with Kurtz against the cynical manager and his colleagues, and having confirmed this decision by his promise to the young Russian trader to protect the dying man's reputation, Marlow accepts his "fate."

By stressing Marlow's feelings of solidarity with the dying agent as well as the young Russian trader and the African natives, and by dramatizing the listeners' reactions, Conrad persuades the reader to make awareness an essential part of moral judgment. We are urged to consider the universal implications of demonic egoism rather than condemn Kurtz, the individual character,—although the values upheld by Marlow (and Conrad) are clearly stated. When Conrad returned to his story about Jim, he used similar techniques to mediate between the outsider and the community of readers. In order to stress the positive aspects of self-idealization, however, he made Marlow's moral position much more ambivalent.

Another method of heightening the egoist's appeal that Conrad adapted from "Heart of Darkness" to *Lord Jim* is the use of supernatural and mythic allusions. In the following passage Marlow's figures of speech invest concrete details with a supernatural aura that seems to transform the human Kurtz into a grotesque phantom:

> I saw the man on the stretcher sit up, lank and with an uplifted arm, above the shoulders of the bearers. "Let us hope that the man who can talk so well of love in general will find some particular reason to spare us this time," I said. I resented bitterly the absurd danger of our situation, as if to be at the mercy of that atrocious phantom had been a dishonouring necessity. I could not hear a sound, but through my glasses I saw the thin arm extended commandingly, the lower jaw moving, the eyes of that apparition shining darkly far in its bony head that nodded with grotesque jerks. Kurtz—Kurtz—that means short in German—don't it? Well, the name was as true as everything else in his life—and death. He looked at least seven feet long. His covering had fallen off, and his body emerged from it pitiful and appalling as from a winding-sheet. I could see the cage of his ribs all astir, the bones of his arm waving. It was as though an animated image of death carved out of old ivory had been shaking its hand with menaces at a motionless crowd of men made of dark and glittering bronze. I saw him open his mouth wide—it gave him a weirdly voracious aspect, as though he had wanted to swallow all the air, all the earth, all the men before him. (133-34)

One can find Gothic romanticizing in many passages throughout Conrad's work (the description of James Wait's arrival on board the *Narcissus,* for example) but this depiction of the dying Kurtz is particularly evocative because it reinforces Marlow's previous allusions to the agent's demonic or supernatural powers. For instance, before we meet him we are told that Kurtz "had taken a high seat amongst the devils of the land," and that the wilderness is like a demon-lover who had taken possession of his soul. The motif prepares us for Marlow's description of his sudden appearance from the station, which suggests the rising of a spirit from the underworld.

As Marlow waits for Kurtz the evening light dies and the station is "in the gloom" and silent. In an ironic echo of the harmony that pervades the first narrator's description of the meditative friends on board the *Nellie* and the "serenity" of the surrounding sky and waters, nature and human beings are united by the profound stillness. From a landscape that does not contain "a living soul" Kurtz and his followers emerge dramatically:

> Suddenly round the corner of the house a group of men appeared, as though they had come up from the ground. They waded waist-deep in the grass, in a compact body, bearing an improvised stretcher in their midst. Instantly, in the emptiness of the landscape, a cry arose whose shrillness pierced the still air like a sharp arrow flying straight to the very heart of the land; and, as if by enchantment, streams of human beings—of naked human beings—with spears in their hands, with bows, with shields, with wild glances and savage movements, were poured into the clearing by the darkfaced and pensive forest. The bushes shook, the grass swayed for a time, and then everything stood still in attentive immobility. (133)

The personification of a "darkfaced and pensive" forest that participates in Kurtz's dying, and the reference to "enchantment" reinforce the ironic allusion to a mythic or ritual order in nature. After Kurtz speaks to his followers the wilderness "moves" again, as if in response to an oracle: "The stretcher shook as the bearers staggered forward again, and almost at the same time I noticed that the crowd of savages was vanishing without any perceptible movement of retreat, as if the forest that had ejected these beings so suddenly had drawn them in again as the breath is drawn in a long aspiration" (134). Because Marlow can communicate neither Kurtz's words nor their sense, the implication of a hidden or latent meaning in the ritual is intensified.

Other examples of romantic heightening in "Heart of Darkness," such as the allusions to the Faust legend, contribute to the complexity and suggestiveness of Conrad's symbolism, for they resist the critic's attempts to fit them neatly within the larger structure of Marlow's quest. Thus, systems like Lillian Feder's Virgilian analogies or Robert O. Evans's elaborate parallels with the *Inferno* tend to limit the range of meanings Conrad implies for Kurtz.[22] The moral implications of the egoist's hollowness are more easily defined, for Conrad's irony emphasizes his criticism of extremism. In the first passage quoted above Marlow uses expressive modifiers like "atrocious," "absurd," and "grotesque" to give his description a sardonic tone. Moreover, the narrator's commentary—especially his reference to the irony of Kurtz's name—controls the reader's response by diverting attention away from the immediate scene. The tone of the second passage is more ambivalent, since the ironic disjunction between Kurtz and the spirit or god with whom he is compared is obscured by the rhythmic intensity of the prose. But immediately following this comes one of Marlow's most sardonic figures of speech: "Some of the pilgrims behind the stretcher carried his arms—two shot-guns, a heavy rifle, and a light revolver-carbine—the thunderbolts of that pitiful Jupiter" (134). The complex blend of irony and romantic heightening allows Conrad to mock the godlike pretensions of a Kurtz without reducing the suggestiveness of his symbolic meaning. Taken as a whole, therefore, the scene illustrates his use of mythic or symbolic allusions to stimulate the reader's imaginative perception while at the same time controlling his moral judgment.

The intense concentration of ghostly and spectral images in the latter part of the story emphasizes the destructive aspect of Kurtz's egoism in a particularly ironic way. Comparing the agent to a vapour, shadow, skeleton, or any other inhuman form without a moral identity or "character" makes a silent comment on the innocently idealistic sentiments about saving souls expressed by Europeans like Marlow's aunt (or, indeed, Kurtz himself). As the narrator discovers, Kurtz's soul is "mad"—consumed by self-love and incapable of moral judgment. Therefore, the encounter in the forest becomes a test of Marlow's inner strength and beliefs rather than a development or transformation of Kurtz's character. The significance of Marlow's ability to act purposefully in spite of the false role he must play in supporting Kurtz's delusions of grandeur is explained by Jacques Berthoud:

> The very sincerity of Kurtz's belief in his humanitarian mission—in other words, the very completeness of his self-deception—provides an insane parody of the values for which Marlow stands. Faith in humanity, as it were, must look into a deranged mirror—and overcome the mocking image. For Marlow, to prevent Kurtz from returning to the jungle is not only necessary for his physical survival; it is also a last-ditch affirmation of the reality of the civilized against that of the primitive. His success in bringing Kurtz back to his cabin, therefore, is some sort of spiritual victory.[23]

Moreover, Conrad points out that Kurtz's inner struggle between the primitive and the civilized does not involve a conflict between essential traits of character. Marlow tells us that "both the diabolic love and the unearthly hate of the mysteries it had penetrated fought for the possession of that soul satiated with primitive emotions, avid of lying fame, of sham distinction, of all the appearances of success and power" (147-48). Here, Conrad equates the "appearances of success and power" in civilized society with the rites of power in the primitive world: both are objects of the egoist's greed. Until Kurtz's deathbed enlightenment, the strange intimacy between the two men yields self-knowledge only for Marlow, the central character of the story and hero of the quest. In contrast, in the Patusan section of *Lord Jim* Conrad uses symbolic images and mythic allusions to emphasize the growth of Jim's moral sense and, consequently, the relationship between moral identity and "exalted" egoism.

When Kurtz finally realizes the truth about his human nature, Marlow interprets his oracular pronouncement, "The horror! the horror!" Only after he has "wrestled with death" himself and found that he would probably have "nothing to say" does he perceive the extraordinary nature of Kurtz's deathbed cry: "Since I had peeped over the edge myself, I understand better the meaning of his stare, that could not see the flame of the candle, but was wide enough to embrace the whole universe, piercing enough to penetrate all the hearts that beat in the darkness. He had summed up—he had judged. 'The horror!' *He was a remarkable man.* After all, this was the expression of some sort of belief. . . ." (151; my italics). As we have seen, Marlow's commentary on "The horror!" carefully avoids speculation about Kurtz's meaning; instead, Conrad uses the narrator's contrasting experience to emphasize the moral significance of the egoist's imaginative vision.

The meaning of the phrase "a remarkable man" shifts according to its context in the story. At the beginning of Marlow's journey the Company's chief accountant calls Kurtz "a remarkable man" because of his reputation as an ivory-collector; at the Inner Station Marlow uses the term politically, to align himself with Kurtz against the Central Station manager and the other Europeans; and in conversation with the Intended, Marlow's "He was a remarkable man" is at least partly ironic. In the passage above the phrase implies a recognition of Kurtz's heroic status at the moment of his death, for his secret knowledge of evil gives him the moral insight to pass judgment on himself and all mankind. Referring to his own "contest" with death, Marlow points out that his experience did not include the final moment of time in which "all truth" is revealed. But the question of whether the morally responsible narrator would have found "something to say" remains unanswered. Paradoxically, it is the man who has been a hollow oracle for his followers in the wilderness who makes the judgment that Marlow calls "an affirmation, a moral victory" because it implies a recognition of civilized values.

Although the different ways in which Kurtz can be viewed are reflected in the shifting meanings of words and phrases such as "a remarkable man," they are more fully illustrated in the conflicting ethical positions of individuals like the brickmaker, the Russian trader, Marlow, and the Intended. To some extent, "Heart of Darkness" anticipates Conrad's exploration of the hero's conduct through multiple points of view in *Lord Jim*. In the shorter fiction, however, Marlow's moral commentary is less ambiguous and controls our response to the other characters' views of the egoist more completely than in the novel. Moreover, Conrad's condemnation of the destructive aspects of human egoism is expressed powerfully and consistently in the narrator's figures of speech, which comprise a symbolic pattern of grotesque images depicting forms without inner substance, such as the ivory skull, the shadow "insatiable of splendid appearances," and so on. The moral implications of this pattern are emphasized by ironic parallels, discrepancies, and sardonic commentary throughout the latter half of the story. Northrop Frye's description of Kurtz as "a study of obsession presented in terms of fear instead of pity" (like a Gothic hero of melodrama) fails to consider the crucial rhetorical effectiveness of irony.[24] Thus, although Conrad frequently modulates Marlow's ironic tone in order to involve the reader, he also subjects Kurtz to a searching moral evaluation that involves sardonic humour rather than melodrama.

Irony plays a lesser role in Marlow's relationship with Jim. The significance of this fact is more apparent when we consider how Conrad's unsympathetic treatment of Jim in the first four chapters of the novel contributes to his investigation of "exalted" egoism. In some ways, the opening of the novel recalls the earlier story "An Outpost of Progress," in which the omniscient narrator ridicules the protagonists' dependence on the European government's "fostering care" by comparing Kayerts and Carlier with children who are absorbed in games of playing house, although the two men adopt a paternalistic attitude towards the African natives. In the opening chapters of *Lord Jim* the narrator emphasizes the ironic disjunction between Jim's deeds and his heroic illusions, juxtaposing his failure to act in an emergency with references to his imaginary deeds of glory. Moreover, recalling Flaubert's ironic technique in *Madame Bovary,* the omniscient summary of Jim's daydreams stresses their conventionality; they belong to "the sea-life of light literature" and have none of the mysterious ineffability that pervades Marlow's description of Jim's fantasizing at Malabar House. The life Jim leads in his imagination is reduced by the narrator's specificity:

> He saw himself saving people from sinking ships, cutting away masts in a hurricane, swimming through a surf with a line; or as a lonely castaway, barefooted and half naked, walking on uncovered reefs in seach of shell fish to stave off starvation. He confronted savages on tropical shores, quelled mutinies on the high seas, and in a small boat upon the ocean kept up the hearts of despairing men—always an example of devotion to duty, and as unflinching as a hero in a book. (6)

Conrad also uses symbolic images, in the manner of Flaubert, to ridicule the protagonist's romanticism. In the following description of Jim's lofty postion in the fore-top of the training ship, he emphasizes the romantic's fatal tendency toward abstraction:

> Having a steady head with an excellent physique, he was very smart aloft. His station was in the fore-top, and often from there he looked down, with the contempt of a man destined to shine in the midst of dangers, at the peaceful multitude of roofs cut in two by the brown tide of the stream, while scattered on the outskirts of the surrounding plain the factory chimneys rose perpendicular against a grimy sky, each slender like a pencil, and belching out smoke like a volcano. He could see the big ships departing, the broad-beamed ferries constantly on the move, the little boats floating far below his feet, with the hazy splendour of the sea in the distance, and the hope of a stirring life in the world of adventure. (6)

In this passage Conrad criticizes Jim's self-idealization by juxtaposing the immediate world of men working in factories, ships, ferries, and small boats with the "hazy splendour" of "the world of adventure." Another form of irony involves the use of free indirect style to reveal Jim's thoughts after his imagination paralyzes him during the rescue episode on the training ship. The following excerpt mocks the young man's egoism because his illusions conflict so dramatically with his recent experience: "He had enlarged his knowledge more than those who had done the work. When all men flinched, then—he felt sure—he alone would know how to deal with the spurious menace of wind and seas. He knew what to think of it" (9). The narrator's irony, which controls the thoughts and feelings of the character, recalls Conrad's equally unsparing criticism of Almayer's dreams and Willems's rationalizations in the opening chapters of *Almayer's Folly* and *An Outcast of the Islands.*

At the beginning of the second chapter Conrad stresses the moral consequences of Jim's inability to reconcile his imaginative dreams with reality. Describing Jim's career at sea before the *Patna* episode, the narrator says:

> After two years of training he went to sea, and entering the regions so well known to his imagination, found them strangely barren of adventure. He made many voyages. He knew the magic monotony of existence between sky and water; he had to bear the criticism of men, the exactions of the sea, and the prosaic severity of the daily task that gives bread—but whose only reward is in the perfect love of the work. This reward eluded him. (10)

The training ship episode immediately before this passage dramatizes the visible effect of Jim's imagination during a crisis when, anticipating the events on board the *Patna,* he is overwhelmed by a vision of disaster that paralyzes action. Here, the narrator emphasizes the invisible moral implications of Jim's obsession. In one of his later essays Conrad writes, "The mere love of adventure is no saving grace. It is no grace at all. It lays a man under no obligation of faithfulness to an idea and even to his own self."[25] Imagination has deprived Jim of self-knowledge and the chance to realize idealistic social values through his work. In the storm episode that follows the narrator's analysis of Jim's lack of moral growth, the protagonist is temporarily crippled by a falling spar, an event that is metaphorically linked to his state of mind.

I have suggested that Conrad perceived Jim as an egoist before he wrote "Heart of Darkness," perhaps to complement his treatment of Tom Lingard in *The Rescue.* Unlike Lingard's,[26] Jim's self-idealization derives from his imagination, the quality that gives him heroic status in the second half of the novel. As we have seen, however, Conrad's initial conception of the work involved a condemnation of Jim's imagination that was central to the plot and characterization. When he returned to the story after completing "Heart of Darkness," he was (in a sense) committed to the opening chapters because he had sent a rough draft to *Blackwood's* along with the manuscript of "Youth." In February 1899, when he planned to resume his work on "Tuan Jim," he still thought of its length in terms of twenty or thirty thousand words,[27] but on July 6, when he mailed the first two revised chapters and a part of the third, he was already telling Meldrum that "the story will be fully 40,000 words."[28] Although we cannot know exactly when Conrad changed his original intention to make criticism of Jim's imaginative egoism the focus of the story as a whole, we can infer from these letters that once he actually began to revise his work he foresaw Marlow's sympathetic involvement in Jim's affairs. The introduction of Marlow and the development of his relationship with Jim would require considerable expansion from the 20,000 words Conrad had previously contemplated.

With this development in mind, Conrad drafted chapters 3 and 4, which refer to "the facts" of the case from an official, public point of view that does not explore Jim's thoughts and feelings after the event. Marlow's future role as Jim's confessor is implied by the court's inability to assess these private views: "At present he was answering questions that did not matter though they had a purpose, but he doubted whether he would ever again speak out as long as he lived. The sound of his own truthful statements confirmed his deliberate opinion that speech was of no use to him any longer" (33). Similarly, describing the *Patna*'s collision with a submerged object, Conrad gives us a critical, detached impression of Jim's situation and character. Ironic parallels, symbolic imagery, free indirect style, and omniscient analysis—all preclude the reader's sympathy with the hero's imaginative illusions. Thus, Jim's egoism is satirized by the disjunction between his thoughts, which are "full of adventurous deeds" and his languid behaviour, as well as by the ironic parallel between the protagonist, who is "drunk with the divine philtre of an unbounded confidence," and the drunken second engineer, who boasts of his courage "with the enthusiasm of sincere conviction."

Moreover, like the earlier image of the protagonist stationed aloft in the foretop of the training ship, the description of Jim's serene abstraction on the bridge, surrounded by instruments of order, precision, and authority, is symbolic. The details comment ironically on his lack of inner direction or self-knowledge:

> Two Malays, silent and almost motionless, steered, one on each side of the wheel, whose brass rim shone fragmentarily in the oval of light thown out by the binnacle. Now and then a hand, with black fingers alternately letting go and catching hold of evolving spokes, appeared in the illumined part; the links of wheel-chains ground heavily in the grooves of the barrel. Jim would glance at the compass, would glance around the unattainable horizon, would stretch himself till his joints cracked with a leisurely twist of the body, in the very excess of well-being; and, as if made audacious by the invincible aspect of the peace, he felt he cared for nothing that could happen to him to the end of his days. From time to time he glanced idly at a chart pegged out with four drawing-pins on a low three-legged table abaft the steering-gear case. The sheet of paper portraying the depths of the sea presented a shiny surface under the light of a bull's-eye lamp lashed to a stanchion, a surface as level and smooth as the glimmering surface of the waters. Parallel rulers with a pair of dividers reposed on it; the ship's position at last noon was marked with a small black cross, and the straight pencil-line drawn firmly as far as Perim figured the course of the ship—the path of souls towards the holy place, the promise of salvation, the reward of eternal life—while the pencil with its sharp end touching the Somali coast lay round and still like a naked ship's spar floating in the pool of a sheltered dock. "How steady she goes," thought Jim with wonder, with something like gratitude for this high peace of sea and sky. (19–20)

In this passage the narrator creates an ironic impression of order and harmony. Conrad implies a correspondence between the two-dimensional chart (which pretends to represent "the depths of the sea" but only conceals its mystery), the deceptively smooth surface of the waters, and Jim's egoism, which hides an inner moral weakness. Even the author's use of the imperfect tense to convey the unthinking repetitiveness of Jim's actions (he "would glance at the compass, would glance around the unattainable horizon, would stretch himself") contributes to the irony, for the iterative aspect of the verb reflects the protagonist's illusion that his universe is governed by a regular and unchanging sequence of events.[29] Instruments of precision such as the parallel rulers and dividers seem to support this illusion, in which even human beings (the two Malays and Jim) have their allotted roles. At the same time, the narrator tells us that Jim's imaginary life has come to depend upon conditions that promote quiescence and passivity, "that serenity which fostered the adventurous freedom of his thoughts." Therefore, the scene as a whole symbolizes the protagonist's increasing detachment from an active commitment to his work, and his decision to stay in the East, surrounded by "the eternal peace of . . . sky and sea," is revealed as the outward symptom of a crippling addiction to illusory hopes and dreams.

In summary, the first four chapters of the novel elaborate Conrad's original conception of Jim as an egoist whose imaginative faculty inhibits his ability to interrelate the real and the ideal and thereby find moral and social value in his work. Each event, descriptive detail, and image supports this characterization, and the ironic, omniscient narrative mode precludes ambiguity. However, when Marlow begins his narration in chapter 5 certain important parallels between "Heart of Darkness" and *Lord Jim* emerge, which ultimately yield a very different view of Jim. In each case, a narrator who is committed to the traditions that inspire human solidarity undertakes to explore the actions of an egoist who has betrayed these values. At the outset, however, these projects are described in somewhat different terms. In "Heart of Darkness" Marlow insists (perhaps defensively) that he does not wish to excuse Kurtz, but rather to "account to [him]self" for Kurtz's experience (117), whereas in *Lord Jim* the narrator identifies himself much more consciously with the egoist, even to the point of admitting that he "wished to find some shadow of an excuse" for Jim:

> Was it for my own sake that I wished to find some shadow of an excuse for that young fellow whom I had never seen before, but whose appearance alone added a touch of personal concern to the thoughts suggested by the knowledge of his weakness—made it a thing of mystery and terror—like a hint of a destructive fate ready for us all whose youth—in its day—had resembled his youth? I fear that such was the secret motive of my prying. (51)

At about this stage in the composition of the first draft, Conrad wrote to Meldrum that the story might "turn out longer than *H of D* even."[30]

From his study of the manuscript of *Lord Jim,* John D. Gordan concludes that Conrad "groped his way" toward the development of his plot and characters, shaping his material as he wrote.[31] The comment to Meldrum helps us to identify the particular point in the growth of the manuscript when Conrad anticipated a major plot development that would take him beyond the 40,000 words he had planned when he first thought of introducing Marlow as Jim's confessor. That is, Conrad saw that Marlow's loyalty to Jim in spite of the latter's "more than criminal weakness" could involve a parallel investigation of "the sovereign power enthroned in a fixed standard of conduct." From this idea, he developed the episodes concerning Captain Brierly's suicide and little Bob Stanton's heroism, as well as Marlow's meetings with the French lieutenant and Chester. By dramatizing different attitudes toward the code of service, Conrad induces us to take a more comprehensive and understanding view of Jim's dilemma. For example, he arranges Marlow's meetings with the French lieutenant and Chester carefully, placing them immediately before and after Jim is stripped of his professional certificate. Indirectly, this narrative order reveals that Jim's resolve to face the

Court's verdict is an affirmation of the very code he has betrayed, for Chester's realistic view of the certificate as merely "a bit of ass's skin" because "you must see things exactly as they are" (162) emphasizes the common ethical ground between Jim and the French lieutenant, who believe that only "the honour" is "real."

Because Marlow's loyalties are divided between the fixed values of the code and Jim's romantic illusions, his function as a mediator is more complex than in "Heart of Darkness," where the encounter with Kurtz and the wilderness helps to clarify the narrator's ethical priorities. For example, Conrad shows us Marlow's solidarity with the Russian trader and Kurtz, but this solidarity only underlines the profound moral differences between them. In *Lord Jim,* as Martin Prince puts it, "Marlow has . . . unfinished business with romantic dreams,"[32] and Conrad often minimizes the differences between the two men. For example, on the basis of one letter from the friend who has taken Jim into his rice-mill business, Marlow is comically eager to indulge in a flight of fancy that takes very little account of the real situation: "Evidently I had known what I was doing. I had read characters aright, and so on. And what if something unexpected and wonderful were to come of it? That evening, reposing in a deck-chair under the shade of my own poop awning (it was in HongKong harbour), I laid on Jim's behalf the first stone of a castle in Spain" (188). The moral ambiguities of Marlow's position are reflected in the schematic repetitions and antitheses of his language, of which the following two examples are of particular significance.

Surprisingly, the Conradian word "fellowship" appears only twice in this novel about friendship and the code of service: Marlow repeats it as he reflects on Jim's confession at Malabar House. The passage occurs at the beginning of chapter 11, when Jim makes his most impassioned attempt to convince Marlow and himself that his honour is not irretrievably lost. Although the narrator has abandoned his earlier desire to see Jim "overwhelmed, confounded, pierced through and through, squirming like an impaled beetle" and finds himself "swayed" by the younger man, he defends the code against statements like "There was not the thickness of a sheet of paper between the right and wrong of this affair" (130). "How much more did you want?" he replies. The division of Marlow's loyalties is finely expressed in his parallel phrases as he shifts from a discussion of "the fellowship of . . . illusions," which binds him to the young romantic, to "the fellowship of the craft," which precludes a full and final commitment (128–29). Later in the same commentary Marlow substitutes "solidarity" for "fellowship" to invoke "the solidarity of the craft," and his only other use of *this* word is to describe his personal feeling for Jim. Explaining his part in Stein's plan to send Jim to Patusan, he says that "the solidarity of our lives" made indifference or abandonment out of the question (224).

Similarly, Conrad uses antithesis and paradox to emphasize the narrator's ambivalent moral position. When sympathy for Jim's plight causes him to offer money for an escape from the Court's verdict, Marlow discovers that the categories of moral and immoral conduct in this particular case are less clearly defined than they appear to be during the trial. He tells his audience: "In this transaction, to speak grossly and precisely, I was the irreproachable man; but the subtle intentions of my immorality were defeated by the moral simplicity of the criminal" (153). Here, the oppositions of "irreproachable man" and "immorality" to describe Marlow, and "moral" and "criminal" to refer to Jim are compounded by the antitheses that link the two men: "irreproachable man" and "criminal"; "moral simplicity" and "subtle intentions of . . . immorality." Conrad's intensely paradoxical syntax suggests the complexity of Marlow's moral dilemma as he recognizes that Jim's egoism has "a higher origin, a more lofty aim" than his own selfish wish to protect a young officer who is "one of us." In contrast, Marlow's ironic perception of Kurtz in "Heart of Darkness" does not affect his belief in virtues like restraint or solidarity, although by lying to the Intended he sacrifices an ethical principle in order to preserve the girl's redemptive idealism. That is, Marlow finds that loyalty to the nightmare of his choice involves denying the factual truth in order to affirm an exalted illusion that will support humanity's faith in altruistic values. In *Lord Jim* these values (embodied for Marlow by the code of service) would be in some sense compromised by the narrator's affirmation of Jim's exalted egoism.

When Conrad adapted the motif of Marlow's loyalty to an egoistic outsider from "Heart of Darkness" to *Lord Jim*, he replaced the narrator's sardonic irony with a more ambiguous discourse of paradox, antitheses, and rhetorical questions. Marlow's style reflects his moral dilemma. At the same time, Conrad emphasized the redemptive aspect of Jim's actions after the *Patna* by modifying the narrator's tendency to romanticize the egoist. Whereas the Gothic imagery and mythic allusions that give Kurtz his powerful immediacy and universality reveal the ironic disjunction between man and the gods, Marlow's comparisons of Jim with a knight in a medieval legend (312) and a hero of Greek mythology (267) suggest that man is capable of becoming more godlike than he really is.

Similarly, Conrad transformed the ironic allusions to nature's participation in Kurtz's dying into an elegiac solemnization of the hero's death in *Lord Jim*. As Dain Waris's body is carried into Doramin's *campong*, "the sun was sinking towards the forests," and when Jim goes to his death Marlow reports that

> the sky over Patusan was blood-red, immense, streaming like an open vein. An enormous sun nestled crimson amongst the tree-tops, and the forest below had a black and forbidding face.
> Tamb' Itam tells me that on that evening the aspect of the heavens was angry and frightful. I may well believe it, for I know that on that very day a cyclone passed within sixty miles of the coast, though there was hardly more than a languid stir of air in the place. (413)

In place of the ironic incongruities that control our response to Kurtz, the personification of nature and the supernatural overtones in *Lord Jim* increase our sense of tragic inevitability and loss. This elegiac note is sustained by Marlow's heightened rhetoric in the coda, which repeats the formal pattern established in *The Nigger of the "Narcissus"* and "Youth."[33]

Romantic heightening of Jim's role in Patusan is also achieved through Marlow's symbolic impressions of the character, expressed in extended figures of speech. Again, this technique is adapted from the narrator's exploration of Kurtz's significance in "Heart of Darkness," but with an important shift in emphasis. Because Marlow is the central figure in the latter work, his impressions reveal his own evolving moral awareness rather than Kurtz's character. It is the narrator's actions, combined with his unique perspective on events, that gives the story its closely knit thematic and structural coherence. In *Lord Jim,* however, Conrad uses Marlow to focus our attention on Jim's character, which is revealed gradually, partly through the action and partly through the impressions of other people. The symbolic view of Jim develops and defamiliarizes the hero's character by showing us his personality and actions in a different, more universal context; in contrast to the limitation of Kurtz's character in "Heart of Darkness," it adds to the realistic portrayal of Jim throughout the novel. In the following passage Marlow describes his impression of Jim's presence and authority at the height of his success in Patusan:

> He stood erect, the smouldering brier-wood in his clutch, with a smile on his lips and a sparkle in his boyish eyes. I sat on the stump of a tree at his feet, and below us stretched the land, the great expanse of the forests, sombre under the sunshine, rolling like a sea, with glints of winding rivers, the grey spots of villages, and here and there a clearing, like an islet of light amongst the dark waves of continuous tree-tops. A brooding gloom lay over this vast and monotonous landscape; the light fell on it as if into an abyss. The land devoured the sunshine; only far off, along the coast, the empty ocean, smooth and polished within the faint haze, seemed to rise up to the sky in a wall of steel.
>
> And there I was with him, high in the sunshine on the top of that historic hill of his. He dominated the forest, the secular gloom, the old mankind. He was like a figure set up on a pedestal, to represent in his persistent youth the power, and perhaps the virtues, of races that never grow old, that have emerged from the gloom. I don't know why he should always have appeared to me symbolic. Perhaps this is the real cause of my interest in his fate. I don't know whether it was exactly fair to him to remember the incident which had given a new direction to his life, but at that very moment I remembered very distinctly. It was like a shadow in the light. (264–65)

At the beginning of this passage Marlow's description of Jim is realistic, but it soon moves to a symbolic level. The character's boyishness becomes eternal youth and his erect posture suggests a statue created to celebrate heroism. Similarly, Marlow suddenly sees the forest setting from an evolutionary perspective that emphasizes the heroic aspect of Jim's achievements in Patusan. At the same time, the horizon is compared to a "wall of steel" restricting these achievements to Jim's new world, and the dark shadow of the past points out the irony of his attempt to fulfil a personal ideal that he has already betrayed. The shift to a symbolic portrayal of the character makes us see this attempt as significant and memorable. Moreover, the image of Jim elevated above a "great expanse . . . rolling like a sea" recalls the ironic description of the young officer-in-training stationed in the ship's foretop in the opening chapter. Comparison of these two perspectives guides our response to Jim's actions after the *Patna*, for the same imaginative egoism that the omniscient narrator condemns at the beginning of the novel acquires heroic resonance through Marlow's symbolic correspondences.

In this sense, the different narrative modes of *Lord Jim* reflect the protagonist's progression from shallow romanticism to idealistic commitment. Many critics have pointed out that Conrad's work is not a *Bildungsroman*, presumably because Jim's experience fails to alter his original exalted view of the world. However, the egoist's disastrous encounter with reality has moral consequences, for it helps him develop a personal integrity and resolve that win Marlow's qualified approval. In the first four chapters Jim is portrayed with ironic omniscience because before the *Patna* episode there are no significant depths of character to explore; by telling us everything about the protagonist, Conrad reveals the superficiality of his thinking. After the *Patna,* however, he emphasizes the psychological and moral aspects of Jim's internal conflict with "an invisible personality, an antagonistic and inseparable partner of his existence—another possessor of his soul" by using Marlow as a foil. The more the sceptical narrator discovers about Jim's "real" character, the more he is persuaded that his inner life has value and significance.

Once again, Conrad repeats a motif from "Heart of Darkness," for Kurtz, like Jim, struggles to preserve his egoistic dream in the face of the conventional civilized values represented by Marlow. In the novel, however, Jim's understanding of the convention he has broken is acute—the "inseparable partner of his existence" is his conscience or "moral identity"—whereas Kurtz's internal conflict is between civilized and primitive forms of egoism, both equally grotesque. Thus, as we have seen, Kurtz's decision to return to the cabin with Marlow does not imply the development of realistic character traits, whereas Jim's struggle involves us in a personal crisis familiar to most human beings. Here, the reader's gradual discovery of moral qualities that modify both the fixed, ironic impression in the opening chapters and Marlow's unsympathetic judgment at the beginning of his narration reverses the dramatic effect of "Heart of Darkness," where Marlow finds that Kurtz's character is not as complex as he had initially supposed. The different methods of characterization in the two works seem to be closely related to Conrad's moral conception of egoism as both demonic and potentially redemptive.

Conrad's skill in exploring Jim's character indirectly, through Marlow's subjective impressions and the suggestive juxtapositioning of large blocks of narrative, is analyzed in Ian Watt's fine discussion of technique in *Lord Jim.*[34] To his study of how our evaluation of Jim is guided by comparisons with figures like Brierly, the French lieutenant, and even the hospitalized chief engineer, I would add that Conrad often uses Marlow himself to emphasize and develop certain traits in Jim's nature. Thus, whereas the narrator controls our sympathy for Jim by pointing out his attempts to evade the moral issue of responsibility during his confession, Marlow's own words and actions show us the younger man's singlemindedness and courage indirectly. For example, at the end of the long conversation at Malabar House, Marlow persists in counselling Jim to run away from his punishment:

> "Oh! nonsense, my dear fellow," I began. He had a movement of impatience. "You don't seem to understand," he said, incisively; then looking at me without a wink, "I may have jumped, but I don't run away." "I meant no offence," I said; and added stupidly, "Better men than you have found it expedient to run, at times." He coloured all over, while in my confusion I half-choked myself with my own tongue. "Perhaps so," he said at last; "I am not good enough; I can't afford it. I am bound to fight this thing down—I am fighting it *now.*" (154)

Perhaps the most interesting aspect of Marlow's decision to offer Jim a chance to evade his moral responsibility is the fact that he makes this offer in full appreciation of the honourable nature of Jim's resolve to face the court. "There was something fine in the wildness of his unexpressed, hardly formulated hope," he says about Jim's belief in some form of redemption through "the ceremony of execution." The contradiction between Marlow's feelings and his actions, and the contrast between his inconsistency and Jim's decisiveness emphasizes the latter quality and makes it appear in a more favourable light. In fact, throughout this episode (which foreshadows the final "ceremony of execution") Conrad seems to suggest that Marlow's divided loyalties affect his ability to act without reservations, whereas Jim's commitment to his dream enables him to "fight this thing down." In "Heart of Darkness" the narrator opposes Kurtz's egoistic illusions with active resistance, carrying the agent out of the wilderness on his back. Here, Conrad focusses our attention on Jim's purposefulness by assigning a more passive, consultative role to the narrator and stressing the complexity of his moral position.

In the Patusan section of the novel Conrad develops Jim's character more directly and traditionally. Abandoning the radical chronological disruptions and thematic oppositions that characterize chapters 5 through 20, he has Marlow summarize the qualities that have distinguished Jim's performance in Patusan. This summary precedes the narration of Jim's adventures and guides the reader's interpretation of the events:

> It was not so much of his fearlessness that I thought. It is strange how little account I took of it: as if it had been something too conventional to be at the root of the matter. No. I was more struck by the other gifts he had displayed. He had proved his grasp of the unfamiliar situation, his intellectual alertness in that field of thought. There was his readiness, too! Amazing. And all this had come to him in a manner like keen scent to a well-bred hound. He was not eloquent, but there was a dignity in this constitutional reticence, there was a high seriousness in his stammerings. He had still his old trick of stubborn blushing. Now and then, though, a word, a sentence, would escape him that showed how deeply, how solemnly, he felt about the work which had given him the certitude of rehabilitation. That is why he seemed to love the land and the people with a sort of fierce egoism, with a contemptuous tenderness. (248)

The strategic placement of this passage and the fact that Marlow's sympathetic point of view is the only perspective we have on Jim's activities before the arrival of Gentleman Brown give the characterization weight and authority. In effect, each new and surprising trait that Marlow distinguishes reverses the ironic judgment of the protagonist in the opening chapters. Thus, the criticism of Jim's failure to achieve his ideals through "the perfect love of the work" is here offset by the statement linking his egoism to rehabilitative work with the natives of Patusan. Similarly, we can compare Marlow's testimony that Jim has shown remarkable readiness and adaptability with the ironic disjunctions between his conduct and the claims that "there was nothing he couldn't meet" earlier in the novel. Therefore, although Conrad continually casts doubt on the ultimate success of Jim's self-idealization, he insists on the protagonist's moral development; and at the end of his stay in Patusan Marlow attributes this growth to the central trait of determination—now identified as fidelity—that makes Jim "romantic, but none the less true" (334).

Perhaps the most convincing dramatization of this trait that Conrad gives us before Jim goes to his death occurs in chapter 35, which describes Marlow's departure from Patusan. When Jim explains why he must persevere with his work in the community no matter how ignoble it may appear to the outside world, he says: "Tomorrow I shall go and take my chance of drinking that silly old Tunku Allang's coffee, and I shall make no end of fuss over these rotten turtles' eggs. . . . I must go on, go on for ever holding up my end, to feel sure that nothing can touch me" (333–34). Here, Conrad suggests Jim's complete recovery from the romantic disease of abstraction because, for the first time, he associates his "butterfly" illusion that "nothing can touch [him]" with the prosaic work of administration.[35] Jim's "exalted egoism" is still self-inspired, but it gains its moral authority from the people's trust.

Conrad's wish to present Jim in this favourable light determined the length of the novel. The history of his difficulty in completing *Lord Jim* is well documented in the letters to William Blackwood and Meldrum during composition of the manuscript. After submitting chapter 20 (Marlow's consultation with Stein) on February 26, 1900, he sent no copy for some five weeks (except for fourteen pages on March 3, when he announced to Meldrum that he had "got hold" again).[36] Most likely, these pages comprised the better part of chapter 21, in which Marlow introduces the theme of Jim's success in Patusan, and says, "My last words about Jim shall be few." At this time Conrad hints at the redemptive aspect of his hero's romantic imagination, for Marlow claims that Patusan will offer "a totally new set of conditions for his imaginative faculty to work upon" (218). During the month-long interruption before he sent more manuscript Conrad apparently decided to elaborate the details of Jim's experience rather than report in a general way on how he had "got hold of" a new set of circumstances. From April 3 until July 14, when he completed the manuscript, the "last chapter" was continually postponed in order to develop his characterization of Jim more fully and realistically.

As I have indicated, the narrative mode that shapes this material differs from the kaleidoscopic impressionism of chapters 5 through 20. Conrad makes straightforward use of the narrator's conventional authority to summarize a protagonist's characteristics, and then dramatizes the traits in a sequence of actions that precludes ambiguity. Jim's exalted egoism, which will not allow him to come to terms with the "infernal alloy" in his nature, becomes no less problematic, but Conrad emphasizes the heroic qualities that emerge from his experiences—especially the determination to "go on for ever" living up to an ideal he has already betrayed—before the fateful meeting with Gentleman Brown. We know from Conrad's correspondence that this meeting and its consequences had been "thought out" before he began the Patusan section of the novel, and that, as in "Heart of Darkness," he "wrote up to" the ending.[37] Thus, the realistic portrayal of the protagonist's moral growth, heightened by Marlow's symbolic impressions, was probably intended to stress the heroic aspect of the decision Jim makes to honour his word to the people. Writing to William Blackwood several days after completing the novel, Conrad said: "It is my opinion that in the working out of the catastrophe psychologic disquisition should have no place. The reader ought to know enough by that time."[38]

In accordance with this theory, Conrad distances his narrator from Jim in the last section of the novel. Marlow tells the story in written rather than oral discourse, and his material has been gathered from participants in the action such as Brown and Tamb' Itam, to whom Jim's motives are profoundly mysterious. The formal aspects of this narrative method evoke the hero's tragic isolation in Patusan, for although Marlow relates the various reports of the disaster "as though [he] had been an eye-witness" (343), Jim's last acts are interpreted (if at all) by uncomprehending observers. Because of the lack of analysis, the narration is focused almost entirely on the events, which the reader is invited to regard as predetermined not only by circumstances but by the "moral identity" or character of the protagonist. As we have seen, the traits attributed to Jim in Patusan before the catastrophe systematically contradict the characterization of him in the opening chapters, just as the plot structure repeats the chain of events that comprise his failure on the *Patna*, but reverses the outcome.[39] These qualities derive from the chivalric tradition that Conrad celebrates in his essay on Lord Nelson. At the same time, Marlow's uneasiness about Jim's security in Patusan prepares the reader for the final irony of his fate, in which his most generous act—the offer of "a clear road" to Gentleman Brown—brings about his ruin.

Generations of family history had taught Conrad that idealism could not prevail against the "profound and terrifying" logic of fate. When he was in the midst of writing *Lord Jim,* he told Edward Garnett that the members of both his paternal and maternal families were united by a common bond: "all made sacrifices of fortune, liberty and life for the cause in which they believed; and very few had any illusions as to its success."[40] This attitude is reflected in Marlow's scepticism, which implies that Jim's death may have been a fruitless gesture of defiance. By leaving the narrator's judgment open-ended, Conrad urges us to continue thinking about Jim and the meaning of his last act. Again, comparison with "Heart of Darkness" reveals schematic parallels and oppositions between the two works. In "Heart of Darkness" Marlow's most explicit statement about Kurtz affirms that at the moment of death the egoist is redeemed by his imaginative vision: "He had summed up—he had judged. . . . He was a remarkable man." The practical implications of this vision, however, are worked out by the narrator, who must reconcile "the horror!" with the Intended's illusions. To accomplish this, he denies the real Kurtz.

In *Lord Jim* Marlow conspicuously evades an affirmation of Jim's ultimate redemption through his imagination, but he tells us repeatedly that Jim's mysterious opacity as a character has more "reality of . . . existence" than the solid facts of everyday life. In fact, in the context of Stein's definition of Jim's romanticism, the truthfulness of the hero's inner life acquires metaphysical overtones:

> "What is it that by inward pain makes him know himself? What is it that for you and me makes him—exist?"
>
> At that moment it was difficult to believe in Jim's existence—starting from a country parsonage, blurred by crowds of men as by clouds of dust, silenced by the clashing claims of life and death in a material world—but his imperishable reality came to me with a convincing, with an irresistible force! I saw it vividly, as though in our progress through the lofty silent rooms amongst fleeting gleams of light and the sudden revelations of human figures stealing with flickering flames within unfathomable and pellucid depths, we had approached nearer to absolute Truth, which, like Beauty itself, floats elusive, obscure, half submerged, in the silent still waters of mystery. (216)

The more difficulty Marlow has in penetrating the mystery of Jim's romantic commitment, the more certain we are of its depth and significance. Moreover, as the characterization of Jim in the Patusan sections is based on realistic evidence of this commitment, Conrad emphasizes the virtues of idealism within the thematic framework of the novel. In a sense, therefore, *Lord Jim* presents an affirmative view of the egoist that includes the tragic knowledge revealed in "Heart of Darkness." Whereas Kurtz's deathbed insight concerns the fundamental amorality of human nature and the enormity of his own self-deception, Jim goes to his death asserting the ideal value of his "real" self in spite of an amoral universe and his own past conduct.

In this chapter I have tried to show how the writing of "Heart of Darkness" influenced Conrad's original conception of Jim's romantic self-idealization. Specifically, certain techniques and motifs that focus on the character of the egoist were adapted from the story to the novel. In the shorter fiction the symbolic and mythic allusions are foregrounded; like Henry James, Conrad used the "long-short-story" to stress universal paradigms of experience rather than describe the realistic characteristics of men in a particularized social environment. Thus, the parabolic aspect of *Lord Jim,* in which the egoist redeems the past through his imaginative exaltation of an ideal self, is more clearly perceived when we compare Jim's career with Kurtz's loss of selfhood and his deathbed redemption.

6
"The Secret Sharer" and *Under Western Eyes*

The links between "The Secret Sharer" and *Under Western Eyes* provide us with another example of Conrad's unique, dialectical approach to a problem. Like "The Planter of Malata,"[1] "The Secret Sharer" was written with unusual speed while he was working on a longer and more complex piece of fiction. In November 1909 Conrad was at a critical stage in his composition of *Under Western Eyes;* that is, part way into the last section (Part Fourth).[2] At this point in the novel Razumov's apparent loyalty to the revolutionary cause has been confirmed by a report of Ziemianitch's suicide, which Sophia Antonovna and the other political exiles interpret as proof of the peasant's betrayal of Victor Haldin. Conrad ends Part Third by juxtaposing the young Russian's perverse satisfaction in having duped his fellow countrymen with his realization that he is now spiritually and morally isolated from his kind. Just as Razumov thinks, "There can be no doubt that now I am safe," his attention is caught by the faint sound of water breaking against the point of the island where he has sought privacy to write an official report of his activities as a Czarist secret agent, "and it occurred to him that this was about the only sound he could listen to innocently, and for his own pleasure, as it were. Yes, the sound of water, the voice of the wind—completely foreign to human passions. All the other sounds of this earth brought contamination to the solitude of a soul."[3] Conrad wrote "The Secret Sharer" when he was in the midst of the final section of the novel, in which Razumov must resolve the conflict between his public and private selves. In this chapter I shall explore the close relationship between these two works, for, as in his writing of "Heart of Darkness" and *Lord Jim,* Conrad used similar situations in the short fiction and novel in order to express different aspects of one central idea.

    Comparison of the young captain's predicament in "The Secret Sharer" with that of Razumov in *Under Western Eyes* reveals many clear parallels between the first section of the novel and the short story. In Part First of *Under Western Eyes* Victor Haldin seeks refuge in Razumov's lodgings after he has assassinated Mr. de P——, the minister of state responsible for a "ruthless persecution of the rising generation" that has seemed "to aim at the destruction of the very hope of liberty itself'' (7-8). At first Razumov fails to recognize his fellow student when he finds him in his room; he sees only a "strange figure" looming like a dark shadow against the white tiles of the stove. Afterwards, in a futile attempt to convince himself that he was not responsible for Haldin after he has betrayed him, Razumov overemphasizes the random nature of this meeting. However, the narrator tells us in his preamble that Haldin's choice of a sanctuary was prompted by the manner in which Razumov had presented himself to his colleagues: especially responsible were his reserve and his apparent lack of self-interest. Summarizing the protagonist's reputation among his fellow students, the old teacher of languages says:

> Amongst a lot of exuberant talkers, in the habit of exhausting themselves daily by ardent discussion, a comparatively taciturn personality is naturally credited with reserve power. By his comrades at the St. Petersburg University, Kirylo Sidorovitch Razumov, third year's student in philosophy, was looked upon as a strong nature—an altogether trustworthy man. This, in a country where an opinion may be a legal crime visited by death or sometimes by a fate worse than mere death, meant that he was worthy of being trusted with forbidden opinions. He was liked also for his amiability and for his quiet readiness to oblige his comrades even at the cost of personal inconvenience. (6)

In "The Secret Sharer" Conrad uses a similar *chiaroscuro* effect to describe Leggatt's sudden and mysterious appearance to the captain, who sees the pale, elongated shape of a man and the "dimly pale oval" of his face against the dark shadow of the ship's side.[4] Moreover, like Haldin's choice of Razumov's lodgings for a refuge, Leggatt's presence on board the ship can be related to certain aspects of the protagonist's conduct as well as to the circumstances of fate. Both Razumov and the captain exploit the ambiguity of silence. When Haldin announces, "It was I who removed de P—— this morning," Razumov conceals his thoughts and emotions, saying nothing. Similarly, when Leggatt says, "The question for me now is whether I am to let go this ladder and go on swimming till I sink from exhaustion, or—to come on board here" (99), the captain makes no comment. By his silence, he encourages the fugitive's decision to "come on board." In both cases, the visitor's attempt to seek asylum involves the protagonist's moral sense of responsibility. Moreover, in *Under Western Eyes* Conrad emphasizes Haldin's instinctive trust in his fellow student: he persists in calling Razumov "brother," and explains that "confidence" has led him to seek his assistance. "All I want you to do is to help me to vanish," Haldin says. Relying upon the captain's understanding in "The Secret Sharer," Leggatt makes a similar request. He asks to be marooned when the ship is among the off-shore islands, because "it would never do for me to come to life again" (131).

Like Haldin, Leggatt seeks refuge from a doctrinaire enforcement of "the law of the land." When Captain Archbold arrives on board to search for Leggatt, the captain realizes that his resolve to turn the fugitive over to the shore police "had in it something incomprehensible and a little awful; something, as it were, mystical, quite apart from his anxiety that he should not be suspected of 'countenancing any doings of that sort'" (118). In contrast to this inflexible point of view (which in some ways resembles Razumov's temporary conversion to Czarist absolutism in the novel) Leggatt assumes that his fellow officer will share his own interpretation of the circumstances surrounding the crime. Like Haldin, that is, he appeals to the other man in the name of humane instincts and common experience. Thus, Haldin interprets Razumov's silence in response to his confession as an "English" reserve that masks a sympathetic feeling ("'You have enough heart to have heard the sound of weeping and gnashing of teeth this man raised in the land,'" he says [16]) and the captain describes Leggatt's account of the murder in the following words: "He appealed to me as if our experiences had been as identical as our clothes" (102).

These similarities draw attention to the protagonists' contrasting responses to a moral dilemma that has surprised each of them, although each has unconsciously invited the problem. But there are still more correspondences between the short story and the first part of the novel, which demonstrate how the two narrative situations were linked in Conrad's imagination. Thus, the action in Part First of *Under Western Eyes* is developed chiefly through three characters: Haldin, Razumov, and Councillor Mikulin of the General Secretariat. Representing politically opposite forms of extremism, Haldin (the revolutionary terrorist) and Mikulin (the functionary of an autocratic régime) exert intense pressure on Razumov, who struggles to retain his intellectual independence. In his "Author's Note" to the novel Conrad comments on this arrangement of characters, identifying it with his initial conception of the plot:

> As to the actual creation I may say that when I began to write I had a distinct conception of the first part only, with the three figures of Haldin, Razumov, and Councillor Mikulin defined exactly in my mind. It was only after I had finished writing the first part that the whole story revealed itself to me in its tragic character and in the march of its events as unavoidable and sufficiently ample in its outline to give free play to my creative instinct and to the dramatic possibilities of the subject. (vii)

A letter to John Galsworthy dated "6th of Jan. of the New Year 1908" confirms Conrad's retrospective description of the work's evolution from a short story that he had planned to complete within a month[5] to the full-length novel, *Under Western Eyes*.

In his letter to Galsworthy, Conrad outlined the plot as he had conceived it before he began to write Part Second (which begins the "second movement" of the following synopsis):

> Listen to the theme. The Student Razumov (a natural son of a Prince K.) gives up secretly to the police his fellow student, Haldin, who seeks refuge in his rooms after committing a political crime (supposed to be the murder of de Plehve). First movement in St. Petersburg. (Haldin is hanged of course.)
> 2nd in Genève. The student Razumov meeting abroad the mother and sister of Haldin falls in

love with that last, marries her and, after a time, confesses to her the part he played in the arrest of her brother.

The psychological developments leading to Razumov's betrayal of Haldin, to his confession of the fact to his wife and to the death of these people (brought about mainly by the resemblance of their child to the late Haldin), form the real subject of the story.[6]

G. Jean-Aubry tells us that in the margin of the first of these paragraphs Conrad wrote "done," and "to do" in the margin of the second.[7] As Conrad says in his "Author's Note," it was only after exploring the dramatic conflict involving the three figures of Haldin, Razumov, and Mikulin that the possibilities for further plot development became clear to him. In fact, considering that he originally planned to write a short story consisting of about forty-five manuscript pages,[8] it would seem that the St. Petersburg part of the action proved to be much more complicated than he had anticipated.

As I have suggested, Part First of the novel bears a strong resemblance in theme and structure to "The Secret Sharer." In the latter work, however, the protagonist's response to his situation is diametrically opposed to Razumov's, and the moral contradictions inherent in the first section of Under Western Eyes are thereby "closed" or resolved. As in the opening part of the novel, the central action of "The Secret Sharer" is based on the interrelationship of three characters: Leggatt, the young captain, and Archbold, the captain of the *Sephora*. To emphasize this interrelationship, Conrad contrasts the captain's crucial interview with Archbold, which is conducted in deliberately loud, "bawling" tones, to his recurrent whispered conversations with Leggatt, the murderer concealed in his cabin. The contrast symbolizes the captain's moral and emotional distance from Archbold, as well as his intimacy with Leggatt.

Like the moral and political pressures exerted by Haldin and Mikulin on Razumov, Leggatt and Archbold offer antithetical choices to the central character, who has embarked (like Razumov) on a quest to seek his "real life" or identity reflected in the high opinion of his fellows. Throughout their interview Archbold tries to coerce the captain by various "oblique steps," including indirect references to Leggatt's presence on board ("I reckon I had no more than a two-mile pull to your ship. Not a bit more," he says [120]) and sly allusions to the young captain's responsibility to uphold the maritime law. For example, he asks him to imagine that the crime had been committed on board his own ship (117). In the first section of Under Western Eyes Councillor Mikulin adopts a similarly oblique approach during his interview with Razumov. Recalling Porfiry Petrovich's treatment of Raskolnikov in *Crime and Punishment,* the interrogator insinuates his meaning indirectly until Razumov is driven to exclaim: "I'll tell you what you think . . . You think that you are dealing with a secret accomplice of that unhappy man" (95).

In "The Secret Sharer" Conrad reverses this situation so that the protagonist triumphs over his inquisitor. The young captain uses his feigned deafness and "punctilious courtesy" to defend himself against Archbold's suspicions, and routs the other man completely by forcing a search of the ship: "I had been too frightened not to feel vengeful; I felt I had him on the run, and I meant to keep him on the run. My polite insistence must have had something menacing in it, because he gave in suddenly. And I did not let him off a single item . . ." (121). The captain's strategy at the end of this meeting, when he counters Archbold's weak threats with a triumphant *non sequitur,* makes effective use of the antagonist's indirect tactics in order to gain the upper hand:

> He was a tenacious beast. On the very ladder he lingered, and in that unique, guiltily conscientious manner of sticking to the point:
> "I say . . . you . . . you don't think that—"
> I covered his voice loudly:
> "Certainly not . . . I am delighted. Good-bye." (122)

Thus, in a comic reversal of a key episode in *Under Western Eyes* Conrad justifies his protagonist's decision to protect Leggatt, and opposes it rhetorically to Razumov's betrayal of Haldin.[9]

This dramatization of the captain's loyalty to Leggatt is not as simple as it might appear at first glance. The narrator insists that his psychological bond with the outlaw precludes his lying to Archbold outright: "I could not, I think, have met him by a direct lie . . . for psychological (not moral) reasons. If he had only known how afraid I was of his putting my feeling of identity with the other to the test!" (120). Here, Conrad emphasizes Leggatt's symbolic role as a complementary version of the captain's outward, public identity: to deny his existence would amount to self-mutilation. Thus, the protagonist's bold evasion of Archbold's suspicions permits him to affirm his secret, inner instincts and convictions without betraying Leggatt to "the law of the land." In *Under Western Eyes* Conrad presents an ironic version of the same theme, for only after Razumov has committed his act of self-mutilation does he acknowledge its real significance. Before he confesses the betrayal to the revolutionaries in Geneva, he writes to Natalia Haldin: "In giving Victor Haldin up, it was myself, after all, whom I have betrayed most basely" (361).

The various ways in which Conrad explores Razumov's discovery of this truth comprise Parts Second, Third, and Fourth of *Under Western Eyes.* In Part First the young Russian chooses autocracy in order to protect his self-interest, although he has intellectual and emotional doubts about individual servants of the Czar, such as General T——. He accepts the official ramifications of his decision, but refuses to acknowledge its "mysterious and secret sides."[10] Most significantly, by making Razumov protest to Councillor Mikulin that he "thinks like a Russian" (that is, "faithfully"), Conrad emphasizes the tragic conflict between political extremism and the individual's need to preserve his independence of thought and action. In this respect, the interview between Mikulin and Razumov points out the direction in which the latter's character will change and develop in response to the pressures of his activities as a secret agent.

Throughout the first section of the novel we see that Razumov's claim to be intellectually independent is largely unproven. In ironic contrast to his defiant statement in Councillor Mikulin's office—"I beg you to allow me the superiority of the thinking reed over the unthinking forces that are about to crush him out of existence" (89)—we have his declaration that he thinks "faithfully," his conviction that "obscurantism is better than the light of incendiary torches" (34), and the narrator's revealing description of his conduct with fellow students: "in discussion he was easily swayed by argument and authority" (5). Only after he struggles with the conflicting claims of Czarist autocracy and revolutionary ideology in the succeeding chapters of the novel does Razumov gradually acquire true independence of thought. At the end of his confession to Natalia Haldin he says: "it is they [the revolutionaries] and not I who have the right on their side!—theirs is the strength of invisible powers. So be it. Only don't be deceived . . . I am not converted. Have I then the soul of a slave? No! I am independent—and therefore perdition is my lot" (361-62). In "The Secret Sharer" the process of individuation is telescoped and given a richly symbolic form, presenting a mirror-image of Razumov's struggle. That is, the captain gains his independence without forfeiting his integrity, although he is "converted" almost immediately by the outlawed "other self."

A good example of the way in which the short story mirrors and reverses the moral and psychological themes of *Under Western Eyes* is Conrad's presentation of the dilemma confronting the young captain when Leggatt appears alongside his ship. First, however, let us consider how Conrad brings this dilemma[11] to the reader's attention. Just before Leggatt emerges mysteriously from the sea "as if he had risen from the bottom," the captain indulges in a typically Conradian contrast between the two worlds of land and sea:

> And suddenly I rejoiced in the great security of the sea as compared with the unrest of the land, in my choice of that untempted life presenting no disquieting problems, invested with an elementary moral beauty by the absolute straightforwardness of its appeal and by the singleness of its purpose.
> The riding-light in the fore-rigging burned with a clear, untroubled, as if symbolic, flame, confident and bright in the mysterious shades of the night. (96)

Although this passage recalls similar thematic oppositions in works like *The Nigger of the "Narcissus"* between the moral clarity of life at sea and the corruption of men's ideals on land, Conrad's ironic intention is evident. The young captain's naïveté is revealed in his overemphatic use of modifiers to describe the "absolute straightforwardness" of life at sea, as well as in the symbolic image of the riding-light, which he invests with his own "clear, untroubled" confidence. From the opening paragraph of the story, when the narrator describes the sea as looking "solid" and "stable" lying below his feet, Conrad stresses the captain's innocent tendency to take appearances for reality.

When he notices the rope ladder still hanging over the side of the ship and realizes that his own actions have prevented the anchor watch from being properly set, the captain's response is predictably uncomplicated: "I asked myself whether it was wise ever to interfere with the established routine of duties even from the kindest of motives" (97). Against this background of confident single-mindedness, Conrad introduces the grotesque, ambiguous figure of the swimmer:

> The side of the ship made an opaque belt of shadow on the darkling glassy shimmer of the sea. But I saw at once something elongated and pale floating very close to the ladder. Before I could form a guess a faint flash of phosphorescent light, which seemed to issue suddenly from the naked body of a man, flickered in the sleeping water with the elusive, silent play of summer lightning in a night sky. With a gasp I saw revealed to my stare a pair of feet, the long legs, a broad livid back immersed right up to the neck in a greenish cadaverous glow. One hand, awash, clutched the bottom rung of the ladder. He was complete but for the head. A headless corpse! The cigar dropped out of my gaping mouth with a tiny plop and a short hiss quite audible in the absolute stillness of all things under heaven. At that I suppose he raised up his face, a dimly pale oval in the shadow of the ship's side. But even then I could only barely make out down there the shape of his black-haired head. However, it was enough for the horrid, frost-bound sensation which had gripped me about the chest to pass off. The moment of vain exclamations was past, too. I only climbed on the spare spar and leaned over the rail as far as I could, to bring my eyes nearer to that mystery floating alongside. (97–98)

Here, Conrad presents the captain with a problem that cannot be solved by consulting a ship's manual, and makes the reader participate in the deciphering process. First, he involves us in the narrator's dreamlike apprehension of the "mystery" by withholding the logical explanation for the presence of "something elongated and pale" in the water. Through "delayed decoding," which renders visual impressions directly, he makes startlingly vivid comparisons of the strange object with a nonhuman, eel-like form, a cadaver, and finally, a "headless corpse."[12] Even after the shape has been identified as a living man, the reason for Leggatt's presence remains a mystery. The narrator cannot even be sure that the stranger has swum to the ship: "As he hung by the ladder, *like* a resting swimmer, the sea-lightning played about his limbs at every stir; and he appeared in it ghastly, silvery, fish-like" (98; my italics). In ironic contrast to his confident distinction between the worlds of land and ocean, the "great security of the sea" has already presented the young captain with a "disquieting problem": that is, an object that seems to belong to both elements at once, and that threatens the "elementary moral beauty" of an existence governed by exact rules and regulations. For the narrator's resolve not to interfere with "the established routine of duties" on board the ship is complicated by his "pure intuition" and the "mysterious communication" that is immediately established between Leggatt and himself.

Thus, in the opening pages of "The Secret Sharer" Conrad introduces a conflict between reason and feeling that is similar to Razumov's moral dilemma in the first part of *Under Western Eyes*. In the novel Razumov betrays Haldin because he cherishes the illusion of living a "normal" life—that is, an existence governed by common sense and rational conduct. He creates an "established routine" rather like a ship's duty roster, partly to protect himself from examining the real conditions of his life under a cynical autocracy. At his "usual hour" he rises, attends morning lectures faithfully, studies in the library during the afternoon, and spends his evening working on the prize essay. To Haldin, who puts forth the claims of fellowship and idealistic feeling, he describes himself as "just a man. . . . A man with a mind" (61).

Like Leggatt, the revolutionist is the protagonist's alter-ego, unrecognized at first sight: he is "not one of the industrious set," is "hardly ever seen at lectures," and has been marked by the authorities as "restless" and "unsound" (14–15). Jacques Berthoud points out that the two young Russians "have the interdependence of complementaries" because "where Razumov represents the spirit of criticism, Haldin, generous, ardent, and brave, stands for the spirit of idealism."[13] In fact, Razumov displays an emotional need for the very type of fellowship that Haldin offers, and this need conflicts with his persistent attempts to rationalize his conduct. With considerable irony, Conrad describes the young man's desire "to pour out a full confession in passionate words that would stir the whole being of that man [Haldin] to its innermost depths; that would end in embraces and tears; in an incredible fellowship of souls—such as the world had never seen" (39–40). During his interview with Councillor Mikulin Razumov's repressed feelings will not allow him to deny this bond completely, and he speaks (and thinks) compulsively about walking over phantoms. In this way Conrad reminds us of the young man's earlier sense of trampling over the ghost of Haldin stretched on its back in the snow—a symbolic affirmation of his moral feelings.

At last, Mikulin seems to sense a secret meaning or emotion beneath Razumov's words:

> "But I protest against this comedy of persecution. The whole affair is becoming too comical altogether for my taste. A comedy of errors, phantoms, and suspicions. It's positively indecent. . . ."
> Councillor Mikulin turned an attentive ear.
> "Did you say phantoms?" he murmured.
> "I could walk over dozens of them." (99)

In this passage Conrad dramatizes, with great economy and effect, the ongoing conflict between Razumov's common sense, which rejects the irrational aspects of his involvement by calling the events "a comedy of errors, phantoms, and suspicions," and his inner feelings, which reject the cynically practical solution to his dilemma. Councillor Mikulin's question—"Where to?"—in response to Razumov's decision to "retire" from the affair leaves the entire action of the novel balanced between the poles of this opposition.

In "The Secret Sharer" Conrad minimizes the captain's inner conflict by undermining the claims of reason and affirming the role of intuition or feeling. Almost immediately after Leggatt appears at the side of his ship, the captain allows his instinct to guide his conduct, and the author tacitly approves. Thus, in the very first conversation with Leggatt Conrad points out the preeminence of feeling over a sober consideration of the facts:

> I felt this was no mere formula of desperate speech, but a real alternative in the view of a strong soul. I should have gathered from this that he was young; indeed, it is only the young who are ever confronted by such clear issues. But at the time it was pure intuition on my part. A mysterious communication was established already between us two—in the face of that silent, darkened tropical sea. I was young, too; young enough to make no comment. (99)

Here, Conrad contrasts the captain's intuition, by which he "felt" the other man's intention, to the logic by which he "should have gathered" the correct answer. The "mysterious" communication between the two is based on the former.

In "The Secret Sharer" Conrad also uses comic juxtapositions to criticize the single-minded adherence to logic or reason. Consider the captain's frequent references to the "absurd" chief mate, who likes to "account for" everything and constructs elaborate theories to explain commonplace events: "Meantime the chief mate, with an almost visible effect of collaboration on the part of his round eyes and frightful whiskers, was trying to evolve a theory of the anchored ship. His dominant trait was to take all things into earnest consideration. He was of a painstaking turn of mind. As he used to say, he 'liked to account to himself' for practically everything that came in his way . . . ." (94). In this episode Conrad undercuts the mate's logical conclusion concerning the anchored ship. Suddenly the junior officer produces all the facts of the matter, which he has learned effortlessly, without using his reason, from the tugboat skipper. The affair ends with the chief mate's comic attempt to "account for" the junior officer's delay in telling his colleagues "all about it."

The captain's choice of feeling and instinct over "established routine" and rational thought is dramatized most strikingly in his crucial meeting with Archbold. As I have pointed out, Conrad uses the same configuration of characters in the short story as he does when he places Razumov between Haldin and Mikulin in the first part of *Under Western Eyes*. Specifically, the numerous correspondences between the two interviews indicate that Conrad may have had Razumov's suppressed feelings about Haldin in his mind when he described the captain's anxiety to protect Leggatt against Archbold. For example, the secret presence of Leggatt in the cabin, which affects the captain's thoughts and actions more and more strongly as the interview progresses, recalls Razumov's self-revealing attempts to deny Haldin. As Razumov stares at Councillor Mikulin "with enormous wide eyes," he imagines the dead man in concrete detail as he had last seen him alive: "Haldin had been hanged at four o'clock. There could be no doubt of that. He had, it seemed, entered upon his future existence, long boots, Astrakhan fur cap and all, down to the very leather strap round his waist" (94).

In "The Secret Sharer" the captain is similarly obsessed with the details of Leggatt's physical appearance and posture as he imagines him on the other side of the bulkhead during the interview: "I looked politely at Captain Archbold . . . but it was the other I saw, in a grey sleeping-suit, seated on a low stool, his bare feet close together, his arms folded, and every word said between us falling into the ears of his dark head bowed on his chest" (117). Consequently, he reacts emotionally to Archbold's hostility, exactly as if he were Leggatt himself: "I had become so connected in thoughts and impressions with the secret sharer of my cabin that I felt as if I, personally, were being given to understand that I, too, was not the sort that would have done for the chief mate of a ship like the *Sephora*" (119). Notice the rhythmical repetitions, which are calculated to draw the reader in and involve him in the captain's emotional identification with the outlaw. In contrast, Razumov's sense of involvement in Haldin's fate is expressed indirectly, in a manner that distances the reader. After he has experienced the vision of Haldin in Mikulin's office, Razumov thinks: "A flickering, vanishing sort of existence. It was not his soul, it was his mere phantom he had left behind on this earth" (94). Through free indirect style, Conrad reproduces the character's self-defensive, mocking tone. At the same time, he exposes the ironic disjunction between the concrete details noted earlier and Razumov's evaluation of Haldin's image as "vanishing" and "flickering."

In summary, comparison of the short story with the first section of *Under Western Eyes* demonstrates how Conrad adapted his original design of three representative figures (Haldin, Razumov, and Councillor Mikulin) to dramatize the captain's resolution of a moral dilemma. In one of the best articles written on "Falk," Tony Tanner points out a similar geometric correspondence between that story and *Victory,* in which Heyst and Falk are in identical triangular situations but at opposite poles: one represents the Schopenhauerian denial of the will, and the other is the incarnation of the "will to live."[14] As we have seen in the preceding chapters of this study, Conrad often explored the dialectical aspects of his ideas by repeating situations, characters, and motifs from one work to another. In the case of "The Secret Sharer" and *Under Western Eyes,* for example, the schematic oppositions of reason and feeling as potential guides of the young captain's conduct provide a critical commentary on Razumov's claim that his rejection of Haldin is dictated by "cool, superior reason." In fact, Razumov's decision is based on emotion just as much as is the captain's. However, in contrast to the captain's altruistic conduct toward Leggatt Razumov acts solely on his egoistic desire for a predictable, orderly future. He represses his moral feelings for Haldin.

These and other dialectical correspondences between the two works emphasize Conrad's criticism of the political conditions that influence Razumov's conduct. Because neither the autocratic state nor the revolutionary movement offers the individual Russian citizen a solid moral foundation for his actions, Razumov's ambition to create a sane, rational future for himself is doomed from the outset. In an effort to escape the extremism represented by Haldin's terrorist activity, the young Russian chooses the only alternative that seems available to him; that is, an equally extremist Messianic Czarism:

> Of course he was far from being a moss-grown reactionary. Everything was not for the best. Despotic bureaucracy . . . abuses . . . corruption . . . and so on. Capable men were wanted. Enlightened intelligences. Devoted hearts. But absolute power should be preserved—the tool ready

for the man—for the great autocrat of the future. Razumov believed in him. The logic of history made him unavoidable. The state of the people demanded him. "What else," he asked himself ardently, "could move all that mass in one direction? Nothing could. Nothing but a single will." (35)

Like the young Russian trader in "Heart of Darkness," Razumov falls under the powerful spell of autocracy because his social environment provides no traditions of compromise, free co-operation, or tolerance. Thus, his failure to acknowledge a concrete personal responsibility for Haldin is symptomatic of a national malaise.[15] Lacking a practical, moral code of conduct, Razumov opts for a mystical "mother Russia" and chooses a hypothetical "forty million brothers" instead of the real "brother" lodged in his student's quarters. As we shall see shortly, this figure of speech becomes an important motif linking the short story to the novel.

Although the captain's situation in "The Secret Sharer" is similar in many respects to Razumov's, the ideological framework for the hero's actions is completely different. Whereas the Russian must choose between complementary forms of extremism, the captain's decision to ally himself with Leggatt is based on the spirit, if not the letter, of the maritime code of solidarity. Moreover, to gain the reader's approval of the hero's conduct, Conrad uses an "I" narrator and draws on the mythic appeal of the Cain and Abel Biblical story. The persuasiveness of the first-person point of view is displayed when the captain first learns that Leggatt has killed a man on board the *Sephora*. In the following passage the narrator pleads the outlaw's case for him: "And I knew well enough the pestiferous danger of such a character where there are no means of legal repression. And I knew well enough also that my double there was no homicidal ruffian. I did not think of asking him for details, and he told me the story roughly in brusque, disconnected sentences. I needed no more" (102). To emphasize the extenuating circumstances of Leggatt's crime, Conrad uses repetition ("And I knew well enough") and a strategically placed short sentence, in the manner of Flaubert ("I needed no more"). These techniques increase the rhetorical effectiveness of the limited narrative perspective, which allows Conrad to present the captain's personal experience and intuition as conclusive proof of Leggatt's claims. In *Under Western Eyes* Razumov's point of view is qualified and interpreted by the English teacher of languages who narrates the story.

Unlike Marlow in *Lord Jim,* whose paradoxical language when he relates Jim's confession at Malabar House reveals deeply divided loyalties, the captain argues passionately for Leggatt's protection under the unwritten laws of the maritime code of service. Not only is Leggatt a fellow officer with a social background and experiences similar to the narrator's, but his performance of Archbold's duties in exceptional circumstances commands respect. As the outlaw confesses his crime, the special difficulties of this performance—a violent storm at sea and the absence of any form of "legal repression" when dealing with a deliberate challenge to the officer's authority—are factors which create a bond between teller and listener.

Again, the dialectical aspect of the parallel situations in "The Secret Sharer" and *Under Western Eyes* emphasizes the lack of moral traditions illustrated by the characteristic Russian response to events. In the novel Haldin assumes that Razumov will sympathize with his crime because he has a "heart"; therefore, the two men must share a common attitude toward Mr. de P——'s repressive tactics. Haldin intuits the existence of a bond of solidarity, but this bond is not based on mutually perceptible concepts of honourable conduct. In contrast, the captain's professional judgment that Leggatt was performing an act of service to the ship and her men just before he killed the mutinous sailor allows him to advance the opinion that the outlaw's strength "recoiled" on "an unworthy . . . existence" (125).

In "The Secret Sharer" Conrad uses the first-person perspective to persuade the reader that the captain's instinct and intuition are valid because they are based on a foundation of morally civilized traditions. Comparison with *Under Western Eyes* reveals that without this foundation, instinct cannot be trusted to promote real solidarity. Throughout the novel Conrad's irony reinforces this view; consider, for example, Sophia Antonovna's intuitive perception of Razumov. Mistaking the secret agent for a "comrade" in the struggle against autocracy, she says: "You understand me, Razumov . . . *I felt it* from the first, directly I set my eyes on you" (260; my italics). Moreover, in "The Secret Sharer" Conrad repeats and develops the implied references to the Cain and Abel story in *Under Western Eyes*, emphasizing indirectly Razumov's inability to distinguish real from illusory solidarity. In the first section of the novel Razumov responds to Haldin's insistent use of the term "brother" by claiming to have forty million brothers: "Is not this my country?" he says. "Have I not got forty million brothers?" (35). As he continues to rationalize his decision to betray Haldin, Razumov's rhetorical questions recall the Biblical response made by Cain to the Lord: "Am I my brother's keeper?" For example, he asks himself: "By what bond of common faith, of common conviction, am I obliged to let that fanatical idiot drag me down with him?" (37-38). When he returns to his lodgings after sending Haldin to a certain death, Razumov recapitulates the allusion, with savage irony. "I am responsible for you," he shrieks at the revolutionist (60).

This oblique reference to the Biblical story becomes explicit in "The Secret Sharer."[16] At the same time, however, the thematic implications of the allusions shift dramatically. Whereas in *Under Western Eyes* the mythic overtones make us feel that Razumov's failure to recognize Haldin's real claims on his loyalty is a serious crime against humanity, in "The Secret Sharer" the parallel between Cain and Leggatt evokes our sympathy for the outlaw. For example, the "Abel" of Conrad's story is a sailor who, as we have seen, transgresses the maritime code of service and threatens the safety of the ship. Because the narrator supports Leggatt's intensely critical view of this man without qualification or irony, the slaying does not seem to merit the punishment of exile, let alone imprisonment or death. In fact, Conrad directs us to this interpretation when he has Leggatt say: "The 'brand of Cain' business, don't you see. That's all right. I was ready enough to go off wandering on the face of the earth—and that was price enough to pay for an Abel of that sort'' (107).

Later in the story Conrad repeats the motif, using a direct reference to the passage from *Genesis*[17] to enhance the pathos of Leggatt's situation:

> "What does the Bible say? 'Driven off the face of the earth.' Very well. I am off the face of the earth now. As I came at night so I shall go.''
> "Impossible!'' I murmured. "You can't.''
> "Can't?' . . . Not naked like a soul on the Day of Judgment. I shall freeze on to this sleeping-suit. The Last Day is not yet. . . .'' (132)

Notice the rhythm and evocative imagery of Leggatt's statement, "As I came at night so I shall go,'' which makes a rhetorical appeal to the reader. At the climax of the story the motif reappears for the last time, making an even stronger bid for our sympathy: "But I hardly thought of my other self, now gone from the ship, to be hidden for ever from all friendly faces, to be a fugitive and a vagabond on the earth, with no brand of the curse on his sane forehead to stay a slaying hand . . . too proud to explain'' (142). Here, Conrad exploits the difference between the Biblical Cain, who could rely on the Lord's intervention to preserve him from human wrath, and Leggatt, who goes into the wilderness unprotected. In this way, the myth is used to concentrate our attention on Leggatt's punishment rather than his crime and to emphasize the extenuating circumstances, which he is "too proud to explain.'' The contrast between Conrad's use of the Cain and Abel story in "The Secret Sharer'' and the ironic allusions to being responsible for one's brother in *Under Western Eyes* points out the lack of moral solidarity that afflicts Russian society. On the other hand, Conrad insists that to understand the circumstances of Leggatt's crime is to endorse the captain's solidarity and affirm the values upon which it is based.

The unusually close relationship between "The Secret Sharer'' and *Under Western Eyes* is expressed through many other connecting motifs, images, and verbal echoes. One of the most Dostoevskian of these links is the symbolic image of the room that shelters and confines both the protagonist and his "secret sharer.''[18] In *Under Western Eyes* Razumov locks Haldin inside his room while he searches for Ziemianitch, imprisoning his visitor in order to protect himself. We find a dialectical correspondence to this motif in "The Secret Sharer,'' where the captain would *like* to lock Leggatt inside his cabin, but for the outlaw's protection as well as his own. When Razumov returns to his room after betraying Haldin, he reveals his inner conflict by duplicating his fellow student's movements: "The room grew dark swiftly though time had seemed to stand still. How was it that he had not noticed the passing of that day? Of course, it was the watch being stopped. . . . He did not light his lamp, but went over to the bed and threw himself on it without any hesitation. Lying on his back, he put his hands under his head and stared upward. After a moment he thought, 'I am lying here like that man'" (69–70). In this passage Razumov's identification with the man whom he has betrayed and his psychological withdrawal (which is symbolized by the darkness and lack of chronological sequence within the room) suggest his spiritual imprisonment by feelings of remorse. The image of the restricted space from which Razumov cannot escape until he confesses pervades the later sections of the novel, forming an ironic parallel to his earlier confinement of Haldin. In "The Secret Sharer," written concurrently with the last part of *Under Western Eyes,* the rhythm of confinement and release seems to shape the entire story. Because of the brief, concentrated scope of the work, the change of mood and tempo at the climax—when Leggatt's release affirms the captain's independence and command—constitutes a movement that controls the rhythm of the whole. The same movement is repeated several times in the novel, so that Razumov's increasing self-imprisonment continually alternates with his need to escape.

In Razumov's letter to Natalia Haldin Conrad describes the sense of entrapment from the protagonist's point of view: "I sat alone in my room, planning a life, the very thought of which makes me shudder now, like a believer who had been tempted to an atrocious sacrilege. But I brooded ardently over its images. The only thing was that there seemed to be no air in it" (360). Like Dostoevsky's Raskolnikov, Razumov is increasingly tortured by the need to draw a breath of fresh, uncontaminated air. Thus, when the narrator and Natalia search for him on the night of Razumov's confession the shopkeeper tells them that the young man has unexpectedly left his room:

> Mr. Razumov, after being absent all day, had returned early in the evening. He was very surprised about half an hour or a little more ago to see him come down again. Mr. Razumov left his key, and in the course of some words which passed between them had remarked that he was going out because he needed air.
> From behind the bare counter he went on smiling at us, his head held between his hands. Air. Air. But whether that meant a long or a short absence it was difficult to say. The night was very close, certainly. (333–34)

Conrad intensifies the rhythm of confinement and release as Razumov returns to his room after confessing to Natalia, only to escape again at midnight in a last reenactment of Haldin's movements: "He was the puppet of his past, because at the very stroke of midnight he jumped up and ran swiftly downstairs as if confident that, by the power of destiny, the house door would fly open before the absolute necessity of his errand" (362). The symbolism of this action is foregrounded when the narrator, anticipating Razumov's confession to the revolutionaries, refers to his "escape from the prison of lies" (363).

In the first section of *Under Western Eyes* Conrad describes Razumov's horror at the prospect of sheltering his visitor for an indefinite length of time: "it was despair—nothing less—at the thought of having to live with Haldin for an indefinite number of days in mortal alarm at every sound" (32). At the climax of the novel, however, Razumov acknowledges that the dead man's spirit, which has haunted him longer and more relentlessly than did the live Haldin, has actually "saved" him:

> He could have gone out at once, but the hour had not struck yet. The hour would be midnight. There was no reason for that choice except that the facts and the words of a certain evening in his past were timing his conduct in the present. The sudden power Natalia Haldin had gained over him he ascribed to the same cause. "You don't walk with impunity over a phantom's breast," he heard himself mutter. "Thus he saves me," he thought suddenly. "He himself, the betrayed man." (362)

When Razumov leaves his rooms for the last time to confront the revolutionaries he recovers his self-respect and gains true independence.

In "The Secret Sharer" Conrad emphasizes much more clearly the ultimately redemptive aspect of the protagonist's bond with a "secret self." Again, the "room" image suggests in a concrete form the symbiotic relationship between the two men. In this case, there are symbolic implications as well: the captain's cabin is shaped "L" for Leggatt. Releasing Leggatt from his hiding place at the end of the story proves that the young captain has finally gained the moral independence that allows him to achieve "the perfect communion of a seaman with his first command" (143). In fact, Conrad repeats the key word "save," which Razumov uses to describe Haldin's role in his redemption, at the climactic moment of revelation in "The Secret Sharer": "And I watched the hat—the expression of my sudden pity for his mere flesh. It had been meant to save his homeless head from the dangers of the sun. And now—behold—it was saving the ship, by serving me for a mark to help out the ignorance of my strangeness" (142).

The thematic link between "The Secret Sharer" and *Under Western Eyes*—in which the protagonist discovers his authentic self by recognizing his responsibility for another individual—is thereby reinforced by a concrete image (the room, or confining space) that functions as a controlling metaphor in both works. Similarly, the network of "phantom" images and references that Conrad creates to emphasize Razumov's moral bond with Haldin in *Under Western Eyes* is also found in "The Secret Sharer." From the moment Leggatt comes on board the ship, the captain is conscious of the ghostly quality of his visitor's presence. In fact, he tries to imagine the first mate's reaction were he suddenly to catch sight of the two men on deck, "the strange captain having a quiet confabulation by the wheel with his own grey ghost" (103). As the protagonist identifies himself more and more closely with Leggatt, he tends to confuse reality with fancy or illusion: "When at last I did [turn around] I saw him standing bolt-upright in the narrow recessed part. It would not be true to say I had a shock, but an irresistible doubt of his bodily existence flitted through my mind. Can it be, I asked myself, that he is not visible to other eyes than mine? It was like being haunted" (130). Razumov experiences the same confusing blend of reality and illusion when he returns to his room after giving Haldin up to the authorities: "He dropped the pencil and turned abruptly towards the bed with the shadowy figure extended full length on it—so much more indistinct than the one over whose breast he had walked without faltering. Was this, too, a phantom?" (57).

The duplication of "phantom" references from novel to short story involves many key words such as "invisible" and "vanish," which pervade both texts. Other significant echoes pertain to the protagonist's secret relationship with another "self." In Part Third of *Under Western Eyes* Conrad takes us inside Razumov's tortured mind and emphasizes his sensations of doubleness. Thus, his "silent thinking" is "like a secret dialogue with himself," and after his ordeal with Madame de S—— and Peter Ivanovitch he feels "as though another self, an independent sharer of his mind, had been able to view his whole person very distinctly indeed" (230). Here, Conrad represents the struggle between Razumov's conscience and his determination to offer intellectual resistance to the revolutionaries in words and images very similar to those he used not very long afterwards to express the captain's sense of Leggatt's being a complementary, secret part of his own identity. The phrase "another self, an independent sharer" seems to have made its way almost directly from the novel to the short story. And in fact, Razumov's inner conflict illustrates the dichotomy between reason and feeling that Conrad explores in both works.

In summary, the close relationship between "The Secret Sharer" and *Under Western Eyes* extends from large formal elements, such as configurations of representative characters and controlling metaphors, to much smaller elements, such as the repetition of key words.[19] Conrad uses the parallels between the two works as starting points from which to explore different aspects of his ideas. For example, in some respects "The Secret Sharer" can be read as a critique of the moral and political conditions that affect Razumov's conduct at the beginning of *Under Western Eyes*. Moreover, the fact that Conrad wrote the short story before he had completed the novel suggests that "The Secret Sharer" may have had an indirect influence on the ending of the longer work. In order to explore this possibility, let us recall that Part Third of *Under Western Eyes* ends with the narrator's description of Razumov's moral isolation at the very moment when he has been accepted by the revolutionaries in Geneva, and that the short story was written part way through Part Four, when Conrad was exploring the implications of this isolation.

Looking at the opening of "The Secret Sharer," one is immediately struck by certain similarities between the captain's situation and Razumov's at the end of Part Third. Conrad depicts both men as solitary human beings who are, in different ways, strangers to themselves. In both cases the specific details of the landscape draw our attention to the protagonist's isolated condition: Razumov feels that the voices of wind and water are the only sounds on earth with which he can commune, and the captain uses words like "abandoned" and "barren" to describe his view from the ship's deck. Even the islets remind him of "stone walls, towers, and blockhouses" built by a vanished tribe of men, and there is "no sign of human habitation as far as the eye could reach" (91).[20] Moreover, the captain is "disturbed" by the only human sounds that interrupt his attempt to commune with the ship; he feels that he knows "very little" of his officers and even less of the crew. "All these people had been together for eighteen months or so, and my position was that of the only stranger on board," he says (93). In the next few sentences Conrad indicates that the captain's alienation is directly related to a lack of self-knowledge. "But what I felt most was my being a stranger to the ship," he tells us, "and if all the truth must be told, I was somewhat of a stranger to myself" (93). Because the captain is not sure if he will "turn out faithful to that ideal conception of one's own personality every man sets up for himself secretly," he cannot communicate effectively with his ship. The appearance of Leggatt, his "other self," leads to the captain's symbolic self-integration, and, consequently, his social integration into the ship's hierarchy as commander.

In this respect, "The Secret Sharer" constitutes an affirmative response to the ironic paradox confronting Razumov at the end of Part Third. Whereas the young Russian betrays himself by turning in Haldin and becoming a secret agent for the autocratic regime, thereby creating an intolerable disjunction between his public and private selves and severing all meaningful communication with his fellows, the captain discovers himself by supporting Leggatt, thus overcoming his secret doubts and alienation and asserting his true place within the ship's community. At this point, we should notice that Conrad's writing of "The Secret Sharer" before he had completed *Under Western Eyes* contributes to a recurring pattern that emerges when one surveys the entire range of his works.

After completing a sea story such as *The Nigger of the "Narcissus,"* Conrad had a tendency to choose a landscape as his next setting, like the tropical hills and plains of "Karain." Often, there would be a corresponding shift in mode from tragic or exalted to comic. For example, immediately after completing *Lord Jim,* whose tragic action in Patusan comprises the entire second half of the novel, he wrote two comic sea stories, "Typhoon" and "Falk." These stories were followed by "Amy Foster" and "To-morrow," which recall Hardy's use of a rural setting combined with mythic overtones and situational irony to convey a tragic view of man's condition. This pattern suggests that Conrad, like Virginia Woolf, relied upon cyclical changes of subject matter and treatment to restore and sustain his creative energies. By shifting the setting of the action from land (in *Under Western Eyes*) to sea in "The Secret Sharer," and adopting a comic rather than tragic mode, Conrad was following a rhythm of composition that was undoubtedly therapeutic for him. However, other factors may also have inspired his creation of an alternative, affirmative version of Razumov's tragedy.

In October 1909 Conrad wrote to Pinker that he had had a visit from an officer of the Merchant Marine, Captain Carlos M. Marris, who had sailed in the Malayan area at the same time as he: "It was like the raising of a lot of dead—dead to me, because most of them live out there and even read my books and wonder who devil [*sic*] has been around taking notes. My visitor told me that Joshua Lingard made the guess; 'It must have been the fellow who was mate in the *Vidar* with Craig.' That's me right enough. And the best of it is that all these men of 22 years ago feel kindly to the Chronicler of their lives and adventures. They shall have some more of the stories they like."²¹ The immediate outcome of this visit was "The Secret Sharer," the earliest-written story in the volume *'Twixt Land and Sea,* which Conrad dedicated to Captain Marris "in memory of those old days of adventure."

The tone of Conrad's remarks to Pinker reveals the storyteller's pleasure in rediscovering a specific audience—the same audience for whom he had created Marlow in "Youth." His reference to people who "live out there and . . . read my books" is especially significant because in recent years Conrad had not been pleased by the critical reception of his work in English newspapers. Most reviews of *The Secret Agent* had been unsympathetic, and the author was sensitive to the critics' references to his foreign origins. Writing to Garnett, he complained: "I've been so cried up of late as a sort of freak, an amazing bloody foreigner writing in English (every blessed review of S.A. had it so—and even yours) that anything I say will be discounted on that ground by the public—that is if the public, that mysterious beast, takes any notice whatever—which I doubt."²² As Conrad suggests, even Garnett had acquired the offensive habit of calling him a Slav in print.

Najder argues that one article in particular—Robert Lynd's review of *A Set of Six,* published in *The Daily News* on August 10, 1908—disturbed Conrad so much that he conceived *A Personal Record* as a project that would respond to the criticism and explain his life and work to the English public.²³ In Lynd's article Conrad is referred to as a man "without either country or language." Moreover, the reviewer uses Conrad's foreignness as an excuse to attack the quality of his writing: "A writer who ceases to see the world coloured by his own language—for language gives colour to thoughts and things in a way that few people understand—is apt to lose the concentration and intensity of vision without which the greatest literature cannot be made."²⁴ It is even possible that the old language teacher who translates Razumov's diary owes some of his ironic self-consciousness to Lynd's ludicrous suggestion that Conrad's work would be more "valuable" if it were written in Polish.

Although Conrad also complained about his public's insatiable desire for sea stories with exotic settings (especially after *The Mirror of the Sea*'s favourable reception),²⁵ his description of Captain Marris's visit suggests that he welcomed the thought of writing fiction for an audience who shared his experiences and values. Eleven years earlier, the prospect of writing for *Blackwood's* ("a good sort of public") had resulted in the creation of a specific narrative point of view, an English seaman persona whose habits of speech and patriotic sentiments could appeal to the reader. In 1909 Conrad no longer needed a Marlow to mediate in this way between himself and his audience. Also, for the first time in his writing career (except for "Karain") he used a first-person narrator without the "framing" commentary of a dramatized audience, limiting the point of view solely to the young captain who expresses some of his own anxieties when faced with his first command. Unlike Marlow in "Youth," the narrator of "The Secret Sharer" does not indulge in patriotic commentary and uses few colloquial expressions or nautical terms. Of course, the more reflective tone of the narration in this story can be explained partly by the fact that Conrad is not imitating oral discourse. Lacking a dramatized audience, the narrator is less likely to exploit the jargon and other forms of rhetoric that promote group solidarity. Generally, however, Conrad uses the first-person perspective in "The Secret Sharer" in a profoundly introspective and confessional way; that is, he represents the captain's emotional and moral responses directly (and, for the most part, without irony) as a means of exploring the anarchic aspects of his own nature.

Albert Guerard describes "The Secret Sharer" as a "willed descent" into Conrad's unconscious feelings and motives, an "archetypal journey into self."[26] His celebrated conclusion is that "Conrad apparently detected in himself a division (possibly damaging, possibly saving) into a respectable traditional rational seaman-self and a more interior outlaw-self that repudiated law and tradition; and again, a division into a seaman-self operating from 'unconscious alertness' and an introspective, brooding-self of solitary off-duty hours." As some critics have pointed out, this theory is supported by Conrad's own description of himself as "Homo duplex."[27] Guerard also claims that in this story Conrad sought to prove that "the self-analytic, introspective bent . . . has *not* crippled the seaman and active human being." Earlier in this chapter I suggested that the captain's self-integration (and subsequent social integration) could be interpreted as an affirmative response to the tragic paradox confronting Razumov at the end of Part Third in *Under Western Eyes*. Considering Guerard's statement that "a highly subjective work of art necessarily reflects . . . the time when it was written," it is surprising that he failed to associate the introspective nature of the short story with Conrad's almost simultaneous work on the novel. Instead, Guerard connects the author's fears and preoccupations at that time with the uncongenial living conditions at Aldington. He also makes the general observation that 1908 and 1909 were "bad years."

Conrad's letters to friends like Galsworthy and William Rothenstein during the year 1909 testify to his nervous depression,[28] and we have already noted that the act of writing "The Secret Sharer" was probably therapeutic because of its contrasting style and setting and the prospect of gaining sympathetic readers. In fact, the self-revelatory mode may have been facilitated by Conrad's consciousness of the moral and professional bond with his audience. Certainly, the unusually high degree of correspondence between "The Secret Sharer" and *Under Western Eyes* suggests that the author's imagination sought to create, in a shorter, more concentrated form, a consolatory alternative to the novel's pessimistic vision of autocracy and revolution. Analyzing the reasons for Conrad's breakdown after completing *Under Western Eyes,* Najder concludes that the novel was "neither his biggest nor the one that took him the longest to write, but it was perhaps the one that caused him more anguish than anything else he ever wrote."[29] Najder relates the extremity of Conrad's emotional stress to the painful content of the book (which deals with the impossibility of reforming the Czarist autocracy, and therefore, the death of

Polish hopes for independence) and to Conrad's continuous struggle to maintain a self-defensive objectivity. He argues that "even the book's narrator, the English teacher of languages, had not set up a protective barrier between the author and his work."

In "The Secret Sharer" Conrad could express more directly some of the thoughts and feelings that are rigorously controlled in the longer fiction. Like *The Secret Agent, Under Western Eyes* belongs to the subgenre of the political novel—a form of writing in which the author's views about specific social and political conditions are represented in poetic terms. In the "Author's Note" to *Under Western Eyes* Conrad reflects the typical modernist scepticism about the validity of politics in art, and emphasizes his commitment to aesthetic objectivity:

> My greatest anxiety was in being able to strike and sustain the note of scrupulous impartiality. The obligation of absolute fairness was imposed on me historically and hereditarily, by the peculiar experience of race and family, in addition to my primary conviction that truth alone is the justification of any fiction which makes the least claim to the quality of art or may hope to take its place in the culture of men and women of its time. I had never been called before to a greater effort of detachment: detachment from all passions, prejudices and even from personal memories. (viii)

Here, the author's self-consciousness about the political nature of his work is evident, but not as obvious is the fact that, in this case, "detachment" was psychologically necessary for the artist. Conrad used the old language teacher to distance himself from his material as well as to explore it more comprehensively, and perhaps the feelings of helplessness generated by his uncompromising analysis of Russian society demanded release. In "The Secret Sharer" the almost schematic reversal of important motifs from the novel and the development of others in symbolic form, combined with a subjective point of view, suggests that Conrad achieved this release (up to a point) by writing the story.

Did Conrad's writing of "The Secret Sharer" before he completed *Under Western Eyes* affect the overall form of the novel? A close relationship between the plots of both works helps us perceive the redemptive aspect of Razumov's punishment more clearly. First, let us look at the ending of "The Secret Sharer." After the captain's self-identification with Leggatt is confirmed by the meeting with Archbold, he is increasingly "haunted" by the phantomlike presence of the outlaw. According to Cedric Watts, the intensification of supernatural allusions in the second half of the story points to the existence of a hidden "metaphysical" plot.[30] Leggatt is like a spirit from another world, a strange being "appearing as if he had risen from the bottom of the sea" (98), who cannot rest until an important truth has been acknowledged. At the climax of the story some of the circumstances of the *Sephora* incident are reversed in an uncanny and ironic manner. That is, in both cases the ship is in grave danger of foundering, but whereas the *Sephora*'s captain succumbs to nerves and abandons his command to Leggatt, the first mate, the young captain responds to the crisis with authority while his mate collapses:

Then stillness again, with the great shadow gliding closer, towering higher, without light, without a sound. Such a hush had fallen on the ship that she might have been a bark of the dead floating in slowly under the very gate of Erebus.

"My God! Where are we?"

It was the mate moaning at my elbow. He was thunderstruck, and as it were deprived of the moral support of his whiskers. He clapped his hands and absolutely cried out, "Lost!"

"Be quiet," I said, sternly.

He lowered his tone, but I saw the shadowy gesture of his despair. "What are we doing here?"

"Looking for the land wind."

He made as if to tear his hair, and addressed me recklessly.

"She will never get out. You have done it, sir. I knew it'd end in something like this. She will never weather, and you are too close now to stay. She'll drift ashore before she's round. O my God!"

I caught his arm as he was raising it to batter his poor devoted head, and shook it violently. (140–41)

The captain continues to shake his terrified mate until the officer is capable of following orders, but the hierarchical chain of command is not completed until the mate can assume his own professional authority: "The foreyards ran round with a great noise, amidst cheery cries. And now the frightful whiskers made themselves heard giving various orders" (143). In the *Sephora* incident this chain of command is broken when Archbold is unable to give the crucial order to reef the foresail, a maneuver that corresponds in significance to the protagonist's command to shift the ship's helm at exactly the right moment. Like the mate on the young captain's ship, the *Sephora*'s captain "forgets his place": he "whimpers" and speaks despairingly, but most importantly, he fails to take action. Leggatt is forced to usurp the commanding role. "I just took it into my own hands," he says (124). In the Koh-ring crisis the mate "moans" and speaks despairingly. Most significantly, however, he trusts his own judgment rather than the captain's: "She will never get out. You have done it, sir. I knew it'd end in something like this." At this point the younger man acts, affirming his rightful place in the hierarchy and preparing the mate to assert his.

Most critics regard the captain's action in risking his ship and crew as a sign of professional immaturity. Some even question Conrad's conclusion that he has achieved "perfect communion" with his command, or that this communion goes beyond a "limited" and "egocentric" sense of authority.[31] But the links between the Koh-ring crisis and the *Sephora* episode contradict these interpretations. They stress the young captain's ability to include his men in the chain of command, suggesting that without the deliberately risky maneuver a true solidarity among officers and crew would not have been achieved. In a large part, Archbold is responsible for Leggatt's violence, because by abandoning his natural place in the chain the captain commits the entire ship to anarchy and chaos. In contrast, the young captain refuses to allow such a disruption, and his crew makes a single-minded and harmonious response: "On the overshadowed deck all hands stood by the forebraces waiting for my order" (143).

The uncanny aspect of these parallels and contrasts enhances Leggatt's symbolic role in the hero's self-assertion. If the protagonist has been haunted by a sense of the outlaw as a phantom or spirit, the plot sequence, in which Leggatt is freed as a result of an identical yet contrasting recapitulation of the original crime, suggests a metaphysical logic, or even exorcism. In his concluding sentence Conrad persuades us that this exorcism is reciprocal:

> Walking to the taffrail, I was in time to make out, on the very edge of a darkness thrown by a towering black mass like the very gateway of Erebus—yes, I was in time to catch an evanescent glimpse of my white hat left behind to mark the spot where the secret sharer of my cabin and of my thoughts, as though he were my second self, had lowered himself into the water to take his punishment: a free man, a proud swimmer striking out for a new destiny. (143)

The emphatic repetitions and word order in the first part of this sentence add weight to the syntactical object—the symbolic white hat that represents reciprocity between the two "selves." Moreover, the image (a rounded white shape against the black shadow of Koh-ring) recalls the "pale oval" of the swimmer's face against the ship's darkness at the beginning of the story. As Leggatt returns to the water to complete the exorcism of his violence by "taking his punishment," the captain's disabling anxieties and isolation from his crew are finally resolved.

Conrad's introduction of a similar plot sequence in *Under Western Eyes* foregrounds the reciprocity between Razumov and Victor Haldin. When Razumov meets Natalia Haldin suddenly in the garden of the Château Borel, he experiences a shock of delayed recognition that recalls his fateful encounter with Haldin:

> But he did not recognize her at once. Coming up with Peter Ivanovitch, he did observe her; their eyes had met, even. He had responded, as no one could help responding, to the harmonious charm of her whole person, its strength, its grace, its tranquil frankness—and then he had turned his gaze away. He said to himself that all this was not for him; the beauty of women and the friendship of men were not for him. He accepted that feeling with a purposeful sternness, and tried to pass on. It was only her outstretched hand which brought about the recognition. It stands recorded in the pages of his self-confession, that it nearly suffocated him physically with an emotional reaction of hate and dismay, as though her appearance had been a piece of accomplished treachery. (167)

In his study of the manuscript Roderick Davis points out that Conrad may have originally planned to have Razumov and Natalia meet through the old teacher of languages, who (in the first draft) "had Mr. Razumov for a pupil." This meeting was not to involve Razumov's shock of recognition, with its suggestive allusions to the supernatural. Davis tells us that the manuscript reads: "He had not guessed . . . He had not the slightest idea of the girl's identity."[32] After he had written "The Secret Sharer" (probably at the typescript stage), Conrad revised the episode so that it recalls Razumov's initial crime against Haldin: "But Razumov had guessed. The trustful girl! Every word uttered by Haldin lived in Razumov's memory. They were like haunting shapes; they could not be exorcised" (167).

Moreover, in Razumov's confession to Natalia in Part Fourth (which was almost certainly written after the short story),[33] Conrad draws our attention to the sequence of meetings and its "metaphysical" logic:

> And when you stood before me with your hand extended, I remembered the very sound of his voice, and I looked into your eyes—and that was enough. . . . I remembered that he had looked to you for the perpetuation of his visionary soul. . . . Hate or no hate, I felt at once that, while shunning the sight of you, I could never succeed in driving away your image. I would say, addressing that dead man, "Is this the way you are going to haunt me?" It is only later on that I understood . . . You were appointed to undo the evil by making me betray myself back into truth and peace. You! And you have done it in the same way, too, in which he ruined me: by forcing upon me your confidence. Only what I detested him for, in you ended by appearing noble and exalted. (358–59)

Surprised by Natalia as he had once been surprised by her brother, Razumov is tempted, but refuses to take advantage of an "exalted" confidence. Like the recapitulation in "The Secret Sharer," which reverses events in order to affirm a true solidarity and order, the plot of *Under Western Eyes* has Razumov betray himself rather than Victor Haldin, who "haunts" him in the person of Natalia.

The redemptive elements of Razumov's tragedy are heavily qualified by the ironies and ambiguities of their social and political context. Nowhere is the dialectical aspect of these two works more dramatically illustrated than in their contrasting narrative perspectives. In contrast to "The Secret Sharer," which is a double confession to the reader,[34] *Under Western Eyes* is narrated by an observer who interprets and translates the thoughts and feelings of other characters, and who mistrusts Razumov's motives in writing a diary. On the other hand, Razumov's confessional letter to Natalia is strategically placed at the climax of the novel, where the correspondences with an earlier betrayal emphasize the theme of redemption. As we have seen, Conrad's writing of "The Secret Sharer" concurrently with the novel provides an interpretive gloss for this and other aspects of *Under Western Eyes*.

7
Conclusion

In the end, the attempt to demonstrate that some of Conrad's shorter fictions are related to specific novels emphasizes the striking duality of this writer's mind and imagination. The divided and at times conflicting loyalties of a "homo duplex" are most clearly seen in the dialectical exploration of moral problems. But even in the case of works which do not directly illustrate this method—such as "An Outpost of Progress" or "The Lagoon"—we can fully understand Conrad's intentions only by considering a shorter fiction together with its related novel. And the overall pattern that is composed of these links reinforces our impression of duality, chiefly because of the innovative techniques Conrad developed from the time of his earliest short stories. The pattern also brings into relief Conrad's tendency to seek correspondences between different events and situations, a tendency that is evident in his autobiographical writings as well. Finally, it reveals a creative rhythm of alternating modes and subjects that was undoubtedly therapeutic for the author.

In the early period of Conrad's writing career the short stories were testing grounds for his later works. Most critics have overemphasized the derivative nature of the fiction in *Tales of Unrest,* arguing that Conrad was influenced excessively by Maupassant, Flaubert, Kipling, Henry James, and the early-nineteenth-century writers of romantic adventure stories. By relating "An Outpost of Progress," "The Lagoon," and "Karain" to *The Secret Agent* and *Lord Jim,* we can see clearly that Conrad was experimenting with themes and techniques which distinguish his mature work from that of other writers. Thus, although he was influenced by Maupassant and Flaubert when he wrote "An Outpost of Progress," he is unlike those authors because at some points in the story the narrator abandons his objectivity and speaks directly to the reader about political and moral concerns. Comparison with *The Secret Agent* reveals how distinctively Conradian many of his techniques in "An Outpost of Progress" are, and how (unlike the irony of Maupassant and Flaubert) they focus on involving the reader as well as controlling and directing him. The sudden shift in narrative perspective at the climax of the plot and the use of grotesque elements throughout are two formal features of "An Outpost of Progress" which are also found in *The Secret Agent.*

"An Outpost of Progress" also anticipates some of the ironic techniques that control the reader's responses in *The Secret Agent* and in Conrad's later fiction in general. The revisions to this story show careful attention to parallelisms and other aspects of sentence structure, the selection of concrete details, and the juxtaposition of characters and events in order to sharpen the ironic impact of the narrative and invite our moral judgment. In general, the same techniques are developed and refined in *The Secret Agent*, accounting for the range and power of the narrator's sardonic voice. A close study of the short fiction, therefore, helps us to see how Conrad achieves his effects in the novel.

In "The Lagoon" and "Karain" Conrad experimented with a narrative technique reminiscent of the Polish gawęda and other literary imitations of the oral narrative. Comparison of these two stories with *Lord Jim* shows how Conrad developed the "told-tale" device from a simple "teller and listener" framework in "The Lagoon" through "Karain" (where the listener becomes a teller himself) to the multiple perspectives of the novel. Again, relating the short fiction to a later novel emphasizes the originality of Conrad's writing. By stages, he developed a complex, impressionistic version of a simple literary convention based on communal values and traditions. However, even in his earliest stories he did not merely "borrow" a technique that had been popularized during the first half of the nineteenth century. The relationship between the "teller" (or protagonist) and listener in "The Lagoon" and "Karain" suggests both elegiac affirmation and sceptical impressionism, anticipating (in a simpler form) the multiple ambiguities of *Lord Jim*.

A larger pattern can be perceived by comparing this ambiguity with the ironic mode of "An Outpost of Progress." Thus, the three or four earliest short stories reflect the essential duality of Conrad's work as a whole. According to Andrzej Busza, Conrad's perception of man's role in the natural universe is characterized by the coexistence of "affirmative thinking" with "modern negative consciousness." At the heart of Conrad's affirmative thinking, Busza writes, lies the concept of the "saving illusion," while "the locus of his modern negative consciousness" is irony.[1] In these experimental stories the opposition of two different modes of writing reveals Conrad's search for appropriate techniques to express a conflict that was deeply rooted in his outlook. Whereas the ironic mode emphasizes the disjunction between human ideals and reality and the individual and his community, the "told-tale" type of narration imitates man's attempts to integrate his personal experiences with the social order and to affirm certain moral values or "saving illusions."

The formal links between these short stories and novels reflect important thematic correspondences. Comparison of "An Outpost of Progress" with *The Secret Agent* brings some of Conrad's concerns in the novel into sharper focus: for example, his criticism of materialism in a "progressive" society and his investigation of the individual's blind dependence on various social systems. Similarly, an analysis of the thematic links between "The Lagoon," "Karain," and *Lord Jim* reveals the importance of illusions as a means of introducing order and purposeful action into one's life and the crucial role of the imagination in creating or destroying these ideals.

The earliest examples of Conrad's short fiction are interesting to the critic primarily because they foreground certain themes and techniques. Conrad's experiments with irony in "An Outpost of Progress" seem crude in comparison with *The Secret Agent*, although they alert us to the parallels, oppositions, and modulations in tone that comprise the rhetoric of the novel. "Youth," on the other hand, is a more successful and original piece of fiction in spite of the fact that it lacks the scope and complexity of later stories like "Heart of Darkness" and "The Secret Sharer." On the whole, Conrad's use of the dramatized narrator to elaborate on symbolic implications and his development of other impressionist techniques fit the elegiac mood of the story. Moreover, because these formal innovations influenced his writing of "Heart of Darkness" and *Lord Jim* to a significant degree, "Youth" can provide us with some insights into the longer works.

Conrad's invention of Marlow as an English ex-seaman persona is linked to his preoccupation in "Youth" with the virtues of national solidarity. The revisions to the story show that he made several additions to Marlow's commentary to persuade us of the English crew's inherent discipline and spirit. The use of a dramatized narrator to direct the reader's interpretation of moral issues is also an important feature of Conrad's "affirmative thinking" in "Heart of Darkness" and *Lord Jim*. In "Heart of Darkness" Marlow endorses the virtues of work and human fellowship in spite of the moral chaos that he finds in the wilderness; and in *Lord Jim* the narrator insists on "the solidarity of our lives," which binds him to Jim in spite of the irremediable fact that "he was guilty . . . guilty and done for." Many of Marlow's moral statements in the novel gain their rhetorical effectiveness from the techniques rehearsed in "Youth": a good example is the well-known passage in chapter 21 which celebrates "the spirit that dwells within the land."

In his revisions to "Youth" Conrad also emphasized Marlow's relationship with his audience, another formal aspect of the story which anticipates an important technique in "Heart of Darkness" and *Lord Jim*. He added a fourth listener to the group, introduced concrete details to describe the setting and made the narrator's language more informal and colloquial. The dramatized audience draws our attention to Marlow's role as a mediator between contrasting views of the world: past and present, romantic and sceptical, youthful and middle-aged. In "Heart of Darkness" and *Lord Jim* Conrad developed this aspect of the shorter fiction so that the narrator functions as a link between the "outsider" and the human community. Thus "Youth" displays in a simple form the essentially integrative nature of the "teller and listener" mode in the longer works. In "Heart of Darkness" Marlow interprets Kurtz's experience in the wilderness for an audience of ex-seamen who represent the foundations of modern capitalist society: law, bureaucracy, and finance.[2] In *Lord Jim* the narrator illuminates Jim's romantic idealism for a group of "respectable" listeners who have traded their "illusions" for profit.

"I do not mean to be offensive," says Marlow to provoke his audience, "it is respectable to have no illusions—and safe—and profitable—and dull" (225). In both cases the narrator mediates between an outcast or "straggler" and society's "establishment."

To the extent that Marlow's mediation between contrasting worlds in "Youth" anticipates the narrator's complex solidarity with Kurtz and Jim, it suggests an aspect of Conrad's "affirmative thinking." At the same time, however, Conrad used the role of Marlow in "Youth" to control the reader's sympathy for the protagonist and point out the disjunction between youthful dreams and reality. The revisions to the story show that he was careful to keep the tone of Marlow's irony genial so that the romantic illusions of youth are not seriously undercut; however, the coexistence of irony with affirmation throughout this story anticipates one of the ways in which Conrad expresses a "negative consciousness" in "Heart of Darkness" and *Lord Jim*. Thus, Marlow's sardonic statements about Kurtz emphasize the disjunction between idealistic words and actions, and in *Lord Jim* the narrator continually draws our attention to the tragic irony that controls Jim's destiny.

Conrad's addition of the *Celestial* episode at the typescript stage of his revisions is further indication that the writing of "Youth" was an important transition between the earliest stories of the "told-tale" type of narration and the later works.[3] In "The Lagoon" and "Karain" his narrative technique is undeveloped and the protagonist's situation lacks universality. In "Youth" Conrad introduces symbolic elements, using Marlow to point out correspondences to the reader. With the addition of the *Celestial* episode, the mythic structure of the quest, which gives young Marlow's comic experiences a metaphysical order and significance, acquires an ironic twist. Thus, "Youth" provides us with a relatively uncomplicated example of Conrad's "affirmative thinking"; that is, it depicts an individual whose ideals are perceived to be "true" in spite of reality and the passing of time. In this way, the short fiction anticipates the symbolic methods by which Conrad insists on the need for "saving illusions" in "Heart of Darkness" and *Lord Jim*.

The concentrated form of the short story brings into relief other aspects of Conrad's technique which are developed in complex and ambiguous forms in the longer works. For example, in each episode of "Youth" the protagonist's limited perspective involves the reader in decoding sense impressions, and the "mysteries" are easily explained by the mature narrator. In "Heart of Darkness" and *Lord Jim* Conrad uses similar impressionist techniques to involve us in Marlow's ongoing exploration of inner truths which resist definition. This movement toward larger, ambiguous implications illustrates another aspect of Conrad's symbolism. In a letter written in 1918 he described the literary work of art as "very seldom limited to one exclusive meaning . . . and this for the reason that the nearer it approaches art, the more it acquires a symbolic character."[4] In order to multiply the meanings suggested by the narrator in "Heart of Darkness" and *Lord Jim*, Conrad developed techniques which he had introduced in a simple form in "Youth," such as the role of the dramatized audience. An understanding of how these techniques are used in the shorter fiction enhances our perception of different shades of meaning in the major works.

A close study of "An Outpost of Progress," "The Lagoon," "Karain," and "Youth" indicates that their most significant links with Conrad's novels are formal rather than thematic. On the other hand, in the case of "Heart of Darkness" and "The Secret Sharer" there are important thematic ties with *Lord Jim* and *Under Western Eyes*. By adapting certain basic situations and motifs from one work to the other, Conrad could explore different aspects of a central idea or theme. Thus, in "Heart of Darkness" and *Lord Jim* he treats Kurtz and Jim as complementary illustrations of idealistic egoists, while in "The Secret Sharer" and *Under Western Eyes* he depicts contrasting responses to a plea for understanding and assistance.

Conrad's dialectical exploration of moral problems reflects the structure of his creative imagination. In his autobiographical writings he continually sought correspondences between different phases of his life and between his life and his art. In *A Personal Record,* for example, we find this characteristic passage:

> And I have carried my notion of good service from my earlier into my later existence. I, who have never sought in the written word anything else but a form of the Beautiful—I have carried over that article of creed from the decks of ships to the more circumscribed space of my desk, and by that act, I suppose, I have become permanently imperfect in the eyes of the ineffable company of pure esthetes.[5]

In a similar way but within the sphere of art, the thematic parallels between his short fiction and the novels illustrate Conrad's tendency to create situations that mirror and illuminate each other. By probing these correspondences, we can understand the full implications of his meaning in each work.

Because of the more concentrated form of the short fiction, symbolic elements and mythic allusions are emphasized. In "Heart of Darkness" and "The Secret Sharer" Conrad stresses universal paradigms of experience which shed light on the complementary episodes of the longer works. In chapter 5 I have tried to show how Conrad opposes Kurtz's demonic loss of selfhood and deathbed redemption to Jim's exaltation of an ideal self through redemptive work in Patusan. Similarly, the captain's symbolic self-realization through an act of solidarity in "The Secret Sharer" helps us to perceive Razumov's tragedy as a loss of moral identity, resulting from irremediable political conditions, which can only be redeemed by his refusal to betray Haldin a second time. In both cases the dialectical aspects of the narrative situations bring Conrad's thematic statements about self-idealization and human solidarity into sharper focus.

In "Heart of Darkness" and *Under Western Eyes* the protagonist's redemption is heavily qualified by Conrad's use of ironic techniques, such as grotesque elements, which stress the disjunction between professed ideals and reality. Looking at the pattern comprised by the two short fictions and their corresponding novels, we can conclude that to different degrees *Lord Jim* and "The Secret Sharer" act as affirmative counterpoints to the more pervasive "negative consciousness" in the parallel works. In this respect, they contribute to the larger design of alternating modes and subjects that characterizes Conrad's work as a whole. In the "Author's Note" to *The Secret Agent* Conrad comments on a small part of this design— the interrelationship of *Nostromo* and *The Mirror of the Sea:*[6]

> The inception of *The Secret Agent* followed immediately on a two years' period of intense absorption in the task of writing that remote novel, *Nostromo,* with its far-off Latin-American atmosphere; and the profoundly personal *Mirror of the Sea*. The first an intense creative effort on what I suppose will always remain my largest canvas, the second an unreserved attempt to unveil for a moment the profounder intimacies of the sea and the formative influences of nearly half my lifetime.[7]

Here, Conrad juxtaposes the "remote" novel and the "personal" collection of essays, the "intense creative effort" and the "unreserved" flow of memories,[8] the landscape "atmosphere" and the sea setting. Although the therapeutic aspect of his creative rhythm is most obvious in the case of "The Secret Sharer" and *Under Western Eyes,* it undoubtedly influenced Conrad's choice of the dialectical approach to his other material as well.

Like some aspects of Conrad's style, this underlying rhythm recalls Flaubert. Writing to Edward Garnett in praise of Garnett's play, Conrad suggested that he follow this romantic work with something in the ironic mode: "You know that it was from the discussion of the *Tentation de St Antoine* that the idea of *Mme Bovary* sprang up in Flaubert's mind. A complete turn about. Why should you also not execute a change of front and take up a subject where your irony could find its opportunity, your wit an aim for its shafts?"[9] Here, Conrad's use of Flaubert's work to illustrate a pattern that clearly describes his own creative process reveals the depth of his involvement with the French writer. No doubt unconsciously, he adopted the same rhythm of alternating modes and settings to express his unique, paradoxical world view.

Finally, the study of "Heart of Darkness" and "The Secret Sharer" in relationship to *Lord Jim* and *Under Western Eyes* sheds valuable light on the formal aspects of Conrad's dialectical method. Thematic correspondences and oppositions led him to adapt specific narrative techniques, symbols, image patterns, and mythic allusions from one work to the other. In chapter 5 I have indicated how Conrad's "romantic realism" in the characterization of Jim was influenced by his earlier portrayal of Kurtz. In the case of "The Secret Sharer" and *Under Western Eyes* basic similarities in plot between the two works suggest that the writing of the short fiction led Conrad to emphasize the redemptive reciprocity between Razumov and the spirit of Victor Haldin at the end of the novel. Conrad's creative process during the period of his major work involved considerable "cross-fertilization."

It is not surprising, then, that the links between some of his stories and novels should reveal so much about Conrad's intentions. They show us a writer who, in the early stages of his career, experimented with techniques to express his highly original, bifocal vision. They illuminate some important aspects of the psychological, moral, and political concerns that characterize his work as a whole. They demonstrate that the shorter form can be used to interpret the related, but less clearly perceived, aspects of the corresponding novel. In the end, by emphasizing how each fiction contributes to Conrad's investigation of a specific issue (such as the nature of imaginative egoism, or the virtues and limitations of patriotism), they give us fresh insight into both the shorter works and the major novels.

Notes

Chapter 1

1. Joseph Conrad, *Tales of Unrest* (1898; London: J. M. Dent, 1947), v. Subsequent page references follow quotations.
2. See Conrad's letter dated July 14, 1923. Richard Curle, ed., *Conrad to a Friend: 150 Selected Letters from Joseph Conrad to Richard Curle* (Garden City, N.Y.: Doubleday, 1928), 147-50.
3. Joseph Conrad, *Youth, Heart of Darkness and The End of the Tether: Three Stories* (1902; London: J. M. Dent, 1946), v-vi. Similarly, Conrad evaded an interviewer's attempt to pin him down by pretending that his method of writing was entirely instinctual and without thought for artistic effect: "I got into *Lord Jim* and I just had to get out. I had to invent Marlow to carry on the story. It seemed the best way. . . . I have too much to think of when I am writing to invent new forms." See Dale B. J. Randall, "Conrad Interviews #2," *Conradiana* 2 (1969-70): 83-91.
4. See Conrad's letter dated August 22, 1899 in Frederick R. Karl and Laurence Davies, eds., *The Collected Letters of Joseph Conrad* (Cambridge: Cambridge University Press, 1986), II, 193-94.
5. Hence the somewhat misleading reference to *Lord Jim*'s being "more like *Youth*," for the earlier story's success had cemented Conrad's good relations with his publisher.
6. Joseph Conrad, *The Nigger of the "Narcissus"* (1897; London: J. M. Dent, 1947), viii. Subsequent page references follow quotations.
7. Conrad uses this expression in reference to Maupassant in his essay "Guy de Maupassant," *Notes on Life and Letters* (1921; London: J. M. Dent, 1949), 25. Conrad's ethical view of art and its relationship to the visible world rather than to "the authority of a school" is fully expressed in his essay "Books" (*Notes on Life and Letters*, 3-10). For example, he says: "It is in the impartial practice of life, if anywhere, that the promise of perfection for . . . art can be found, rather than in the absurd formulas trying to prescribe this or that particular method of technique or conception."
8. Lawrence Graver begins his study of Conrad's short fiction with this statement and, essentially, he agrees with it. See *Conrad's Short Fiction* (Berkeley: University of California Press, 1969), vii.
9. *The Collected Letters*, I, 124. In chapter 5, I shall refer to this statement again in more detail.
10. *The Collected Letters*, II, 332.
11. For example, consider the narrative continuity between "Barn Burning" and *The Hamlet*.
12. Ian Watt, *Conrad in the Nineteenth Century* (Berkeley: University of California Press, 1979), 134.

13. Ted Boyle, *Symbol and Meaning in the Fiction of Joseph Conrad* (London: Mouton, 1965), 60–63.
14. Joseph Conrad, "Guy de Maupassant," *Notes on Life and Letters*, 28.
15. See Conrad's letter dated October 9, 1899 in *The Collected Letters*, II, 199–202.
16. Unpublished letter to J. B. Pinker dated July 30, 1907. Berg Collection, New York Public Library.
17. See letter dated March 18, 1917 in G. Jean-Aubry, *Joseph Conrad: Life and Letters* (London: William Heinemann, 1927), II, 184.
18. *Joseph Conrad: A Chronicle* (New Brunswick, N.J.: Rutgers, 1983), 424.

Chapter 2

1. The most comprehensive comparisons of the two stories are D. C. R. A. Goonetilleke's "Conrad's African Tales: Ironies of Progress," *Ceylon Journal of the Humanities* 2 (January 1971): 64–97 and Cedric Watts's analysis in *Conrad's "Heart of Darkness": A Critical and Contextual Discussion* (Milan: Mursia International, 1977), 33–36.
2. Examples of Conrad's revisions to "An Outpost of Progress" in this chapter derive from collations of the autograph manuscript (The Beinecke Rare Book and Manuscript Library, Yale University) with the serial version published in *Cosmopolis* (June–July 1897), and the English book text in *Dent's Collected Edition*. The typescript of the story has not survived.
3. Joseph Conrad, *Tales of Unrest*, 61. Subsequent page references follow quotations.
4. In his essay written in 1904 as a preface to Ada Galsworthy's translation (*"Yvette" and Other Stories*), Conrad praises Maupassant for his "scrupulous, prolonged and devoted attention to the aspects of the visible world," but comments that "his talent is not exercised for the praise and consolation of mankind." Although in this essay Conrad scorned "the mediocrity of an obvious and appealing tenderness," he implies that detachment can be too rigorous. "Guy de Maupassant," *Notes on Life and Letters*, 25–31. As critics have pointed out, Conrad was also influenced by Flaubert's *Madame Bovary* when he wrote "The Idiots," especially in his description of the wedding at the Bacadou farm.
5. Although Kayerts and Carlier are Belgian, the narrator's references to "masquerading philanthropy," "the pioneers of trade and progress," and so on, apply to European colonizing nations in general.
6. Joseph Conrad, *The Secret Agent: A Simple Tale* (1907; London: J. M. Dent, 1947), 33. Subsequent page references follow quotations.
7. Robert Hobson, "A Textual History of Conrad's 'An Outpost of Progress,'" in *Conradiana* 11 (1979): 143–63 provides a summary of the various stages of Conrad's textual revisions.
8. Writing to Conrad for the first time after having read "An Outpost of Progress," R. B. Cunninghame Graham contrasted the two stories and attacked Kipling's ideology. See C. T. Watts's comments in *Joseph Conrad's Letters to R. B. Cunninghame Graham* (Cambridge: Cambridge University Press, 1969), 20.
9. Wayne Booth, *A Rhetoric of Irony* (Chicago: The University of Chicago Press, 1974).
10. D. C. Muecke, *Irony* (London: Methuen, 1970), 50–51.
11. Lawrence Graver, *Conrad's Short Fiction* (Berkeley: University of California Press, 1969), 10–14.
12. See letter dated July 22, 1896 in *The Collected Letters*, I, 291–92.
13. Quoted by C. T. Watts in *Joseph Conrad's Letters to R. B. Cunninghame Graham*, 20.

14. See Conrad's preface to *The Secret Agent* ("Author's Note") and also Norman Sherry, ed., *Conrad: The Critical Heritage* (London: Routledge and Kegan Paul, 1973), 186–89, 194, 199–200, and 201–2.
15. Watts, *Conrad's "Heart of Darkness": A Critical and Contextual Discussion*, 7.
16. In his letter to Fisher Unwin describing the story, Conrad wrote: "All the bitterness of those days, all my puzzled wonder as to the meaning of all I saw—all my indignation at masquerading philanthropy have been with me again while I wrote." See letter dated July 22, 1896 in *The Collected Letters*, I, 293–94.
17. "I remember perfectly well the inflexible and solemn resolve not to be led astray by my subject. I aimed at a scrupulous unity of tone, and it seems to me that I have attained it there." Conrad's remarks about "An Outpost of Progress" when it appeared in *The Grand Magazine* in 1906 are reprinted in an article by A. T. Tolley: "Conrad's 'Favorite' Story," *Studies in Short Fiction* 3 (Spring 1966): 314–20.
18. He writes to Mrs. Helen Sanderson: "I am like a tight-rope dancer who in the midst of his performance should suddenly discover that he knows nothing about tight-rope dancing. He may appear ridiculous to the spectators but a broken neck is the result of such untimely wisdom." *The Collected Letters*, II, 90–91.
19. In a letter to Cunninghame Graham about *The Secret Agent*, Conrad wrote, "All these people are not revolutionaries—they are Shams." See *Joseph Conrad's Letters to R. B. Cunninghame Graham*, 170.
20. See letter to Fisher Unwin dated August 14, 1896 in *The Collected Letters*, I, 199. Conrad uses the same figurative expression (attributed originally to Maupassant) in a letter to E. L. Sanderson, when he writes, "I told the unspeakable idiots that the thing halved would be as ineffective as a dead scorpion." *The Collected Letters*, I, 318–20.
21. In his article Hobson concludes that the lost typescript must have closely resembled a pamphlet set from the first proofs of the story, and the pamphlet contains the revision.
22. For interesting confirmation of this practice, see Conrad's letter to Garnett concerning *The Rescue* in *The Collected Letters*, I, 286–87, and Emily K. Dalgarno, "Conrad, Pinker, and the Writing of *The Secret Agent*," *Conradiana* 9 (1977): 47–58. In his letter to J. B. Pinker dated March 1912 (Berg Collection, New York Public Library), Conrad confirms (prematurely) Austin Harrison's acceptance of *Chance* for publication in the *English Review*, saying "He's scared at there being no chapters! I promised to shorten it, chapter it, etc. etc.—making it look ever so nice and so on."
23. Conrad may have been thinking of the several occasions in *The Time Machine* (1895) when the Time Traveller solemnly burns his matches to astonish the Eloi. If so, there is an implied ironic comparison between the resourceful, Wellsian Time Traveller and the completely helpless Carlier.
24. As Muecke points out, sarcasm conveys the intended meaning so unequivocally that the pretense of innocence, a basic feature of irony, disappears.
25. See especially, the letter to Garnett dated June 10, 1896 (*The Collected Letters*, I, 286–87) in which he says, "I doubt the sincerity of my own impressions."
26. See his letters to Sanderson, Galsworthy, Douglas, and H. G. Wells in Jean-Aubry, *Joseph Conrad: Life and Letters*, II, 21–26.
27. See Alan Wilde, Introduction, *Horizons of Assent* (Baltimore: The Johns Hopkins University Press, 1981), 1–16 and Charles I. Glicksberg, *The Ironic Vision in Modern Literature* (The Hague: Martinus Mijhoff, 1969).

Notes for Chapter 3

28. Northrop Frye, *Anatomy of Criticism: Four Essays* (Princeton: Princeton University Press, 1957), 40–41.

29. In this we can see the influence of Flaubert on Conrad's writing. See Flaubert's letter to Louise Colet in *Correspondance de Gustave Flaubert*, II, Deuxième série: 1847–1852 (Paris: Nationale, 1968), 469, in which he imagines a style which would have "la consistance du vers" and says: "une bonne phrase de prose doit être comme un bon vers, *inchangeable,* aussi rhythmée, aussi sonore."

30. Jacques Berthoud points out that Verloc's meeting with Vladimir anticipates Heat's interview with the Assistant Commissioner. *Joseph Conrad: The Major Phase* (Cambridge: Cambridge University Press, 1978), 144.

31. See letter dated August 14, 1896 in *The Collected Letters,* I, 300–301.

32. Ian Watt, *Conrad in the Nineteenth Century,* 75.

33. This passage was revised at both manuscript and typescript stages to make the sense impression more concrete. For example, "A tremendous explosion took place between them; red fire, smoke" (*MS* 31) became "A loud explosion took place between them; a roar of red fire, thick smoke."

Chapter 3

1. Conrad finished "An Outpost of Progress" on July 21 and was already writing "The Lagoon" on August 5. See his letter to Garnett dated August 5, 1896 in *The Collected Letters,* I, 295–97.

2. Joseph Conrad, *Tales of Unrest,* 203. Subsequent page references for both "The Lagoon" and "Karain: A Memory" follow quotations.

3. See Albert J. Guerard, *Conrad the Novelist* (Cambridge, Mass.: Harvard University Press, 1958) and Ian Watt, *Conrad in the Nineteenth Century* (Berkeley: University of California Press, 1979), 63–65.

4. Joseph Conrad, *Almayer's Folly* (1895; London: J. M. Dent, 1947), 8.

5. Like Henry James and Virginia Woolf, Conrad uses narrated monologue (free indirect style in which the narrator is present, but words and tone are the character's) rather than interior monologue, in which the character's mental voice is heard directly, as in parts of *Ulysses.* See Seymour Chatman's *Story and Discourse: Narrative Structure in Fiction and Film* (Ithaca, N.Y.: Cornell University Press, 1978) for full descriptions and examples of these terms, as well as "internal analysis."

6. Albert J. Guerard, *Conrad the Novelist,* 67.

7. Joseph Conrad, *Lord Jim* (1900; London: J. M. Dent, 1946), 81. Subsequent page references follow quotations.

8. Because Arsat "goes back" to justify the death of a brother whom he has left "in the midst of enemies," it is tempting to connect the plot of "The Lagoon" to Conrad's mixed emotions about Poland. One of the many biographical facts to support such a speculation concerns an event that took place four years before Conrad wrote the story. Tadeusz Bobrowski had informed him that his cousin Stanislaw (like Apollo Korzeniowski) had been arrested and imprisoned for political "crimes" in the Warsaw citadel. Zdzisław Najder tells us that Conrad inquired "repeatedly" about Stanislaw and speculates that the event left a deep impression on him. See *Joseph Conrad: A Chronicle* (New Brunswick, N.J.: Rutgers University Press, 1983), 155.

9. See letter dated August 14, 1896 in *The Collected Letters,* I, 300–301.

10. See Bruce E. Teets and Helmut Gerber, eds., *Joseph Conrad: An Annotated Bibliography of Writings about Him* (De Kalb, Ill.: Northern Illinois University Press, 1971). The review is quoted on page 16.

11. Although we cannot know to what extent Conrad revised "The Lagoon" (the manuscript has not survived and the location of the typescript is unknown), a comparison of the book and serial versions proves that he eliminated at least one sequence of parallel structures, rewriting the description of the mist that follows the climax of Arsat's story.

12. An interesting debate about the ending of "The Lagoon" ran for five issues of *The Explicator* between January 1956 and May 1960.

13. My reading of the revision differs from Graver's (*Conrad's Short Fiction*, 27), Elmer Ordoñez's (*The Early Joseph Conrad: Revisions and Style* [Quezon City: University of Philippines Press, 1969], 49), and George Whiting's ("Conrad's Revisions of Six of His Short Stories," *PMLA* 48 [1933]: 552-57), all of whom interpret the book version as more sombre than the earlier serial one.

14. Lawrence Graver notes that the white listener "appears to embody a moral position" and "is a shadowy precursor of a later, more familiar, figure." *Conrad's Short Fiction*, 29.

15. David Thorburn, *Conrad's Romanticism* (New Haven and London: Yale University Press, 1974), 49.

16. Letter from Charles L. Graves in the Lilly Library, University of Indiana. Quoted in Lawrence Graver's *Conrad's Short Fiction*, 17-18.

17. See Ian Watt's instructive analysis of Marlow's investigation in *Conrad in the Nineteenth Century*, 269-304.

18. Roy Pascal, *Kafka's Narrators* (Cambridge: Cambridge University Press, 1982), 1.

19. Ian Watt, *Conrad in the Nineteenth Century*, 281-85.

20. Jacques Berthoud, *Joseph Conrad: The Major Phase* (Cambridge: Cambridge University Press, 1978), 91.

21. I can find only one instance when Marlow is ironic at Jim's expense during his retelling of this episode. When he relates Jim's description of the skipper and engineers working to free the boat, he comments drily on Jim's stoic attitude: "They had no leisure to look back upon his passive heroism, to feel the sting of his abstention."

22. The effect of authenticity and immediacy created by the first-person point of view had particular appeal for the nineteenth-century English magazine reader, who favoured an anecdotal style combined with exotic material. Many of the stories published in *Blackwood's* during the 1890s are either "true" episodes related by military or colonial figures, or sentimental plots in which strange customs and topographic details are reported as if by an eye-witness traveller to the area. The opening sentences of "Karain" would have found an immediate response in such readers.

23. Lawrence Graver, *Conrad's Short Fiction* (Berkeley: University of California Press, 1969), 32.

24. "Conrad's Polish Literary Background and Some Illustrations of the Influence of Polish Literature on His Work," *Antemurale* 10 (Rome and London, 1966): 209-15.

25. See Bruce M. Johnson, "Conrad's 'Karain' and *Lord Jim*," in *Lord Jim: An Authoritative Text*, ed. Thomas Moser (New York: Norton, 1968), 462-70 and Paul Bruss, "Narrative Irony in 'Karain: A Memory,'" *Conrad's Early Sea Fiction: The Novelist as Navigator* (Lewisburg, Penn.: Bucknell University Press, 1979), 47-57.

26. The narrator's invocation of the past and its spiritual claims on the present is echoed in a letter Conrad wrote to Edward Garnett six days after the completed, rewritten copy of "Karain" had

been sent to Fisher Unwin. The occasion was the death of Garnett's friend, Eustace Hartley: "Wisdom says: do not fill the vacated place—never! This is the only way to a life with phantoms who never perish; who never abandon one; who are always near and depart only when it is time also for yourself to go. I can tell for I have lived during many days with the faithful dead." *The Collected Letters*, I, 352–53.

27. "Conrad's 'Karain' and *Lord Jim*," 466–67.

28. The issue of the narrator's national identity becomes more significant in "Youth" and will be discussed in the next chapter.

29. Dorothy Van Ghent, *The English Novel: Form and Function* (New York: Rinehart, 1953), 191.

Chapter 4

1. Like John D. Gordan and Rosalind Walls Smith, Zdzisław Najder cites June 3 as the completion date because of a letter written to Helen Sanderson and the posting of copy to Meldrum at the time. However, I see no reason to dispute the date on the autograph manuscript as the month in which Conrad completed the first draft. See Najder's *Joseph Conrad: A Chronicle* (New Brunswick, N.J.: Rutgers University Press, 1983), 248 and Rosalind Walls Smith, "Dates of Composition of Conrad's Works," *Conradiana* 11 (1979): 63–90.

2. For example, in Conrad's letter to William Blackwood on October 29, 1897, he criticizes the "sweeping assertion" made by an ultra-conservative reviewer and refers to *Blackwood's* with considerable irony: "In this combat 'Maga' is to the front. In this time of fluid principles the soul of 'Maga' changeth not. It informs every page and knows no compromise. It is something. It is, indeed, everything." *The Collected Letters*, I, 401–2.

3. Unpublished letter to J. B. Pinker dated November 1911 (Berg Collection, New York Public Library).

4. Examples of Conrad's revisions to "Youth" in this chapter derive from collations of the autograph manuscript (entitled "A Voyage," Colgate University Library, Colgate University) with the serial version published in *Blackwood's Edinburgh Magazine*, September 1898, 309–30 and the English book text in *Dent's Collected Edition*. The manuscript is complete except for one page, the loss of which Conrad was evidently unaware when he sold the document to John Quinn, because there is no number missing from his pagination. The "Youth" manuscript consists of forty-two pages cut from an exercise book and written on both sides. The verso pages are followed by "b" in the parenthetic references throughout this chapter. Unless otherwise indicated (by "*B*" for *Blackwood's*) the serial and book versions are identical, and the page reference is to the *Youth* volume of *Dent's Collected Edition*. References to "Heart of Darkness" are also to this edition.

5. Najder offers the persuasive evidence of a note concerning the part of *The Rescue* Conrad was writing in April, found on the back of one of the "Tuan Jim" pages. *Joseph Conrad: A Chronicle*, 544.

6. These sections generally deal with events (such as young Marlow's joining the ship, the pumping during the storm, and the abandoning of the *Judea*) rather than descriptions, although the most dramatic episode—the explosion—is heavily revised.

7. Najder, *Joseph Conrad: A Chronicle*, 229.

8. Joseph Conrad, "Tales of the Sea," *Notes on Life and Letters*, 55. Subsequent page references follow quotations.

9. *The Collected Letters*, I, 346–47.

10. This episode reflects Conrad's tendency to separate any form of work, including writing, from the pragmatic or material value it might have.

11. To Kazimierz Waliszewski, who had written an article claiming that Conrad's works portrayed the relative inferiority of some races, he protested "Quand [sic] à 'l'infériorité des races,' je me permets de protester,— quoique évidemment la faute est à moi si je vous ai donné une fausse idée de mon intention. C'est la *différence* des races que j'ai voulu indiquer." December 16, 1903. G. Jean-Aubry, ed., *Joseph Conrad: Lettres françaises* (Paris: Gallimard, 1929), 64.

12. *The Collected Letters*, II, 346–49.

13. Although Ian Watt finds that in this episode "light has been degraded to a cold and artificial brightness . . . contrary to the positive values of human life," most critics interpret the "glow" of the Intended's "great and saving illusion" as the symbol of positive human values, opposing the dark truth represented by the allusions to Kurtz's reign in the wilderness. *Conrad in the Nineteenth Century*, 251–52.

14. See his letter to H. G. Wells, dated September 6, 1898 in *The Collected Letters*, II, 91–93.

15. See Albert B. Lord's comments on the cultural and religious roots of oral narrative in *The Singer of Tales* (Cambridge, Mass.: Harvard University Press, 1960).

Andrzej Busza argues that Conrad's use of a dramatized narrator derives from the *gawęda* or "literary yarn," which first appeared in Polish literature during the romantic period. He concludes that the technique "lent itself especially to Conrad, since much of his narrative material was based either on his own memories, or on yarns which he heard from other people." The *gawęda* technique is elegiac in nature, for it records and celebrates the traditions and values of the past. See "Conrad's Polish Literary Background and Some Illustrations of the Influence of Polish Literature on His Work," *Antemurale* 10 (1966): 208.

16. Jean-Aubry, G., *Joseph Conrad: Life and Letters* (London: William Heinemann, 1927), I, 67.

17. John Dozier Gordan, *Joseph Conrad: The Making of a Novelist* (Cambridge, Mass.: Harvard University Press, 1941), 38–39.

18. Najder, *Joseph Conrad: A Chronicle*, 78.

19. Conrad's revisions to the manuscript include a cancelled reference to a member of this last crew to board ship, who is not from Liverpool. He is "an old sailor called Jennings the only man in Falmouth who had the courage to ship with us" (*MS* 38a). Conrad must have decided that to include a native of the region would diminish the force of his statement that "the story of the ship was known, by this [the departure of the *Judea*'s rats] all up the Channel from Land's End to the Forelands, and we could get no crew on the south coast." Moreover, by drawing the old sailor to the reader's attention, as he does in the first draft when he tells us that Jennings owns a monkey, "an ugly old little brute liked by none but its owner," the writer obscures the most important fact in Marlow's account; that is, that a new crew had to be sent "all complete" from Liverpool.

20. Two exceptions to this rule are Lawrence Graver and Juliet McLauchlan. See Graver's *Conrad's Short Fiction*, 70–77, and McLauchlan's "Conrad's 'Three Ages of Man': The 'Youth' Volume," *The Polish Review* 20 (1975): 189–202.

21. The only detailed treatment of the humour in "Youth" is by Stanton de Voren Hoffman in *Comedy and Form in the Fiction of Joseph Conrad* (The Hague: Mouton, 1969), 99–107. Hoffman concludes that the comedy in the story is "a device of skepticism" which, by mocking all aspects of the journey, allows Conrad to "step away from moral responsibility." I believe that exactly the opposite is true. Marlow's humour involves us in a reexamination of the fundamental virtues of youth, an age that is often disparaged in maturity.

22. Jean Starobinski explores this point in his article "The Style of Autobiography," *Literary Style: A Symposium,* ed. Seymour Chatman (London: Oxford University Press, 1971), 285–96.

23. Najder, *Joseph Conrad: A Chronicle,* 230–31.

24. *The Collected Letters,* I, 357–59.

25. Lord, *The Singer of Tales,* 49.

26. José Ortega y Gasset, "Notes on the Novel," *The Dehumanization of Art and Other Essays on Art, Culture, and Literature* (1948; Princeton: Princeton University Press, 1968), 92.

27. Cedric Watts discusses this aspect of the story in detail. See his *Conrad's "Heart of Darkness": A Critical and Contextual Discussion* (Milano: Mursia International, 1977).

28. *The Collected Letters,* I, 302–4.

29. Ibid. 430.

30. J. Wilkes Berry and Marion C. Michael, "The Typescript of 'The Heart of Darkness,'" *Conradiana* 12 (1980): 147–55.

31. Quoted in George Whiting's article, "Conrad's Revision of Six of his Short Stories," *PMLA* 48 (1933): 552.

32. The only revision Conrad made to this passage for the book edition closely resembles the original wording in the manuscript, which is characteristic of the changes from serial to book version. He substituted "as if inviting us to walk the plank at once and be done with our ridiculous troubles" (26) for "as if inviting us to walk the plank at once and thus end the poignant comedy of that voyage," possible because the diction of the latter was too literary.

33. Ian Watt, *Conrad in the Nineteenth Century,* 176–77.

34. For a complete account of how Conrad's conception of Marlow's function changed from the manuscript to the book version, see Ernest W. Sullivan's "The Genesis and Evolution of Joseph Conrad's 'Youth': A Revised and Copy-Edited Typescript Page," *The Review of English Studies* 36 (November 1985): 522–34.

35. See chapter 5 in *A Personal Record,* 92.

36. Examples are James W. Mathews, "Ironic Symbolism in Conrad's 'Youth,'" *Studies in Short Fiction* 11 (1974): 117–23 and J. H. Wills, "A Neglected Masterpiece: Conrad's 'Youth,'" *Texas Studies in Literature and Language* 4 (1963): 591–601. There have been several other articles of this nature published within the last twenty years.

37. The difficulty of determining how closely Conrad supports Marlow's views was first raised by William York Tindall in "Apology for Marlow," *From Jane Austen to Joseph Conrad: Essays Collected in Memory of James T. Hillhouse,* ed. Robert C. Rathburn and Martin Steinmann, Jr. (Minneapolis: University of Minnesota Press, 1958).

38. "From 'Youth' to *Lord Jim:* The Formal-Thematic Use of Marlow," *The Play and Place of Criticism* (Baltimore: The Johns Hopkins Press, 1967), 98.

39. E. M. Forster, *Aspects of the Novel* (New York: Harcourt, Brace and Co., 1927), 27.

40. This term is used by Robert Kiely to describe the antirealistic nature of the adventure novel. *Robert Louis Stevenson and the Fiction of Adventure* (Cambridge, Mass.: Harvard University Press, 1964).

41. Donald C. Yelton, *Mimesis and Metaphor: An Inquiry into the Genesis and Scope of Conrad's Symbolic Imagery* (The Hague: Mouton and Co., 1967), 123.

42. The alterations and additions also affect the cadence, since periodic sentences and parallel structures give the passage more weight and ceremony. At least seventy-five of Conrad's substantive revisions to the story are concerned with improving either the euphony or the rhythm of the prose.

43. J. Hillis Miller and Donald Yelton have illustrated this point in some detail. See Miller's "*Lord Jim:* Repetition as Subversion of Organic Form," *Fiction and Repetition: Seven English Novels* (Cambridge, Mass.: Harvard University Press, 1982), 22–41 and Yelton's *Mimesis and Metaphor,* chapter 6.

44. The captain's outburst reaches its peak in his statement, "If you had to take a valuable steamer along this God-forsaken coast you would want a light, too" (40). The motif of materialism is recapitulated in the coda.

45. Najder, *Joseph Conrad: A Chronicle,* 78.

46. This aspect of the writer's realism was foreshadowed by James Fenimore Cooper, whose accurate representation of sea life earned Conrad's praise in "Tales of the Sea." Cooper wrote his first sea novel partly in reaction to Walter Scott's *The Pirate.* He wanted to give a "truer picture of the ocean and ships" by "letting the landsman into the secrets of the seaman's manner of life." See his preface to *The Pilot: A Tale of the Sea* (Boston: Colonial Press, 1823).

47. In the latter type of revision, for example, Conrad would add "There was no time to cast off the lashings" to explain why Marlow and Mahon had to cut the towrope.

Chapter 5

1. See Conrad's letter dated May 19, 1900 in *The Collected Letters,* II, 271–73. Conrad also thought of "Typhoon" and *The Nigger of the "Narcissus"* as companion pieces, and there are significant thematic correspondences between the two works. Jessie Conrad reports that during an interview with an American journalist he referred to "Typhoon" as "one of my storm pieces. *The Nigger of the "Narcissus"* is the one on a sailing ship in a storm. Having done that I felt that I should do the steamship—'Typhoon.'" See Jessie Conrad, *Joseph Conrad and His Circle* (New York: E. P. Dutton, 1935), 252.

2. The manuscript is reproduced by Thomas Moser in his *Lord Jim: An Authoritative Text,* 276–91. In April or May of 1898 Conrad abandoned this early attempt to write a story about Jim, and resumed the work in the summer of 1899 after completing "Heart of Darkness."

3. See Eloise Knapp Hay, "*Lord Jim:* From Sketch to Novel" in *Lord Jim: An Authoritative Text, Background, and Sources,* ed. Thomas Moser (New York: W. W. Norton, 1968), 418–37.

4. Hay, "*Lord Jim:* From Sketch to Novel," 419.

5. Zdzisław Najder also comes to this conclusion in *Joseph Conrad: A Chronicle* (New Brunswick, N.J.: Rutgers University Press, 1983), 248. Working with the "Youth" manuscript, I found that pages 49 and 78 contain paragraphs that belong to much earlier episodes or descriptions. The appearance of these pages indicates very strongly that they were once separated from the main text, for Conrad wrote all around the original paragraphs as his story grew and he needed more paper. Therefore, if he had worked on extra pages of manuscript for "Tuan Jim" that were subsequently lost, this would have been entirely consistent with his methods of composition.

6. This probability illustrates Flaubert's influence on Conrad's original conception of the work. In the serial and book versions the brief outline of Jim's background recalls the summaries in the first chapters of *Madame Bovary* and *Bouvard et Pécuchet.*

7. Thomas Moser makes this point in his footnote linking the sketch to the novel. See *Lord Jim: An Authoritative Text,* 276.

8. Hay, "*Lord Jim:* From Sketch to Novel," 434.
9. Joseph Conrad, *The Rescue: A Romance of the Shallows* (1920; London: J. M. Dent, 1949), 106.
10. On the back of page 28 of the "Tuan Jim" manuscript Conrad wrote a note concerning chapter 6, part 3 in *The Rescue*. At this point in the novel, Hassim and Immada arrive on board the Travers' yacht, and Lingard's two worlds converge.
11. *The Collected Letters*, II, 157–61. This statement should perhaps be compared with an earlier letter to Paul Briquel (July 3, 1895) in which Conrad warns the younger man against egoism, and sounds a little like his uncle, Tadeusz Bobrowski, in his devotion to duty rather than self: "Et ne pensez pas que je prêche l'égoïsme. Il faut accomplir des tâches ennuyeuses, pénibles et répugnantes, il faut faire marcher le monde. . . ." *The Collected Letters*, I, 231–32.
12. *The Collected Letters*, II, 29–31.
13. Ibid., 346–49.
14. Avrom Fleishman, *Conrad's Politics: Community and Anarchy in the Fiction of Joseph Conrad* (Baltimore: The Johns Hopkins Press, 1967), 107. See chapter 4, "Colonists and Conquerors," for the argument in full.
15. Conrad stresses Kurtz's tyranny over the minds of others when the Russian trader tells Marlow, "You don't talk with that man—you listen to him" (123).
16. Joseph Conrad, "The Heroic Age," *The Mirror of the Sea* (1906; London: J. M. Dent, 1946).
17. See *Notes on Life and Letters*, 98.
18. Ian Watt, *Conrad in the Nineteenth Century*, 205.
19. For some eccentric interpretations of the connection between Marlow and the young trader, see C. F. Burgess's "Conrad's Pesky Russian," *Nineteenth Century Fiction* 18 (September 1963): 189–93 and John W. Canario's "The Harlequin," *Studies in Short Fiction* 4 (1967): 225–33.
20. Albert J. Guerard, *Conrad the Novelist* (Cambridge, Mass.: Harvard University Press, 1958), 37–48.
21. "I did say the right thing, though indeed he could not have been more irretrievably lost than he was at this very moment, when the foundations of our intimacy were being laid. . . ." (143).
22. See Feder's "Marlow's Descent into Hell," *Nineteenth Century Fiction* 9 (March 1955): 280–92 and Evans's "Conrad's Underworld," *Modern Fiction Studies* 2 (May 1956): 56–62.
23. Jacques Berthoud, *Joseph Conrad: The Major Phase* (Cambridge: Cambridge University Press, 1978), 58.
24. Northrop Frye, *Anatomy of Criticism: Four Essays* (Princeton: Princeton University Press, 1957), 40.
25. "Well Done," *Notes on Life and Letters*, 189.
26. Conrad links Tom Lingard's egoism to his "sentimental pity" for the natives (in other words, his paternalism) rather than romantic imagination.
27. See Conrad's letter to Blackwood, dated Feb. 14, 1899 in *The Collected Letters*, II, 166–68.
28. Ibid., 184–85.
29. Conrad's use of the imperfect is another example of Flaubert's influence on the opening of *Lord Jim*.

30. See Conrad's letter dated July 31, 1899 in *The Collected Letters*, II, 190.

31. John Dozier Gordan, *Joseph Conrad: The Making of a Novelist* (Cambridge, Mass.: Harvard University Press, 1941), 173.

32. Martin Prince, "Conrad: The Limits of Irony," *Forms of Life: Character and Moral Imagination in the Novel* (New Haven and London: Yale University Press, 1983), 244.

33. The distinctive features of this coda include a return to the fictive present and a first-person narrator who retrospectively affirms a vanished tradition or spirit. In this case, the affirmation is qualified by Marlow's doubts.

34. See "The Narrative Progress and Its Methods," in Ian Watt, *Conrad in the Nineteenth Century*, 269–310.

35. The prhase "Nothing can touch me" is one of the leitmotifs that Conrad uses to emphasize his major ideas in the novel. It appears no fewer than ten times. Conrad first uses the phrase in free indirect style, to stress Jim's condescension toward his fellow officers on the *Patna:* "They could not touch him" (25) is ironic. The last use of the motif affirms the hero's acceptance of his fate: "'Nothing can touch me,' he said in a last flicker of superb egoism" (413). The significance of the phrase changes each time it appears.

36. *The Collected Letters*, II, 253–54.

37. Ibid., 164–65 and 252.

38. See letter dated July 19, 1900 in ibid., 283–84.

39. Jacques Berthoud lists these parallels in *Joseph Conrad: The Major Phase*, 90.

40. See the letter dated January 20, 1900 in *The Collected Letters*, II, 243–47.

Chapter 6

1. Conrad wrote "The Planter of Malata" in November and early December of 1913, when he was a little over halfway through *Victory*. There are significant links between the two works. Like the novel, the short story describes the effect of a love relationship on the sceptical hero, who lives apart from society and tries to maintain an aloof self-sufficiency. Certain motifs, such as the island retreat, are repeated from one narrative to the other. More significantly, Conrad explores the "supreme illusion" of love dialectically, by opposing Felicia Moorsom's egoistic conception of "a sacred debt—a fine duty" in "The Planter of Malata" to Lena's redemptive self-sacrifice in *Victory*.

    In her excellent study of "The Planter of Malata" Juliet McLauchlan comments that "in the middle of trying to portray a given complex relationship [Heyst's and Lena's], there came to [Conrad's] mind another which is remarkable for its contrasts rather than its similarities." "Conrad's Heart of Emptiness: 'The Planter of Malata,'" *Conradiana* 18 (1986): 180–92.

2. In his letters to Pinker dated October 1909 and December 20, 1909 (Berg Collection, New York Public Library), Conrad estimated that he had written about 100,000 words of *Razumov* by October 1909. Since the novel was originally almost 145,000 words long (see Zdzisław Najder, *Joseph Conrad: A Chronicle* (New Brunswick, N.J.: Rutgers University Press, 1983), 569), he must have completed at least three-quarters of the first draft by the time he began "The Secret Sharer" in late November.

3. Joseph Conrad, *Under Western Eyes* (1911; London: J. M. Dent, 1947), 291. Subsequent page references follow quotations.

Notes for Chapter 6

4. Joseph Conrad, "The Secret Sharer," *'Twixt Land and Sea* (1912; London: J. M. Dent, 1947), 98. Subsequent page references follow quotations.

5. In his letter to Pinker dated December 4, 1907 Conrad announced that he had started a short story ("the one about the revolutionist who is blown up with his own bomb") that would be finished "after Xmas." Berg Collection, New York Public Library.

6. G. Jean-Aubry, *Joseph Conrad: Life and Letters* (London: William Heinemann, 1927), II, 64–65.

7. Ibid., 64–65.

8. In his letter to Pinker dated December 1907 (Thursday), Conrad wrote, "I send you in a hurry 10 pp. of Razumov. . . . It is quite possible that you will get the rest (say 35 pp) by Monday or Tuesday." Berg Collection, New York Public Library.

9. In his influential study of "The Secret Sharer" Albert Guerard writes that "it is entirely wrong to suppose, as some readers do, that Conrad unequivocally *approves* the captain's decision to harbour Leggatt." Some of Guerard's reasons for this interpretation are not very convincing; for instance, he claims that Leggatt is "a rather questionable seaman" and quotes Archbold's remark that he "wasn't exactly the sort for the chief mate of a ship like the *Sephora.*" Of course, this particular statement is clearly invalid because of its source. Moreover, as we saw in the protagonist's triumph over Archbold, Conrad uses many rhetorical techniques to guarantee the reader's sympathy with the captain's decision. See Albert J. Guerard, *Conrad the Novelist* (Cambridge, Mass.: Harvard University Press, 1958), 14–33.

10. Returning to his rooms after he has betrayed Haldin to Prince K—— and General T——, Razumov thinks, "What must be must be. Extraordinary things do happen. But when they have happened they are done with. Thus, too, when the mind is made up. That question is done with. And the daily concerns, the familiarities of our thought swallow it up—and the life goes on as before *with its mysterious and secret sides quite out of sight,* as they should be. Life is a public thing" (54; my italics).

11. Cf. Jocelyn Baines in *Joseph Conrad: A Critical Biography* (London: Weidenfeld and Nicolson, 1959), 354–59. Baines finds no indication whatsoever of a moral dilemma involving the captain.

12. In his notes to the critical edition, Bruce Harkness provides a few tantalising examples of the revisions one might find were the manuscript of "The Secret Sharer" accessible. One of these is Conrad's addition of the exclamation "A headless corpse!"—probably at the typescript stage—for the serial version. This revision prolongs the process of decoding sense-impressions because the captain's first guess is wrong. Cedric Watts analyzes this aspect of Conrad's technique in *The Deceptive Text: An Introduction to Covert Plots* (Sussex: The Harvester Press, 1984), 43–46. Harkness provides eight examples of Conrad's revisions in his "Textual Note," *Conrad's "Secret Sharer" and the Critics* (Belmont, Calif.: Wadsworth, 1965), 151–61. I shall refer to one or two of these revisions a little later, as well as to the facsimile of the first page of manuscript, which is included in Harkness's textual notes.

13. Jacques Berthoud, *Joseph Conrad: The Major Phase* (Cambridge: Cambridge University Press, 1978), 171.

14. "'Gnawed Bones' and 'Artless Tales': Eating and Narration in Conrad," *Joseph Conrad: A Commemoration,* ed. Norman Sherry (London: Macmillan, 1976), 17–36.

15. Donald Yelton comments on the "imagery of disease and narcosis" in *Under Western Eyes,* pointing out that it refers to Russia and Russians in general as well as to Razumov in particular. *Mimesis and Metaphor: An Inquiry into the Genesis and Scope of Conrad's Symbolic Imagery* (The Hague: Mouton, 1967), 193–95.

16. Cedric Watts comments on Conrad's use of the Cain-Abel story in his discussion of "The Secret Sharer" (*The Deceptive Text: An Introduction to Covert Plots*, 87–88). He argues that the allusions are paradoxical and ambiguous because in the Bible God punishes Cain yet seems benevolent when he gives him the protective mark on the brow. However, in "The Secret Sharer" Conrad writes *against* the latter part of the legend, in order to minimize Leggatt's guilt.

17. Gen. 5: 13-15: And Cain said unto the Lord, My punishment is greater than I can bear.

    Behold, thou hast driven me out this day from the face of the earth; and from thy face shall I be hid; and I shall be a fugitive and a vagabond in the earth; and it shall come to pass that every one that findeth me shall slay me.

    And the Lord said unto him, Therefore whosoever slayeth Cain, vengeance shall be taken on him sevenfold. And the Lord set a mark upon Cain, lest any finding him should kill him.

18. See "The Double" (1846). In Dostoevsky the emphasis is psychological, whereas Conrad uses the concept of the double and the motif of confinement to introduce important moral themes.

19. Other significant verbal echoes include the key words "confidence" and "secret."

20. Thanks to Bruce Harkness's reproduction of the first page of the manuscript, we can see that Conrad's intention was to heighten the impression of the captain's isolation through the different stages of his revisions. The first sentence originally read: "On my right hand there were lines of fishing-stakes resembling a mysterious system of half-submerged bamboo fences; to the left a group of islets." In the manuscript Conrad added "as if abandoned for ever by *some* nomad tribe *of brown* fishermen now removed to the other end of the earth." For the serial version, he added "for there was no sign of human habitation as far as the eye could reach." See *Conrad's "Secret Sharer" and the Critics*, 161.

21. Letter to J. B. Pinker, dated Monday [October 1909]. Berg Collection, New York Public Library.

22. Letter to Garnett, dated Friday, October 1907. Edward Garnett, ed., *Letters from Joseph Conrad: 1895-1924* (Indianapolis: Bobbs-Merrill, 1928), 212.

23. Najder, *Joseph Conrad: A Chronicle*, 341.

24. Robert Lynd's review is reprinted in Norman Sherry's *Conrad: The Critical Heritage* (London: Routledge and Kegan Paul, 1973), 210-11.

25. See letter to Davray, dated November 8, 1906, G. Jean-Aubry, *Joseph Conrad: Lettres françaises* (Paris: Gallimard, 1929), 78, and also Richard Curle, ed., *Conrad to a Friend: 150 Selected Letters from Joseph Conrad to Richard Curle* (Garden City, N.Y.: Doubleday, 1928), 147.

26. Guerard, *Conrad the Novelist*, 14-33.

27. In a letter to Kazimierz Waliszewski, a Polish historian, Conrad wrote, "Homo duplex has in my case more than one meaning. . . ." Zdzisław Najder, ed., *Conrad's Polish Background: Letters to and from Polish Friends* (London: Oxford University Press, 1964), 240-41.

28. See G. Jean-Aubry, *Joseph Conrad: Life and Letters*, II, 103-6.

29. Najder, *Joseph Conrad: A Chronicle*, 356.

30. Cedric Watts, *The Deceptive Text: An Introduction to Covert Plots*, 88-90.

31. See Carl Benson, "Conrad's Two Stories of Initiation," *PMLA* 69 (March 1954): 46-56, Donald Yelton, *Mimesis and Metaphor*, 272-98, and Porter Williams, "The Matter of Conscience in Conrad's 'The Secret Sharer,'" *PMLA* 79 (Dec. 1964): 626-30.

32. Roderick Davis, "*Under Western Eyes:* 'The Most Deeply Meditated Novel,'" *Conradiana* 9 (1977): 59-75.

33. See Najder, *Joseph Conrad: A Chronicle*, 353–54.
34. That is, the captain's and Leggatt's.

Chapter 7

1. Andrzej Busza, "Conrad's Rhetoric of Affirmation and the Moderns," Paper presented to the Joseph Conrad Society (U.K.), London, July 8, 1976.
2. One of the listeners is a Director of Companies; another is a lawyer; the third is an accountant.
3. In this episode the young protagonist's romantic first impressions of the East are undercut by the crass materialism of the steamer's captain.
4. See G. Jean-Aubry, *Joseph Conrad: Life and Letters* (London: William Heinemann, 1927), II, 205.
5. Joseph Conrad, "A Familiar Preface," *A Personal Record,* xvii.
6. These two works were written concurrently.
7. Joseph Conrad, *The Secret Agent,* viii-ix.
8. Like all of Conrad's autobiographical writings, *The Mirror of the Sea* is actually highly structured. However, Conrad is comparing the book with *Nostromo,* which is a densely complex work of fiction.
9. See Conrad's letter dated March 1911 in *Letters from Joseph Conrad,* 228.

Bibliography

Manuscript Material

Letters from Joseph Conrad to J. B. Pinker. Berg Collection, New York Public Library.
"An Outpost of Progress." The Beinecke Rare Book and Manuscript Libarary, Yale University.
"Youth: A Narrative" ("A Voyage"). Colgate University Library, Colgate University.

Serial Publications of Conrad's Works

"Heart of Darkness." *Blackwood's Edinburgh Magazine*, February–April 1899.
"Karain." *Blackwood's Edinburgh Magazine*, November 1897.
"The Lagoon." *The Cornhill*, January 1897.
"An Outpost of Progress." *Cosmopolis*, June–July 1897.
"Youth: A Narrative." *Blackwood's Edinburgh Magazine*, September 1898.

Conrad's Works

Conrad, Joseph. *Congo Diary and Other Uncollected Pieces*. Ed. Zdzisław Najder. New York: Doubleday, 1978.
———. *Dent's Collected Edition of the Works of Joseph Conrad*. 22 vols. London: J. M. Dent, 1946–55.
———. *Heart of Darkness: An Authoritative Text, Background and Sources*. Edited by Robert Kimbrough. New York: W. W. Norton, 1963.
———. *Lord Jim: An Authoritative Text, Background, and Sources*. Edited by Thomas Moser. New York: W. W. Norton, 1968.
———. *The Sisters: An Unfinished Story*. With an introduction by Ford Madox Ford. Edited by Ugo Mursia. 1928; rpt. Milan: U. Mursia, 1968.

Conrad's Letters

Blackburn, William, ed. *Joseph Conrad: Letters to William Blackwood and David S. Meldrum*. Durham, N. C.: Duke University Press, 1958.
Curle, Richard, ed. *Conrad to a Friend: 150 Selected Letters from Joseph Conrad to Richard Curle*. Garden City, N.Y.: Doubleday, 1928.
Garnett, Edward, ed. *Letters from Joseph Conrad: 1895–1924*. Indianapolis: Bobbs-Merrill, 1928.
Gee, John A., and Paul J. Sturm, trans. and eds. *Letters of Joseph Conrad to Marguerite Poradowska, 1890–1920*. New Haven: Yale University Press, 1940.
Jean-Aubry, G. *Joseph Conrad: Lettres françaises*. Paris: Gallimard, 1929.
———. *Joseph Conrad: Life and Letters*. 2 vols. London: William Heinemann, 1927.

Karl, Frederick R., and Davies, Laurence, eds. *The Collected Letters of Joseph Conrad.* 2 vols. to date. Cambridge: Cambridge University Press, 1983– .

Najder, Zdzisław, ed. *Conrad's Polish Background: Letters to and from Polish Friends.* Translated by Halina Carroll. London: Oxford University Press, 1964.

———, ed. *Conrad under Familial Eyes.* Translated by Halina Carroll-Najder. Cambridge: Cambridge University Press, 1983.

Randall, Dale B. J. *Joseph Conrad and Warrington Dawson: The Record of a Friendship.* Durham, N.C.: Duke University Press, 1968.

Rapin, Rene, ed. *Lettres de Joseph Conrad à Marguerite Poradowska.* Geneva: Université de Lausanne, 1966.

Watts, C. T., ed. *Joseph Conrad's Letters to R. B. Cunninghame Graham.* Cambridge: Cambridge University Press, 1969.

Selected Critical and Background Books and Articles

Baines, Jocelyn. *Joseph Conrad: A Critical Biography.* London: Weidenfeld and Nicolson, 1959.

Bender, Todd K. "Conrad and Literary Impressionism." *Conradiana* 10 (1978): 211–24.

Benson, Carl. "Conrad's Two Stories of Initiation." *PMLA* 69 (1954): 46–56.

Berry, J. Wilkes, and Michael, Marion C. "The Typescript of 'The Heart of Darkness.'" *Conradiana* 12 (1980): 147–55.

Berthoud, Jacques. *Joseph Conrad: The Major Phase.* Cambridge: Cambridge University Press, 1978.

Bonheim, Helmut. *The Narrative Modes: Techniques of the Short Story.* Cambridge: D. S. Brewer, 1982.

Booth, Wayne C. *The Rhetoric of Fiction.* Chicago: The University of Chicago Press, 1961.

———. *A Rhetoric of Irony.* Chicago: The University of Chicago Press, 1974.

Boyle, Ted E. *Symbol and Meaning in the Fiction of Joseph Conrad.* London: Mouton, 1965.

Braun, Andrzej. "The Myth-Like Kingdom of Conrad." *Conradiana* 10 (1978): 3–16.

Bruss, Paul. *Conrad's Early Sea Fiction: The Novelist as Navigator.* Lewisburg, Penn.: Bucknell University Press, 1979.

Burgess, C. F. "Conrad's Pesky Russian." *Nineteenth Century Fiction* 18 (1963): 189–93.

Burjorjee, Dinshaw M. "Comic Elements in Conrad's 'The Secret Sharer.'" *Conradiana* 7 (1975): 51–61.

Busza, Andrzej. "Conrad's Polish Literary Background and Some Illustrations of the Influence of Polish Literature on His Work." *Antemurale* 10 (1966).

———. "Conrad's Rhetoric of Affirmation and the Moderns." Paper presented to the Joseph Conrad Society (U.K.), London, July 8, 1976.

———. "Rhetoric and Ideology in Conrad's *Under Western Eyes.*" *Joseph Conrad: A Commemoration.* Papers from the 1974 International Conference on Conrad. Ed. Norman Sherry. London: Macmillan, 1976: 105–18.

———. "The Rhetoric of Conrad's Non-Fictional Political Discourse." *Annales de la Faculté des Lettres et Sciences humaines de Nice* 34 (1978): 159–70.

Canario, John W. "The Harlequin." *Studies in Short Fiction* 4 (1967): 225–33.

Carlyle, Thomas. *Sartor Resartus and On Heroes, Hero-Worship, and the Heroic in History.* 1841; London: J. M. Dent, 1908.

Chatman, Seymour, ed. *Literary Style: A Symposium.* London: Oxford University Press, 1971.

———. *Story and Discourse: Narrative Structure in Fiction and Film.* Ithaca, N.Y.: Cornell University Press, 1978.

Conrad, Borys. *My Father: Joseph Conrad.* London: Calder and Boyars, 1970.

Conrad, Jessie. *Joseph Conrad and His Circle.* New York: E. P. Dutton, 1935.

———. *Joseph Conrad as I Knew Him.* Garden City, New York: Doubleday, Page and Co., 1926.

Conrad, John. *Joseph Conrad: Times Remembered.* Cambridge: Cambridge University Press, 1981.

Covino, W. A. "Lugubrious Drollery: Humor and Horror in Conrad's Fiction." *Modern Fiction Studies* 23 (1977): 217-25.
Cox, C. B. *Joseph Conrad: The Modern Imagination.* London: J. M. Dent, 1974.
Craig, Randall. "Swapping Yarns: The Oral Mode of *Lord Jim.*" *Conradiana* 13 (1981): 181-93.
Curley, Daniel. "Legate of the Ideal." *Conrad's "Secret Sharer" and the Critics.* Edited by Bruce Harkness. Belmont, Calif.: Wadsworth, 1962.
Current-Garcia, Eugene, and Walton R. Patrick. *What Is the Short Story?* Glenview, Ill.: Scott, Foresman and Co., 1974.
Dalgarno, Emily K. "Conrad, Pinker, and the Writing of *The Secret Agent.*" *Conradiana* 9 (1977): 47-58.
———. "Conrad's Attitude to His Text." *Conradiana* 9 (1977): 3-16.
Davidson, Arnold E. "The Abdication of Lord Jim." *Conradiana* 13 (1981): 19-34.
———. "The Open Ending of *The Secret Agent.*" *Ariel* 7 (1976): 84-100.
Davis, Kenneth W.; Higdon, David Leon; and Rude, Donald W. "On Editing Conrad." *Joseph Conrad: A Commemoration.* Papers from the 1974 International Conference on Conrad. Edited by Norman Sherry. London: Macmillan, 1976: 143-55.
Davis, Roderick. "*Under Western Eyes:* 'The Most Deeply Meditated Novel.'" *Conradiana* 9 (1977): 59-75.
Dilworth, Thomas R. "Conrad's Secret Sharer at the Gate of Hell." *Conradiana* 9 (1977): 201-17.
Eagleton, Terry. "Joseph Conrad and *Under Western Eyes.*" In his *Exiles and Emigrés.* London: Chatto, 1970: 21-32.
Emmett, V. J. "Carlyle, Conrad, and the Politics of Charisma: Another Perspective on 'Heart of Darkness.'" *Conradiana* 7 (1975): 145-53.
Evans, Frank B. "The Nautical Metaphor in 'The Secret Sharer.'" *Conradiana* 7 (1975): 3-16.
Evans, Robert O. "Conrad's Underworld." *Modern Fiction Studies* 2 (1956): 56-62.
Feder, Lillian. "Marlow's Descent into Hell." *Nineteenth Century Fiction* 9 (1955): 280-92.
Fernandez, Ramon. "The Art of Conrad." *Messages.* Translated by Montgomery Belgion. London: Jonathan Cape, 1927: 137-51. Rpt. "The Art of Conrad." Translated by Charles Owen. In *The Art of Joseph Conrad: A Critical Symposium.* Edited by R. W. Stallman. East Lansing, Mich.: Michigan State University Press, 1960: 8-13.
Fleishman, Avrom. *Conrad's Politics: Community and Anarchy in the Fiction of Joseph Conrad.* Baltimore: The Johns Hopkins Press, 1967.
Ford, Ford Madox. *Critical Writings of Ford Madox Ford.* Edited by Frank MacShane. Lincoln: University of Nebraska Press, 1964.
———. *Joseph Conrad: A Personal Remembrance.* 1924; New York: Octagon, 1965.
———. *Return to Yesterday.* New York: Liveright, 1932.
Forster, E. M. *Aspects of the Novel.* New York: Harcourt, Brace and Co., 1927.
Foye, Paul E.; Harkness, Bruce; and Marvin, Nathan L., "The Sailing Maneuver in 'The Secret Sharer.'" *Journal of Modern Literature* 2 (1971): 119-23.
Friedman, Alan. "Conrad's Picaresque Narrator: Marlow's Journey from 'Youth' through *Chance.*" *Joseph Conrad: Theory and World Fiction.* Proceedings of the Comparative Literature Symposium. Vol. VII. Lubbock: Texas Tech Press, 1974: 17-39.
———. *The Turn of The Novel: The Transition to Modern Fiction.* Oxford: Oxford University Press, 1966.
Frye, Northrop. *Anatomy of Criticism: Four Essays.* Princeton: Princeton University Press, 1957.
Geddes, Gary. *Conrad's Later Novels.* Montreal: McGill-Queen's University Press, 1980.
Gilliam, Harriet. "The Daemonic in Conrad's *Under Western Eyes.*" *Conradiana* 9 (1977): 219-36.
Gleckner, Robert F. "Conrad's 'The Lagoon.'" *The Explicator* 16 (1958), item 33.
Glicksberg, Charles I. *The Ironic Vision in Modern Literature.* The Hague: Martinus Nijhoff, 1969.
Goonetilleke, D. C. R. A. "Conrad's African Tales: Ironies of Progress." *Ceylon Journal of the Humanities* 2 (1971): 64-97.

Gordan, John Dozier. *Joseph Conrad: The Making of a Novelist.* Cambridge, Mass.: Harvard University Press, 1941.
Graver, Lawrence. *Conrad's Short Fiction.* Berkeley: University of California Press, 1969.
Guerard, Albert J. *Conrad the Novelist.* Cambridge, Mass.: Harvard University Press, 1958.
Guetti, James. *The Rhetoric of Joseph Conrad.* Amherst, Mass.: Amherst College Press, 1960.
——. *Word-Music: The Aesthetic Aspect of Narrative Fiction.* New Brunswick, N.J.: Rutgers University Press, 1980.
Gullason, Thomas Arthur. "Conrad's 'The Lagoon.'" *The Explicator* 14 (1956), item 23.
——. "The Short Story: Revision and Renewal." *Studies in Short Fiction* 19 (1982): 221-30.
Harkness, Bruce, ed. *Conrad's "Secret Sharer" and the Critics.* Belmont, Calif.: Wadsworth, 1965.
Hawkins, Hunt. "Conrad and Congolese Exploitation." *Conradiana* 13 (1981): 84-99.
——. "Conrad's Criticism of Imperialism in 'Heart of Darkness.'" *PMLA* 94 (1979): 286-99.
Hay, Eloise Knapp. "*Lord Jim:* From Sketch to Novel." *Lord Jim: An Authoritative Text, Background, and Sources.* Edited by Thomas Moser. New York: W. W. Norton, 1968.
Hervouet, Y. "Aspects of Flaubertian Influence on Conrad's Fiction, Part One." *Revue de Littérature Comparée* 1 (1983): 5-24.
——. "Conrad's Relationship with Anatole France." *Conradiana* 7 (1977): 195-224.
Higdon, D. L., and Eddleman, F. E. "Collected Edition Variants in Conrad's *Almayer's Folly.*" *Conradiana* 9 (1977): 77-103.
Hilson, J. C., and Timms, David. "Gobila in London: A Note on 'An Outpost of Progress' and *The Secret Agent.*" *Conradiana* 9 (1977): 189-92.
Hobson, Robert. "A Textual History of Conrad's 'An Outpost of Progress.'" *Conradiana* 11 (1979): 143-63.
Hoffman, Stanton de Voren. *Comedy and Form in the Fiction of Joseph Conrad.* The Hague: Mouton, 1969.
Houze, William C. "*The Secret Agent* from Novel to Play: The Implications of Conrad's Handling of Structure." *Conradiana* 13 (1981): 109-22.
Howe, Irving. *Politics and the Novel.* New York: World Publishing Co., 1957.
James, Henry. *The Art of the Novel.* 1907; New York: Charles Scribner's Sons, 1934.
——. *The Notebooks of Henry James.* Edited by F. O. Matthiessen and Kenneth B. Murdock. 1891; New York: Oxford University Press, 1947.
Jameson, Fredric. *The Political Unconscious: Narrative as a Socially Symbolic Act.* Ithaca, N.Y.: Cornell University Press, 1981.
Johnson, Bruce M. "Conrad's 'Karain' and *Lord Jim.*" *Lord Jim: An Authoritative Text.* Edited by Thomas Moser. New York: Norton, 1968.
Karl, Frederick R. "Conrad and Pinker." *Joseph Conrad: A Commemoration.* Papers from the 1974 International Conference on Conrad. Edited by Norman Sherry. London: The Macmillan Press Ltd., 1976: 156-73.
——. *Joseph Conrad: The Three Lives.* New York: Farrar, Straus and Giroux, 1979.
Kermode, Frank. "Secrets and Narrative Sequence." *On Narrative.* Edited by W. J. T. Mitchell. Chicago: The University of Chicago Press, 1980: 79-97.
——. *The Sense of an Ending: Studies in the Theory of Fiction.* London: Oxford University Press, 1966.
Kiely, Robert. *Robert Louis Stevenson and the Fiction of Adventure.* Cambridge, Mass.: Harvard University Press, 1964.
Kirschner, Paul. *Conrad: The Psychologist as Artist.* Edinburgh: Oliver and Boyd, 1968.
Krieger, Murray. *The Play and Place of Criticism.* Baltimore: The Johns Hopkins Press, 1967.
Lemon, Lee T., and Reis, Marion J., eds. *Russian Formalist Criticism: Four Essays.* Lincoln: University of Nebraska Press, 1965.
Lewitter, L. R. "Conrad, Dostoyevsky, and the Russo-Polish Antagonism." *Modern Language Review* 79 (1984): 653-63.

Lindstrand, Gordon. "Bibliographical Surveys of the Literary Manuscripts of Joseph Conrad." *Conradiana* 2, nos. 1, 2, and 3 (1969-70).
Lord, Albert B. *The Singer of Tales*. Cambridge, Mass.: Harvard University Press, 1960.
McCann, Charles J. "Conrad's 'The Lagoon.'" *The Explicator* 18 (1959), item 3.
McLauchlan, Juliet. "Amy Foster: Echoes from Conrad's Own Experience?" *Polish Review* 23 (1978): 3-8.
———. "Conrad's Heart of Emptiness: 'The Planter of Malata.'" *Conradiana* 18 (1986): 180-92.
———. "Conrad's 'Three Ages of Man': The 'Youth' Volume." *Polish Review* 20 (1975): 189-202.
———. "'Piety' in Joseph Conrad's *A Personal Record*." *Polish Review* 29 (1984): 11-23.
Martin, David M. "The Paradox of Perspective in Conrad's 'The Lagoon.'" *Studies in Short Fiction* 11 (1974): 306-7.
Mathews, James W. "Ironic Symbolism in Conrad's 'Youth.'" *Studies in Short Fiction* 2 (1974): 117-23.
Meyer, Bernard C. "Conrad and the Russians." *Conradiana* 12 (1980): 13-21.
———. *Joseph Conrad: A Psychoanalytic Biography*. Princeton: Princeton University Press, 1967.
Miller, J. Hillis. *Fiction and Repetition: Seven English Novels*. Cambridge, Mass.: Harvard University Press, 1982.
———. *Poets of Reality: Six Twentieth-Century Writers*. Cambridge, Mass.: Harvard University Press, 1965.
Mitchell, W. J. T., ed. *On Narrative*. Chicago: The University of Chicago Press, 1980.
Morf, Gustav. *The Polish Heritage of Joseph Conrad*. London: Astra, 1930.
Moser, Thomas. *Joseph Conrad: Achievement and Decline*. Cambridge, Mass.: Harvard University Press, 1958.
Mroczkowski, Przemyslaw. "A Glance Back at the Romantic Conrad: 'The Lagoon'—A Study in the Technique of the Short Story." *Polish Review* 4 (1959): 15-23.
Muecke, D. C. *Irony*. London: Methuen, 1970.
Najder, Zdzisław. *Joseph Conrad: A Chronicle*. New Brunswick, N.J.: Rutgers University Press, 1983.
Ordoñez, Elmer. *The Early Joseph Conrad: Revisions and Style*. Quezon City: University of Philippines Press, 1969.
Ortega y Gasset, José. *The Dehumanization of Art and Other Essays on Art, Culture, and Literature*. 1948; rpt. Princeton: Princeton University Press, 1968.
Owen, Guy. "Conrad's 'The Lagoon.'" *The Explicator* 18 (1960), item 47.
Pinsker, Sanford. *The Languages of Joseph Conrad*. Amsterdam: Rodopi, 1978.
Price, Martin. *Forms of Life: Character and Moral Imagination in the Novel*. New Haven and London: Yale University Press, 1983.
Pulc, I. P. "Two Portrayals of a Storm: Some Notes on Conrad's Descriptive Style in *The Nigger of the 'Narcissus'* and 'Typhoon.'" *Style* 4 (1970): 49-57.
Randall, Dale B. "Conrad Interviews." *Conradiana* 2, nos. 1, 2, and 3 (1969-70); *Conradiana* 3, no. 2 (1971-72); *Conradiana* 4, no. 1 (1972).
Redwine, Bruce. "Deception and Intention in *The Secret Agent*." *Conradiana* 11 (1979): 253-66.
Ressler, Steve. "Conrad's 'The Secret Sharer': Affirmation of Action." *Conradiana* 16 (1984): 195-214.
Retinger, J. H. *Conrad and His Contemporaries*. New York: Roy, 1943.
Rude, Donald W. "Addenda to Teets and Gerber." *Publications of the Bibliographical Society of America* 72 (1978): 560-62.
———. "An Annotated Checklist of the Works of Joseph Conrad in Author's Corrected Proofs." *Analytical and Enumerative Bibliography* 2 (1978): 87-102.
Said, Edward W. *Joseph Conrad and the Fiction of Autobiography*. Cambridge, Mass.: Harvard University Press, 1966.
Schleifer, Ronald. "Public and Private Narrative in *Under Western Eyes*. *Conradiana* 9 (1977): 237-54.
Schwarz, Daniel R. *Conrad: Almayer's Folly to Under Western Eyes*. London: Macmillan, 1980.

Sherry, Norman, ed. *Conrad: The Critical Heritage.* London: Routledge and Kegan Paul, 1973.
———. *Conrad's Eastern World.* Cambridge: Cambridge University Press, 1966.
———. *Conrad's Western World.* Cambridge: Cambridge University Press, 1971.
———, ed. *Joseph Conrad: A Commemoration.* Papers from the 1974 International Conference on Conrad. London: Macmillan, 1976.
Sickels, Eleanor M. "Conrad's 'The Lagoon.'" *The Explicator* 15 (1956), item 17.
Sizemore, C. W. "A Small Cardboard Box: A Symbol of the City and of Winnie Verloc in Conrad's *The Secret Agent.*" *Modern Fiction Studies* 24 (1978): 23–39.
Smith, J. Oates. "The Existential Comedy of Conrad's 'Youth.'" *Renascence* 16 (1963): 22–28.
Smith, Rosalind Walls. "Dates of Composition of Conrad's Works." *Conradiana* 11 (1979): 63–90.
Stallman, R. W., ed. *The Art of Joseph Conrad: A Critical Symposium.* East Lansing, Mich.: Michigan State University Press, 1960.
Starobinski, Jean. "The Style of Autobiography." *Literary Style: A Symposium.* Edited by Seymour Chatman. London: Oxford University Press, 1971: 285–96.
Steiner, Joan E. "Conrad's 'The Secret Sharer': Complexities of the Doubling Relationship." *Conradiana* 12 (1980): 173–86.
Sullivan, Ernest W. "The Genesis and Evolution of Joseph Conrad's 'Youth': A Revised and Copy-Edited Typescript Page." *The Review of English Studies* 36 (November 1985): 522–34.
Tanner, Tony. *Conrad: Lord Jim.* London: Edward Arnold, 1963.
———. "'Gnawed Bones' and 'Artless Tales': Eating and Narration in Conrad." *Joseph Conrad: A Commemoration.* Edited by Norman Sherry. London: Macmillan, 1976: 17–36.
———. "Nightmare and Complacency: Razumov and the Western Eye." *The Critical Quarterly* 4 (1962): 197–214.
Teets, Bruce E., and Gerber, Helmut, eds. *Joseph Conrad: An Annotated Bibliography of Writings about Him.* De Kalb, Ill.: Northern Illinois University Press, 1971.
Thomas, Lloyd Spenser. "Conrad's 'Jury Rig' Use of the Bible in 'Youth.'" *Studies in Short Fiction* 17 (1980): 79–82.
Thorburn, David. *Conrad's Romanticism.* New Haven and London: Yale University Press, 1974.
Tindall, William York. "Apology for Marlow." *From Jane Austen to Joseph Conrad: Essays Collected in Memory of James T. Hillhouse.* Edited by Robert C. Rathburn and Martin Steinmann, Jr. Minneapolis: University of Minnesota Press, 1958: 274–85.
Todorov, Tzvetan, *The Poetics of Prose.* Translated by Richard Howard. Ithaca, N.Y.: Cornell University Press, 1977.
Tolley, A. T. "Conrad's 'Favorite' Story." *Studies in Short Fiction* 3 (1966): 314–20.
Trilling, Lionel. "On the Teaching of Modern Literature." *Beyond Culture: Essays on Literature and Learning.* 1965; New York: Harvest/HBJ, 1979: 3–27.
Ullman, Stephen. *Language and Style.* Oxford: Basil Blackwell, 1964.
———. "Stylistics and Semantics." *Literary Style: A Symposium.* Edited by Seymour Chatman. London: Oxford University Press, 1971: 133–52.
Van Ghent, Dorothy. *The English Novel: Form and Function.* New York: Rinehart and Co., 1953.
Watson, Wallace. "'The Shade of Old Flaubert' and Maupassant's 'Art Impeccable.'" *The Journal of Narrative Technique* 7 (1977): 37–56.
Watt, Ian. *Conrad in the Nineteenth Century.* Berkeley: University of California Press, 1979.
———. "Joseph Conrad: Alienation and Commitment." *The English Mind: Studies in the English Moralists Presented to Basil Willey.* Edited by Hugh Sykes Davies and George Watson. Cambridge: Cambridge University Press, 1964: 257–78.
———, ed. *The Secret Agent: A Casebook.* London: Macmillan, 1973.
Watts, Cedric T. "Conrad's Absurdist Techniques: A Terminology." *Conradiana* 9 (1977): 141–48.
———. *Conrad's "Heart of Darkness": A Critical and Contextual Discussion.* Milano: Mursia International, 1977.
———. *The Deceptive Text: An Introduction to Covert Plots.* Sussex: The Harvester Press, 1984.

———. *A Preface to Conrad.* London: Longman, 1982.
Wells, H. G. *Experiment in Autobiography.* London: Victor Gollancz and The Cresset Press, 1934.
Weston, John Howard. "'Youth': Conrad's Irony and Time's Darkness." *Studies in Short Fiction* 11 (1974): 399-407.
Whitehead, Lee Melvin. "The Active Voice and the Passive Eye: *Heart of Darkness* and Nietzsche's *The Birth of Tragedy.*" *Conradiana* 7 (1975): 121-35.
———. "Joseph Conrad and the Vision of Tragedy." Diss., University of Wisconsin 1965.
Whiting, George. "Conrad's Revisions of Six of His Short Stories." *PMLA* 48 (1933): 552-57.
Williams, Porter. "The Matter of Conscience in Conrad's 'The Secret Sharer.'" *PMLA* 79 (1964): 626-30.
Wills, J. H. "A Neglected Masterpiece: Conrad's 'Youth.'" *Texas Studies in Literature and Language* 4 (1963): 591-601.
Willy, Todd Gray. "The 'Shamefully Abandoned' Kurtz: A Rhetorical Context for *Heart of Darkness.*" *Conradiana* 10 (1978): 97-112.
Yelton, Donald C. *Mimesis and Metaphor: An Inquiry into the Genesis and Scope of Conrad's Symbolic Imagery.* The Hague: Mouton, 1967.
Zukerman, Jerome. "The Motif of Cannibalism in *The Secret Agent.*" *Texas Studies in Language and Literature* 10 (1968): 295-99.

Index

Almayer's Folly, 28, 86, 98
"Amy Foster," 7, 127
"Autocracy and War," 91

Barthes, Roland, 31
Beckett, Samuel, 47
Berry, J. Wilkes, 64
Berthoud, Jacques, 35
Bible, 122–23
Blackwood, William, 2–3, 107, 108
Blackwood's Edinburgh Magazine, 10, 128
  "Youth" in, 49, 52, 58, 64, 66, 75, 80
  Lord Jim in, 85, 99
Booth, Wayne, 9, 19
Boyle, Ted, 4
Brontë, Emily, 47
Brooke, Sir James, 88–89
Busza, Andrzej, 43, 136

Céline, Louis-Ferdinand, 47
Colvin, Sidney, 6
Conrad, Joseph
  dialectical method of, 127, 135, 140–41
  "Heart of Darkness," revisions to, 64, 81
  "The Lagoon," writing, 1, 6, 33–34
  Lord Jim, writing, 2, 85–87, 99, 101, 107–8
  on Lord Nelson, 89, 108
  "An Outpost of Progress," revisions to, 8, 17–18, 21–22
  on own works, 1–2, 10, 18–19, 31, 54, 55, 85, 113–14, 140
  on patriotism and foreignness, 51, 60, 128
  philosophy of, 62–63, 68, 87–88
  on politics, 91, 108, 120, 129–30
  seaman, life as, 57, 81, 127–28
  "The Secret Sharer," writing, 111, 129–30
  Under Western Eyes, revisions to, 132
  Under Western Eyes, writing, 111, 113–14, 129

  on writing, 3–4, 5–6, 14, 140
  "Youth," revisions to, 6, 49–50, 51–53, 57–59, 61, 63–68, 72, 74–75, 77–78, 80–83
  "Youth," writing, 49, 50, 60
  See also individual titles
Cooper, James Fenimore, 50, 75
The Cornhill (magazine), 6, 31, 33–34
Cosmopolis (magazine), 8
Crime and Punishment (Dostoevsky), 114, 124
Curle, Richard, 1–2

Dante Alighieri, 95
Davis, Roderick, 132
Dickens, Charles, 82
Dostoevsky, Fyodor, 114, 124

Evans, Robert O., 95

"Falk," 120, 127
Faulkner, William, 4, 19, 62
Faust legend, 95
Feder, Lillian, 95
Flaubert, Gustave, 121, 135, 140
  irony in, 9, 98
  "An Outpost of Progress" and, 7, 18, 23
  "Youth" and, 77, 82
Fleishman, Avrom, 88–89
Ford, Ford Madox, 3–4, 54
Frye, Northrop, 19, 97

Galsworthy, John, 113, 129
Garnett, Edward, 1, 21
  Conrad to, on literature, 108, 128, 140
  Conrad to, on stories, 18–19, 31
Gawęda, 136
Gordan, John D., 57, 101
Graham, Cunninghame, 10, 87–88
Graver, Lawrence, 4–5, 9, 42
Great Expectations (Dickens), 82
Guerard, Albert, 28, 29, 33, 93, 128

166 Index

Hawkes, John, 47
Hay, Eloise Knapp, 85–86
"Heart of Darkness"
  characters in, 16, 24, 43, 89–91, 105
  in Conrad's development, 137, 140
  Czarist autocracy in, 121
  form of, 16, 27–28
  imperialism in, 42–43, 54–55, 88–89
  impressionism in, 25, 69–72, 138
  irony in, 97, 103, 139
  "Karain," compared to, 40, 42
  "The Lagoon," compared to, 27–28
  Lord Jim, compared to, 2, 85, 87, 101, 103–5, 139
  Marlow in, 4, 11, 12, 53–56, 64–65, 90–94, 103, 137–38
  myth in, 94–96
  narration in, 34, 42, 61, 62, 73, 74, 106
  "An Outpost of Progress," compared to, 7, 10–12, 15, 26
  revisions to, 64, 81
  rhetoric in, 53, 59–60, 63–64, 104
  symbolism in, 78–80
  themes in, 40, 59, 87, 88, 108–9, 139
  "Youth," compared to, 55–57, 71, 79, 82–83, 85
Heron, E., 34
Heron, H., 34
Hoffman, E.T.A., 38
Hueffer, Ford Madox. *See* Ford, Ford Madox
Humour, 59–60, 119. *See also* Irony

"The Idiots," 1, 7–8, 18, 27
Imperialism, 8–11, 42–43, 54–55, 88–89
Impressionism, 31
  in "Heart of Darkness," 25, 69–72, 138
  in *Lord Jim*, 25, 138
  in "Youth," 66–69, 83, 138
Inferno (Dante), 95
The Inheritors, 54
Irony
  in "Heart of Darkness," 97, 103, 139
  in "Karain," 38, 40–41
  in *Lord Jim*, 97–98, 100
  in "An Outpost of Progress," 8–9, 21–24, 25–26, 136, 137
  in *The Secret Agent*, 137
  in "The Secret Sharer," 116–17
  in *Under Western Eyes*, 115–16, 139
  in "Youth," 73

James, Henry, 11, 62, 135
  Conrad compared to, 1, 2, 3, 92, 109
Jean-Aubry, G., 57, 114
Johnson, Bruce, 44, 45

"Karain: A Memory," 27, 33
  in Conrad's development, 46–47, 127, 135
  East and West in, 42–47
  form of, 46–47, 139
  "Heart of Darkness," compared to, 40, 42
  irony in, 38, 40–41
  "The Lagoon," compared to, 38, 40, 43
  Lord Jim, compared to, 33, 38, 40, 42–47, 135
  narrative in, 33, 36–42, 51, 128, 136, 138
  themes in, 40, 43, 45–47, 136–37
  "Youth," compared to, 51, 56, 61, 82
Kipling, Rudyard, 8–9, 135
Krieger, Murray, 73

"The Lagoon," 33
  in Conrad's development, 1, 47, 135
  ending of, 32–33
  form of, 47, 139
  "Heart of Darkness," compared to, 27–28
  "Karain," compared to, 38, 40, 43
  Lord Jim, compared to, 4, 28, 29, 30–32, 36–37, 135
  narrative in, 29–30, 33–34, 36–38, 136, 138
  rhetoric in, 31–32
  themes in, 30, 40, 136–37
  writing of, 1, 6, 33–34
Lord, A.J., 61
Lord Jim
  characterization in, 43, 72, 91, 101–2, 105–8
  critical problems concerning, 4, 32
  early version of, 85–87
  "Heart of Darkness," compared to, 2, 85, 87, 101, 103–5, 139
  idealism in, 46–47, 108–9
  illusions in, 32
  imperialism in, 88–89
  impressionism in, 25, 138
  irony in, 97–98, 140
  "Karain," compared to, 33, 38, 40, 42–47, 135
  "The Lagoon," compared to, 4, 28, 29, 30–32, 36–37, 135
  Marlow in, 4, 32, 44, 53, 56–57, 64, 99, 137–38
  moral questions in, 37, 45–46, 53, 98–99
  myth and symbolism in, 78, 94, 96
  narration in, 28, 33, 34–37, 41, 42–47, 61, 73, 74, 76, 121
  rhetoric in, 104–5
  themes in, 33, 40, 43, 46–47, 74, 88, 102–3, 136–37, 139
  writing of, 2, 99, 101, 107–8, 127, 140
  "Youth," compared to, 2, 56–57, 78, 82–83, 85, 103

Lutoslawski, Wincenty, 60
Lynd, Robert, 128

Marlow (character)
    function of, for Conrad, 2, 49, 51–53, 77, 82, 99, 128, 137–38
    in "Heart of Darkness," 11, 12, 53–56, 64–65, 90–94, 103
    in *Lord Jim,* 32, 34, 35–37, 41, 44, 53, 56–57, 64, 99, 105–6
    as mediator, 88, 97, 102–3
    qualities as narrator, 4, 41, 54, 62, 74–75
    in "Youth," 50, 53, 56–57, 71, 73, 74
Marris, Captain Carlos M., 127–28
Marryat, Captain Frederick, 50, 75
Maupassant, Guy de, 9, 14, 54
    Conrad and, 5, 7, 8, 135
McLauchlan, Juliet, 73
Meldrum, David S., 85, 99, 101, 107
Michael, Marion C., 64
Mickiewicz, Adam, 43
Miller, J. Hillis, 19
Mirror of the Sea, 128, 140
Muecke, D.C., 9

Najder, Zdzisław, 6, 50, 60, 128, 129–30
Nelson, Lord, 89, 108
New York Times Saturday Book Review, 54, 88
The Nigger of the "Narcissus," 83, 94, 127
    narration in, 25, 28
    and other works, 38, 56, 103
    preface to, 1, 3, 5, 45, 54, 55
    themes in, 58, 116
Nostromo, 140

Ortega y Gasset, José, 61–62
An Outcast of the Islands, 1, 28, 86, 98
"An Outpost of Progress," 14–15, 18–19
    in Conrad's development, 135–36, 139
    "Heart of Darkness," compared to, 7, 10–12, 15, 26
    irony in, 15–17, 25–26, 136, 137
    "The Lagoon" and "Karain," compared to, 27
    Lord Jim, compared to, 86, 97
    point of view in, 8, 11–12
    revisions to, 8, 17–18, 21–22
    The Secret Agent, compared to, 7, 22, 25–26, 135–36, 139
    themes in, 24–25, 42–43, 136
    writing of, 1, 50

Palestine (barkentine), 57, 73
Pascal, Roy, 34

A Personal Record, 1, 71, 128
Pinker, J.B., 6, 49, 127–28
"The Planter of Malata," 111
Poe, Edgar Allan, 3, 38
Poradowska, Marguerite, 3
Prince, Martin, 102

Quiller-Couch, A., 62

The Rescue, 18, 42–43, 87, 99
"The Return," 50
Rhetoric, 31–32, 53, 104–5
Rothenstein, William, 129

Said, Edward, 4
Sanderson, Ted, 51
The Secret Agent
    in Conrad's development, 6, 137, 140
    irony in, 19–21, 22, 25–26, 137
    "An Outpost of Progress," compared to, 7, 22, 25–26, 135–36
    reviews of, 128
    techniques in, 12–14, 18
    themes in, 8, 130, 136
"The Secret Sharer"
    in Conrad's development, 6, 127–30, 137, 140
    formal elements in, 123–24, 128–29
    irony in, 116–17, 119, 140
    moral questions in, 112–13, 116–19
    themes in, 114–15, 121–22, 130–32
    Under Western Eyes, connections to, 111, 119–20, 125–27, 130, 133, 139
Set of Six, 128
Sissie (steamer), 81
The Sisters, 1, 28, 38
Stevenson, Robert Louis, 75

"Tales of the Sea," 50
Tales of Unrest
    "Author's Note" to, 1, 14, 18–19
    criticism of, 31, 135
    "An Outpost of Progress" in, 18
Tanner, Tony, 120
Thorburn, David, 33
"To-morrow," 127
"Tuan Jim: A Sketch," 49, 85–87, 99
Turgenev, Ivan, 62
'Twixt Land and Sea, 128
"Typhoon," 127

Under Western Eyes
    in Conrad's development, 6, 127, 140
    irony in, 115–16, 139

moral questions in, 111–13, 115–18, 132–33
politics in, 120–21, 130
"The Secret Sharer," connections to, 111, 119–20, 125–27, 130, 133, 139
symbolism in, 123–24
themes in, 114–15, 122–25, 132–33, 139
writing of, 111, 113–14, 129–30, 132
Unwin, Fisher, 62, 68

Van Ghent, Dorothy, 47
Victory, 120
Virgil, 95

Watt, Ian, 23, 92
  on Conrad's technique, 28, 67, 105
  on Marlow stories, 4, 34, 105
Watts, Cedric, 10, 79–80
Wells, H.G., 55
Woolf, Virginia, 1, 31
Wuthering Heights (E. Brontë), 47

Yelton, Donald, 77
"Youth"
  as autobiography, 57, 81
  in Conrad's development, 137, 139
  form in, 27, 103, 139
  "Heart of Darkness," compared to, 55–57, 71, 79, 82–83, 85
  impressionism in, 66–69, 83, 138
  irony and humour in, 59–60, 73, 74
  "Karain," compared to, 51, 56, 61, 82
  Lord Jim, compared to, 2, 56–57, 78, 82–83, 85, 103
  Marlow in, 4, 50, 53, 56–57, 71, 73, 74, 137–38
  narrative in, 38, 40, 61, 65–68, 73, 74, 128, 138
  pace of, 75–76
  patriotism in, 51–53, 54, 60–61
  revisions to, 6, 49–50, 51–53, 57–59, 61, 63–68, 72, 74–75, 77–78, 80–83
  rhetoric in, 53
  symbolism in, 78–79
  themes in, 58–59, 77
  writing of, 49, 99